D1083130

LIVES OF GREAT RELIGIOUS BOOKS

The *Talmud*: A Biography

LIVES OF GREAT RELIGIOUS BOOKS

FORTHCOMING

The *Talmud*

A BIOGRAPHY

Barry Scott Wimpfheimer

PRINCETON UNIVERSITY PRESS

Princeton and Oxford

Copyright © 2018 by Princeton University Press

Published by Princeton University Press,
41 William Street, Princeton, New Jersey 08540

In the United Kingdom: Princeton University Press,
6 Oxford Street, Woodstock, Oxfordshire OX20 1TR

press.princeton.edu

Jacket art: © Andi Arnovitz

All Rights Reserved

ISBN 978-0-691-16184-6
Library of Congress Control Number: 2017963018

British Library Cataloging-in-Publication Data is available

This book has been composed in Garamond Premier Pro

Printed on acid-free paper. ∞

Printed in the United States of America

10 9 8 7 6 5 4 3 2 1

For Shana, Adin, and Amalia

CONTENTS

ACKNOWLEDGMENTS

An announcement in a conference schedule about a decade ago alerted me to a new series from Princeton University Press called "Lives of Great Religious Books." My instant desire to write a volume for this series on the Babylonian Talmud would take several years to come to fruition. Passing mention of my interest to Daniel Boyarin led to an invitation to pitch my idea for this book to Fred Appel. The rest is history.

I am grateful to those who have helped me with this project. Northwestern University has been my scholarly home for eleven years. I feel tremendous support from the Department of Religious Studies and the Weinberg College of Arts and Sciences. The Crown Family Center for Jewish and Israel Studies—which I directed while writing this book—is particularly dear to me; thank you to Nancy Gelman, who administers the Crown Center, for freeing up my time to write this book. My colleagues in both Religious Studies and Jewish Studies have been terrific sounding boards for this project and for scholarship in general. I particularly want to thank three colleagues—Mira Balberg, Sarah Jacoby, and Michelle

Molina—who have often served as a writers collective for this and other projects.

Several friends were very generous with their time and energy and gave me extensive feedback. Thank you to Mira Balberg, Daniel Boyarin, Jeremy Dauber, Shana Gillers, Yohanan Petrovsky-Shtern, and Tzvi Novick for their manuscript annotations and suggested edits. Jonathan Milgram, Daniel Reifman, and Elli Stern are old friends with unique expertise in the Talmud, and their conversations over the years have produced many of the underlying ideas in this book. Sarah Wolf co-taught with me during the period the book was written. Adina Goldman provided valuable research support. Thanks also to Anne Mintz for copyediting and Angela Erisman for indexing.

Family members have encouraged this process. I want to specially thank Susanne and Michael Wimpfheimer, Mina and Bruce Gillers, Jan/Orit, Ahuva/Gershon, David/Rachel, Ben/Tracy, Sara, Chanani/Seth, Yosef/Sara, and their families.

Adin and Amalia have kept me company on this escapade and tolerated those nights on which I couldn't quite let go of the day's work. I thank them for cheering me up and distracting me while serving as concrete reminders to keep things in perspective.

Shana is my confidante and partner who has encouraged and critiqued this project since its inception. I am grateful for her love and her company for so many years. In recognition of my inexpressible gratitude, I dedicate this book in her honor and in honor of our children.

LIVES OF GREAT RELIGIOUS BOOKS

The *Talmud*: A Biography

400BCE	200BCE	1CE	200CE	400CE	600CE	800CE	1000CE

Period

Classical Antiquity			Late Antiquity			
	Tannaitic		Amoraic		Geonic	

Events

- **334-331 BCE** Alexander the Great conquers the Near East
- **167-164 BCE** Antiochus's decree and resultant Maccabean revolt
- **~200 CE** Redaction of Mishnah by R. Judah the Prince
- **70 CE** Second Temple destroyed
- **~30 CE** Jesus's death
- **132 CE** Bar Kokhba Revolt
- **~324 CE** Christianity becomes religion of Roman empire
- **~300 CE** Redaction of Tosefta
- **~400 CE** Redaction of Palestinian Talmud
- **~600-750 CE** Range of possible redaction of Babylonian Talmud
- **Eighth Century CE** Islamic Conquest
- **Tenth Century CE** Oldest extant fragments of Talmud manuscripts
- **987** Letter of Rav Sherira Gaon

People

- **37-100 CE** Josephus (historian) Judea and Rome
- **~ 990-1055** Rabbenu Hananel ben Hushiel (commentator), Qairouan (Tunisia)
- **1013-1103** Rabbi Isaac Alfasi (codifier), Lucena, Cordoba (Spain)

Timeline

1200CE	1400CE	1600CE	1800CE	2000CE
Middle Ages		**Early Modern**		**Modern**
		Renaissance		

1096 First Crusade

1147-1149 Second Crusade

1147 Almohad Oppression of Jews in Cordoba (Spain)

1263 Barcelona Disputation

1240 Paris Disputation

1342 Munich 95 Manuscript of the Talmud written

1414 Tortosa Disputation

1480s Spanish editions of individual tractates printed

1484 Soncino tractate Berakhot, Rashi/Tosafot around central text

1492-1497 Expulsion of Jews from Iberia

1520-1523 First complete printed Talmud (Venice/Bomberg)

1565 First printed edition of *Shulhan Arukh*

1757 Podolia Disputation

1803 Founding of Volozhin Yeshiva

1880-1886 Printing of Vilna Edition by Widow & Brothers Romm

1923 Rabbi Meir Shapira introduces *Daf Yomi*, daily Talmud program

1935-1948 Soncino Press English translation of the Talmud

1949 U.S. Army & JC publish "Survivors' Talmud" in Heidelberg

1967-2010 Steinsaltz vocalized Hebrew-translated edition of the Talmud

1990-2004 Artscroll publishes English translation of the Talmud

1992 Bar Ilan Responsa Project Version 1 released

2012 Artscroll releases Talmud app for IOS and Android

2012 ~600,000 attend parties for completion of the Talmud

1100-1171
Rabbi Jacob Tam
(commentator), Troyes, France

1488-1575
Rabbi Josef Karo
(codifier) Safed, Israel

1720-1797
Vilna Gaon (commentator),
Vilnius, Lithuania

1125-1198
Rabad (commentator),
Posquières, Provence (France)

1240-1305
Moses de Leon, Arévalo, Spain

1040-1105
Rashi (commentator), Troyes, France

1135-1204
Maimonides
(codifier),
Fustat, Egypt

1340-1411
Hasdai Kreskas (philosopher),
Saragosa, Spain

1194-1270
Nahmanides (commentator), Barcelona, Spain

1077-1141
Ri Migash (commentator), Lucena, Cordoba (Spain)

The Talmud—Essential, Enhanced, and Emblematic

The Babylonian Talmud can be accurately defined in three distinct ways:

1. The Babylonian Talmud is a work of religious literature collectively produced by a group of rabbi scholars who lived in two geographic regions (Palestine and Babylonia) between the first and eighth centuries CE.

2. The Babylonian Talmud is the central canonical work of the Judaism that emerged after the destruction of the Temple in Jerusalem; within an idiosyncratically scholastic culture that relied heavily on texts to ground religious meaning, the Talmud has been the text on which scholars have focused their energies.

3. The Babylonian Talmud is a uniquely Jewish scripture and has often come to function as the ultimate symbolic representation of Judaism, Jewishness, and Jews.

The above three definitions are not mutually exclusive. All are true and can work together. It is necessary to delineate these definitions, though, because each implicates a different historical story and each of these stories produces a register of meaning. This book will demonstrate that there are three registers of Talmudic meaning. (Chapter 1 contains a fuller description of the Talmud itself.)

To understand this notion of multiple registers of meaning, the reader who has not yet encountered the Talmud should consider the biblical Ten Commandments or the United States Constitution as comparable foundational texts. These three texts (the two comparators and the Talmud) were produced in historical time and place. The original meaning of the text is the *essential* meaning of the text. There are fundamental problems that affect one's ability to confidently recover the original meaning of a text. And yet we can easily comprehend historical meaning as an ideal to which one might strive. This is the first register of Talmudic meaning.

The three texts we are considering are fundamental to ongoing cultural (including legal and religious) practices of reading and have engendered interpretations and applications (to say nothing of explicit amendments) that exponentially expand the work as each original word or sentence generates exegesis, and becomes the basis for inferences and new applications. From its completion (ca. 750 CE) until today, the Talmud has been at the center of an active culture of reading that has generated an enormous literature of reception that understands, interprets, and applies it. This enormous literature is often understood as the Talmud by cultural insiders and should be considered the *enhanced* Talmud.

Part of what makes the Ten Commandments or the Constitution relevant long after their respective historical moments of production is the potency of their symbolic meaning. This symbolic meaning is sometimes employed without awareness of essential or enhanced meanings and even, occasionally, in contradiction to those meanings. People regularly invoke the Ten Commandments as a symbol of divine legislation and moral justice without knowing the specifics of the commandments themselves. The Constitution is invoked as the basis for liberal democracy and all that is noble about the United States without recourse to its specific words. This book argues that the Talmud also possesses a register of meaning that is only loosely connected with the underlying original content (essential) of the work or the vast apparatus of reception (enhanced). When functioning in this *emblematic* register, the Talmud is sometimes concrete and sometimes abstract. It is concrete when the Talmud embodies tradition and a particular modern Jewish movement attempts to behead the personified Talmud on the way to a repudiation of tradition. It is abstract when the Talmud is made to signify the idea of Judaism or inherent Jewishness.

The three different registers of Talmudic meaning map somewhat neatly on three distinct scholarly fields. Academic scholars of the Talmud are primarily interested in the essential Talmud. Traditional scholars of the

Talmud engage the enhanced Talmud. Historians of all periods take a strong interest in the emblematic Talmud.

Chaim Potok's 1969 bestseller *The Promise* builds on the tension that exists among the essential, enhanced, and emblematic Talmuds.[1] The novel's first-person narrator, Reuven Malter, is a rabbinical student who spends his days immersed in intense study of the Talmud. The Talmud as a work of literature features multiple layers of rabbinic argumentation about law, myth, and theology. Students of the Talmud within a *yeshiva* [traditional learning] environment strive to decipher the Talmud's often messy text. The density and complexity of the Talmud make the reader work actively to produce both basic comprehension and a coherent sense of the whole. Talmudic aptitude is measured by assessing a reader's ability to wring coherence out of the text. Talmudic genius inheres in the ability to reimagine the set of Talmudic variables to resolve a dilemma.

The Promise is set in postwar New York, and its central plot device is a battle over how to read the Talmud. Reuven Malter has been trained by his father to employ the tools of a textual historian to resolve Talmudic difficulties. By altering a problematic text, the text critic can make the Talmud readable. When the correction is based on a text witness—a different version of the original text preserved in a handwritten manuscript or an alternate print edition—it is as if history itself justifies the alteration. According to the Malters' methodology, the scholar is fixing a mistake that has crept into the print editions and caused the textual dilemma. The correction restores the text to its original unblemished form. Implicitly, this methodology argues that the essential meaning of the text—the historically original understanding—is its correct meaning.

For Rav Kalman, Reuven Malter's teacher and his father's nemesis, textual emendation is heretical. It is a cheap solution to an expensive problem. Generations of Talmud scholars sweated over the textual inconsistencies and performed logical calisthenics to circumvent and resolve such issues. Emendation retroactively transforms these creative attempts—part of the literature that constitutes the enhanced Talmud—rendering them mistaken or irrelevant. Rav Kalman resists the alluring historical solution to preserve a vision of the Talmud's reception that understands the millennium-long debate about Talmudic ideas asynchronically, as if all the rabbis from all the periods and cultures participate in a single debate that defies time and space. In defense of the expansive Talmud, Rav Kalman willfully blinds himself to the easy solution of changing the original text. And, as a result, the Talmud is an enhanced text that includes both the original text and the millennium of texts that comment upon the original.

The climactic scene of *The Promise* stages an oral examination to certify Reuven Malter as a rabbi.[2] A tribunal disguised as an exam, the scene finds the book's hero facing a three-person panel of rabbis who test him on his control of the corpus of rabbinic Judaism. The examination stretches over several days. On day one, Reuven handles the panel's questions with aplomb, demonstrating his ability to make both the Talmud and its commentarial texts readable—he demonstrates mastery of the enhanced Talmud. As the exam moves to a second day, though, the panel targets the core methodological divide between Rav Kalman and David Malter. Kalman begins to ask thorny questions of Talmudic exegesis—how to explain a passage's troubling logic and how to resolve apparent contradictions within the Talmudic corpus. Initially reluctant to employ his critical methodology, Reuven eventually demonstrates his aptitude (indeed his creative brilliance) by resolving textual problems through emendation—by correcting the words of the text that appear in the standard print editions. His emendations are progressively more "heretical": his first emendation draws on a variant of the text found in the printed edition of a related passage in another tractate of the Babylonian Talmud; his second derives from a version of the text found in an alternate print edition of the Palestinian Talmud; his third and most egregious draws upon a version of the text found in a handwritten medieval manuscript. This last emendation is simultaneously the most impressive (Reuven had hypothesized the existence of a variant and then discovered it) and the most heretical (from Rav Kalman's perspective). Canceling the final day of exams, Rav Kalman says that he has heard enough and indicates that Reuven will not be ordained. The rabbi relents, with conditions, a day later.

That the central tension of a major American bestselling novel should be about how one reads the Talmud may seem strange. But the conflict encapsulates one of the core dramas of religion in modernity. The Malters, who wish to emend their Talmudic texts, stand on the side of reason, history, and autonomy, while Rav Kalman stands on the side of mystification, tradition, and romanticism. Their clash is a microcosm of the modern post-Enlightenment struggle between traditional religious life and modern scientific modes of thinking. It is precisely because the Talmud is both intellectually sophisticated and religiously essential that it can function for the novelist as the perfect symbol to evoke this tension between the critical scientific method that wishes to recover a rational historical object, and the traditional intellectual methodology that finds comfort in resisting history, and embracing the most expansive version of the Talmud.

The novel is set in the postwar period because it seeks to ask what Jewishness and Judaism will become in the Holocaust's wake. Debates about how to read the Talmud are nothing less than ruminations about the anxiety of Jewish survival after World War II. Rav Kalman's resistance to modernity is buttressed by the deep-seated fear that capitulating to text criticism finishes Hitler's work.[3] On the other side, Reuven Malter's incredulity at his teacher's resistance is a mark of his comfort in American modernity.

Historically, the tension between the essential and enhanced Talmuds in the United States was largely dissipated by the splintering that separated Conservative Judaism from Orthodox Judaism as two different denominations.[4] Today, critical readers of the Talmud and traditional readers of the Talmud in the United

States have retreated into denominational corners. Without the shared religious space of institutions and the shared public space of intellectual journals, the two distinct interpretive communities only rarely intersect.

By making Talmudic reading a stand-in for Judaism in modernity, Chaim Potok transforms the Talmud into a symbolic rope being tugged by two visions of the future of Judaism. The tension between the traditional and critical readers is significant not for its particulars (the novel doesn't really provide the specifics of either the essential or the enhanced Talmudic particulars) but because of its larger ramifications for Judaism and the universal questions of tradition and modernity. For all his originality, Potok did not originate this symbolic usage of the Talmud. For as long as the Talmud has been a canonical work, it has served as a symbol of Judaism, Jewishness, and Jews. It is this Talmudic personification in the emblematic register that most entitles the Talmud to a biography.

This book explores the three different registers of Talmudic meaning both as discrete and as intertwined entities. The opening two chapters provide historical context for understanding the essential Talmud and some examples to introduce the hero of our story. The third chapter describes the processes through which the enhanced Talmud began to be generated, while the fourth includes a large quantity of material about the earliest emblematic uses of the Talmud. The final chapter presents three stories of the Talmud in modernity that provide a thick picture of the Talmud's tremendous success and contemporary popularity.

Gestation and Birth
(Essential Talmud Part One)

Talmud on Fire Liability

The Talmud is a commentary on an earlier law code, the Mishnah, which was published orally by the rabbis around the year 200 CE. Much like other ancient law codes (including the ones found in the Hebrew Bible) the Mishnah writes many of its laws as hypothetical scenarios. A far-fetched hypothetical is grounds for a fascinating Talmudic discussion of the basis of liability for fire that damages a neighbor's property. This brief foray into a Talmudic text introduces a passage about fire liability that this book will return to in greater depth in subsequent chapters.

Mishnah Baba Qamma 2:3b

> A dog who took a cake [baking on top of hot coals] and went to a haystack; it ate the cake and set fire to the haystack:
>
> on the cake [an owner] pays full damages, but on the haystack [an owner pays] half damages.[1]

The owner pays the full value of the eaten cake and half of the value of the burnt haystack. Liability for the full value of the cake follows a basic principle of expectation: since animals can be expected to eat cake, one is responsible to watch them and ensure that they do not do so. For the haystack, the owner of the dog is liable for half of the damages. No rationale is offered in the Mishnah and a reader must work to produce an explanation. One common explanation is that the burning of a haystack is unexpected; since the owner could not have anticipated this form of damage, the owner is only liable for half of the damages. Another common explanation considers fire damage to be a form of secondarily causal damage such as when pebbles projected by an animal's moving feet break a pane of glass.

The Talmud begins its discussion of this mishnah by citing a debate between two rabbis, R' Yohanan and Resh Laqish, who lived in Palestine and were active in the first half of the third century.

Babylonian Talmud Baba Qamma 22a

It was said:[2] R' Yohanan said, "his fire[3] because [it is] his arrow."

And Resh Laqish[4] said, "his fire because [it is] his property."

Though the Babylonian Talmud was produced in Babylonia, it preserves many texts that were first articulated by Palestinian rabbis. Each of the two rabbis explains fire liability by drawing a specific analogy. R' Yohanan says that

CHAPTER I

liability for fire is like liability for an arrow: just as one is liable for the distant damage caused by a launched arrow, one is also liable for the distant damage caused by kindled fire. Resh Laqish analogizes liability for fire to property liability: as one is liable for damage caused by property (such as one's animal), one is also liable for damage caused by a set fire.

The Talmud's anonymous voice teases out the differences between these two analogies by asking after the stakes for each individual rabbi.

Why did Resh Laqish not explain like R' Yohanan?
(He would say to you,)[5] "arrows move from his force, this [fire] did not move from his force."

And why did R' Yohanan not explain like Resh Laqish?
(He would say to you,)[6] "property has tangibility, this [fire] does not have tangibility."

Why does R' Yohanan prefer the analogy to an arrow and Resh Laqish the analogy to property? Resh Laqish rejects the analogy to the arrow because the damage caused by the arrow is directly linked to the energy of the archer's pulling the bow; while fire may share the feature of being able to cause distant damage, it does not share this direct connection between the energy of the person responsible and the damage. R' Yohanan rejects the analogy to property because property is tangible while fire is not; though the two are similar since one is responsible for them, there is a fundamental difference between responsibility for tangible items and intangible ones.

The Talmudic passage continues by connecting this debate about fire liability to the mishnah cited above on which the entire Talmudic passage is something of a commentary. Drawing an inference, the Talmud asserts that the mishnah seems to support the view of R' Yohanan that liability for fire is like liability for the damage of an arrow:

> It was stated in the Mishnah, "A dog who took a cake, etc."[7]
>
> Granted that for [R' Yohanan] who said (fire liability is)[8] like an arrow, the arrow is of the dog[9] [and for this reason the owner is not liable for full damages]. But for [Resh Laqish] who said (fire liability)[10] is like property liability, (this fire)[11] is not the property of the dog's owner?

A hungry dog eats a cake that was cooking on some coals. The cake is still attached to a coal and the dog transports the coal to a haystack, setting the stack on fire and burning it to the ground. The mishnah rules that the owner of the dog pays full damages for the cake and half damages for the haystack. The Talmud's anonymous narrator seeks to determine whether this mishnah about a bizarre case of fire liability holds the clue to the conceptual debate regarding whether fire is like an arrow or like other property. Drawing attention to the idea of half damages for the haystack, the Talmud's anonymous voice suggests that this scenario's law reflects the arrow view more than the property view. For while one can understand a dog owner's responsibility for the secondary effects of the dog as akin to the repercussions of shooting an arrow, the indirect nature of this tort makes any liability for the haystack hard to explain for someone who thinks of fire liability as based on liability for one's property.

The anonymous voice of the Talmud does not concede that this bizarre case of the Mishnah supports R' Yohanan. Rather, it modifies the narrative of the scenario to create space for Resh Laqish's property-based notion of fire liability.

> Here with what are we dealing? [With a scenario in which the dog] threw the coal. For the cake [the dog's owner] pays full damages, for the site of the coal [the dog's owner] pays[12] half damages and for the entire haystack [the dog's owner] is exempt.

In this new version of the story, the dog threw the coal in the air and it landed on the haystack. The owner of the dog is liable for full damages for the cake, half damages for the initial landing spot of the coal and exempt from the damage to the rest of the haystack. By modifying the story such that the dog threw the cake/coal onto the haystack, the Talmud has created space within which to understand the mishnah as agreeing with the conceptual approach of Resh Laqish that fire liability is based on property liability.

The Talmud is replete with passages like this one that explore the intricacies of law (ritual, civil, criminal), metaphysics, and theology. The Talmudic method of drilling down into the underlying bedrock to uncover core doctrines involves a marriage of creative logical deduction with careful analysis of valued canonical texts. The specific way in which the Talmud attempts to maintain the validity of the mishnah as a core textual precedent alongside the conceptual possibility of fire liability as a subset of property liability is thorny, and became the basis for commentarial controversies in the enhanced Talmud. This book will return to further probe this Talmudic passage more extensively in the second chapter, and to unpack the controversies surrounding its interpretation in the third chapter. For now, though, this taste of the Talmud provokes a series of questions:

1. The passage opens with a legal dictum from the Mishnah. What is the Mishnah and in what ways is it central to the Talmud?

2. R' Yohanan and Resh Laqish are two named rabbis whose debate structures the passage. Who were these rabbis, and what was the context in which they debated the conceptual character of fire liability?

3. The original debate is enriched through a seemingly unique idiosyncratic textual discourse. Where did this interesting rhetorical and exegetical project come from, and how did it come to be the quintessence of rabbinic religiosity?

4. The anonymous narrator thickens the respective conceptual approaches of the two named rabbis and draws their debate into conversation with the Mishnah's strange hypothetical of the dog with the cake. Who is this anonymous narrator?

5. The passage about fire liability continues in the Talmud for a few pages in the standard print editions. As we will see in the next chapter, the Talmud uses different scenarios found in rabbinic legal precepts to prove that fire liability is more akin to an arrow than to property liability and each of these is explained away.[13] Then a fourth-century Babylonian rabbi, Abaye, draws attention to a statutory scenario that works better with a property liability understanding and not as well with an arrow liability approach, and the Talmud works extremely hard to explain this problem away. The passage's conclusion is that even those who think that liability for fire is akin to arrow liability must accept, at times, that one is liable for fire because it is one's property. A reader who successfully follows the intricacies of this passage might justifiably wonder about its goals. Is the reader expected to land on a specific understanding of fire liability? If not, does this passage have a specific learning outcome? Do Talmudic passages have goals?

Who Were the Rabbis?

History: Continuity and Disruption

Among its many stories, the Talmud includes a legendary rabbinic origin tale.[14]

Abba Sikra, the head of the *biryoni*[15] in Jerusalem, was the son of the sister of Rabban Yohanan b. Zakkai.

[R. Yohanan] sent (to him)[16] saying, "Come visit me privately."[17]

When [Abba Sikra] came, he said to him, "How long are you going to act this way and kill all the people with starvation?"

[Abba Sikra] replied: "What can I do? If I say something[18] to them, they will kill me."

[R. Yohanan] said: "Devise some plan for me to escape. Perhaps there will be a small salvation."

[Abba Sikra] said to him: "Pretend to be ill, and let everyone come to inquire about you. Bring something evil smelling and put it by you so that they will say you are dead.[19] Let then your disciples get under your bed, (but no others, so that they shall not notice that you are still light,)[20] since they know that a living being is lighter (than a corpse)."[21]

[R. Yohanan] did so, and R. Eliezer went [under the bier] from one side and R. Joshua from the other. When they reached the opening, [some of the people inside the walls] wanted to run a lance through [the bier].

[They][22] said to them: "Shall [the Romans] say. They have pierced their Master?"

They wanted to jostle it.

[They] said to them: "Shall they say that they pushed their Master?"

They opened a town gate[23] for him and (he got out).[24]

When [R. Yohanan] reached [the Romans] he said, "Peace to you, O king, peace to you, O king."

[Vespasian] said: "Your life is forfeit on two counts, one because I am not a king (and you call me king),[25] and again, if I am a king, why did you not come to me (before now)?"[26]

[R. Yohanan] replied: "As for your saying that you are not a king, (in truth you are a king),[27] since if you were not a king Jerusalem would not be delivered into your hand, as it is written (Isaiah 10:34), "And Lebanon shall fall by a mighty one." 'Mighty one' [is an epithet] applied only to a king, as it is written (Jeremiah 30:21), "And their mighty one shall be of themselves etc.;" and Lebanon refers to the Sanctuary, as it says (Deuteronomy 3:25), "This goodly mountain and Lebanon."[28] As for your question, why (if you are a king),[29] I did not come to you (till now),[30] [the answer is that] the *biryoni* among us did not let me."

[Vespasian] said to him: "If there is a jar of honey round which a serpent[31] is wound, would they not break the jar to get rid of the serpent?"

[R. Yohanan] could give no answer.[32] . . .

At this point a messenger came to him (from Rome)[33] saying, "Up, for the Caesar is dead, and the notables of Rome have arranged[34] to establish you as head [of the State]."

[Vespasian][35] had just finished putting on one boot. When he tried to put on the other he could not. He tried to take off the first but it would not come off. (He said: "What is the meaning of this?")[36]

R. Yohanan said to him: "(Do not worry:)[37] the good news has done it, as it says (Proverbs 15:30),

'Good tidings make the bone fat.' What is the remedy? Let someone whom you dislike come and pass before you, as it is written (Proverbs 17:22), 'A broken spirit dries up the bones.'" He did so, [and the boot] went on.

[Vespasian] said to him: "Seeing that you are so wise, why did you not come to me (till now)?"[38]

[R. Yohanan] said: "Have I not told you?"—

[Vespasian] retorted: "I too have told you."

[Vespasian] said: "I am now going, and will send someone [to take my place]. Ask something of me and I will grant it to you."

[R. Yohanan] said to him: Give me[39] Yavneh and its Wise Men, and the [family] chain of Rabban Gamaliel, and physicians to heal R. Zadoq.

The setting for the legend is the Roman siege of Jerusalem in 70 CE. A rabbinic intellectual inside Jerusalem, Rabban Yohanan ben Zakkai, uses the ruse of death to sneak out of the city and speak directly with Vespasian, the Roman general. Fumbling over himself, the rabbi refers to the general as a monarch and the general considers this a blasphemous offense. When an emissary arrives mid-conversation informing Vespasian of a Roman election that has elevated him to the position of Caesar, the newly crowned monarch recognizes the prophetic abilities of his interlocutor. Rabban Yohanan ben Zakkai frames his ability to see the future as a byproduct of a midrashic reading of biblical verses that had predicted Jerusalem's destruction. Vespasian offers him three requests. Rabban Yohanan ben Zakkai asks for the preservation of the Gamaliel family, for a healer to heal Rabbi Zadoq, and for Yavneh (Jamnia) and its rabbis. This last request is often understood as a trade of Jerusalem for rabbinic Judaism.[40]

The Roman siege of the city of Jerusalem[41] was a siege preceding the final battle in a war that had stretched on for more than three years. The war had been triggered by the rise of militant Judean factions who sought the kind of political autonomy enjoyed earlier in the century under the Hasmonean rulers. Such Judean autonomy was not desired by the Romans, who understood the positioning of biblical Israel along the Mediterranean Sea as pivotal.

The rabbis who collectively produced the corpus of writings known as "rabbinic literature" did not produce epic poems like Homer's *Odyssey* or national historiography along the lines of Thucydides' *History of the Peloponnesian War*.[42] On the rare occasion that they produced histories, the rabbis produced short episodic legends that densely capture important themes. The story of Rabban Yohanan Ben Zakkai and Vespasian is one such legend.

In the ancient world, religion was not a separable piece of cultural activity or identity. Religion was closely related to national activity and identity. In the decades leading up to the Temple's destruction, there was sectarian strife that pitted certain sects against the national religious leadership and its ideology, but even these sects still venerated Jerusalem. Rabbinic Judaism was a movement that gave up on the idea of political autonomy in exchange for a portable and robust religiosity. Rabban

Yohanan ben Zakkai's requests explicitly did not include a request for Jerusalem itself or for political power; he was prepared to sacrifice political hegemony for religious opportunity.

The term "sacrifice" gives pause. In giving up Jerusalem, Rabban Yohanan ben Zakkai not only sacrificed political ambition, he also acquiesced to the loss of the Temple—the building that had been the essential space of the Second Temple cult. Judean religiosity in the Second Temple period required the sacrifices that were the nearly exclusive cultic ritual; these could only be performed in Jerusalem's Temple. Rabban Yohanan ben Zakkai chooses a diasporic form of religiosity with no Temple and sacrifices, effectively renouncing the central religious cultic behaviors of prior generations.

To someone schooled in the Hebrew Bible, the story of the rabbi and the general may be surprising for its failure to directly feature God as a character. The God of the Hebrew Bible is incredibly and overwhelmingly present. God's presence is manifest both in communication and action. Within the patriarchal stories of Genesis, God is a character who interacts with other characters, engaging them in dialogue from on high. As one progresses through the historical time of the biblical story, God remains an active presence, but communication is mediated through the person of the prophet, who is distinguished by his or her ability to hear God's messages. Even though communication with God is limited, the biblical narratives continue to understand God to have an active role in historical events. The legendary encounter with Vespasian models a different mode of relating to God than through direct divine communication or manifestation. When God appears in rabbinic texts, that appearance is often the result of human manipulation. Rabban Yohanan ben Zakkai employs *midrash*, a creative mode of reading the Bible, to *read* God into historical events. God's control of the events of the day is less direct; there are neither Egyptian plagues nor the smiting of an Assyrian army. God is present because the Bible is a lens through which to process world events. The rabbi empowers himself to see God in a world which no longer has a direct prophetic line of communication and no longer witnesses miraculous divine intervention.

Midrash, a form of biblical interpretation which will be further explained below, empowers the rabbi to introduce God into a set of historical events from which God is seemingly absent. God's voice is now the voice of the Bible *as read by the rabbi*. The rabbi is the new prophet who produces God's word in the world.[43] The relationship between God and rabbi differs from the relationship between God and prophet. The God-prophet relationship is a unidirectional one in which God overwhelms the prophet with the message; the prophet, however reluctant, accedes and represents God to the people. The God-rabbi relationship is more aptly characterized as rabbi-God; it is the rabbi who produces God in the world through an act of interpretation.

The legend of the rabbi and the Roman general has been popular throughout Jewish history because it prefigures various events in Jewish realpolitik in the medieval and early modern periods.[44] Gauging the limited likelihood of resisting the enemy, Rabban Yohanan Ben Zakkai strikes up a vertical alliance with the most powerful enemy authority and works out a contract.[45] Pragmatism is strange in a legendary text. Rarely do peoples tout their pragmatic compromises. But the rabbis embrace their status as a political minority by creating a legend that extols a rabbi for just that pragmatism.

This rabbinic legend is often employed to assert that *rabbinic Judaism reinvents Judaism in the wake of the Temple's destruction*. This pithy formulation captures a fundamental truth about the rabbinic project. The legend of the encounter with Vespasian is evidence that the rabbis themselves were occasionally aware of this assessment of their project. But the legend is ahistorical, and the historical record is more complicated than the pithy formulation. By shifting to the unreliability of the story as history, we can attend to an alternative understanding of the rabbis that supplements the reinvention claim with an understanding of the rabbis as a continuation of Second Temple realities.

It is difficult to accept the legend as historiography.[46] It is unlikely that the historical factions in Jerusalem shared the strong commitment to the laws of purity that enables the ruse that gets the rabbi outside the city walls. The opening of the gates to the city to remove the body would literally open the door to the enemy. The similar ease with which Rabban Yohanan ben Zakkai can meet and address the Roman general is suspicious.

External historical data also makes the story hard to accept. Roman sources indicate that Vespasian first seized the title of Caesar in the Middle East and only afterwards received Roman consular approval.[47] The episode in the story would have taken place in 69–70 CE, and shows the rabbis' willing to sacrifice political sovereignty for religious space. But in 132 CE, various rabbis supported Simon ben Kosiba (Bar Kokhba) in his military revolt against Roman rule in Judea to restore Jewish self-rule. Historically, it is the crushing of *this* revolt that eliminated Jewish fantasies of sovereignty.

An autobiographical story nearly identical to the legend of Vespasian and Rabban Yohanan appears in the work of Josephus, the first-century Jewish historian who switched from the Judean to the Roman side in the war and wrote various extant works in Greek about those experiences.[48] *The Jewish War* describes how Josephus, the Judean general, was imprisoned by the Romans upon surrendering. As he was led off in chains, Josephus prophesied that Vespasian would be named the Caesar. When the prediction came true a year later, Vespasian informed his son Titus, and Josephus was elevated to Titus' *aide-de-camp*. Josephus spent the rest of the war on the Roman side before retiring to Rome where he wrote his works.

Though Josephus was a contemporary first century eyewitness to the events described, discrepancies between his own versions and his tendency towards self-aggrandizement make scholars suspicious of his work. In this particular case, Josephus' Vespasian story draws on tropes from the biblical Joseph story in which a Jewish character is imprisoned and elevated to an important political post in exchange for an accurate prophetic prediction.[49] Bracketing the question of the historical reliability of Josephus' story about Vespasian, it is clear that a rabbinic writer, working between two to four centuries after Josephus, was familiar with the basic contours of Josephus' story when the Talmudic legend was crafted.[50]

The unreliability of the legend as historiography throws suspicion on its message that rabbinic Judaism is a post-Temple innovation, and pushes for consideration of an opposing characterization—that the rabbis continue the ideological and social realities that were present during the Second Temple period. *The rabbis magnify and unify the energy of the sectarian movements of the Second Temple period.*[51]

The elite populations of first-century Judea produced several different sects of Judaism. These sects self-segregated from the Jewish population at large—and each other—to engage in religious practices and scholarship. They were polemical rivals divided by core fundamental differences with respect to ideology and law. For all their differences, though, the sects had much in common with one another. They were highly scholastic, predominantly male organizations that filtered the world through a primarily religious lens. Their differing theologies all bore the imprint of apocalypticism, and they were staunchly committed, as both producers and consumers, to the idea of a scriptural canon.

The rabbis were a social group that perpetuated many of the values of these earlier sects without preserving the polemical reality of multiple sects.[52] Some of the rabbis were biological descendants of Pharisees. Acts of the Apostles, a New Testament work, features a Pharisee leader named Gamaliel who saves the apostles from execution by a Jewish tribunal, which flogs them instead.[53] Rabbinic texts fill out the genealogy of Gamaliel's family, tracing a distinguished paternal line from the time of the Pharisees to the time of the rabbis. It is this distinguished family of heirs to sectarian Judaism whom Rabban Yohanan ben Zakkai saves with one of his three requests.

Both the sects and the rabbis actively attempted to resist the overwhelming influence of Hellenistic culture. The Hasmonean monarchy that ruled greater Judea for much of the first two centuries BCE was founded on a revolt that had an element of ideological resistance to Hellenic culture. The Maccabean resistance to Hellenism was but a momentary and minority phenomenon. As the centuries wore on, Judean culture became increasingly indistinguishable from other Hellenic subcultures.[54] The Hasmonean monarchs resembled other vassal kings and their children were sent abroad to receive schooling in Hellenistic schools. The sects that emerged in the last two centuries BCE were, in part, a response to increasing majority Hellenization. In this sense, they continued the trajectory of the zealous Maccabees who had revolted against Antiochus IV and set the Hasmonean Era in motion. As the populace and the royal elite were both becoming more Hellenized, the sects isolated themselves within the hermetic confines of the textual and cultic Jewish tradition. The rabbis carried on this mantle after the Temple's destruction.

Many rabbinic texts speak ill of Greek culture and mandate practices—like prohibitions on teaching Greek to one's children—that are designed to keep Jews from being overrun by Greek ideas and inventions.[55] But by the close of the first century CE, Judea had been under Greco-Roman cultural influence for more than four hundred years. Roughly one-third of the vocabulary in rabbinic Hebrew and rabbinic Aramaic is comprised of words with Greek etymologies.[56] Archeological evidence of the period demonstrates the ubiquitous Greek influence on cultural production from pottery to coinage to sculpture.[57] This helps explain how the structure of the rabbis' primary cultural activity—scholarship—was a Jewish facsimile of Greek scholastic culture.

One of the profound transformations wrought by Hellenism within Greek culture was the transition from the centrality of the city to the centrality of education.[58] That form of education was referred to as *paideia*, a term that meant both education and culture.[59] Where once one would want a child brought up as a warrior in service of city, now one aspired to educate a child through (or to) paideia into the leadership class. Paideia instruction was divided into three tiers: teachers of letters, grammar, and rhetoric, respectively. The elite student was one who could rise to the third tier and excel in its rhetorical exercises.

Similarly, the rabbinic educational movement was part of a transformation from the centrality of city (Jerusalem) to the centrality of education (rabbinic learning). A Jewish child would be trained by a teacher of letters before moving on to a teacher of biblical reading and comprehension.[60] The role of the Bible was like the role of classical literature, which was the subject of instruction in the Greek system. Only advanced learners would progress to study rabbinic basic texts and be trained in the specific skills of argumentation and dialogue that contribute so much to the production of the Talmud. Like the Greeks, who understood paideia as a meritocratic way for lower classes to elevate their position in society, the rabbis understood their social practice of Torah study as a meritocratic enterprise open to all strata of society. Some of the most compelling rabbinic legends are rags-to-riches stories of men who start out ignorant, poor, and powerless before becoming wise, wealthy, and powerful through the vehicle of Torah education.[61]

The legend of Rabban Yohanan ben Zakkai and Vespasian testifies to the idea that the rabbis invented something new that replaced the Temple-based Judaism that had been rendered impossible by Jerusalem's destruction. At the same time, critical examination of the legend's limitations as history allows one to see that the rabbis both continued the legacy of the sects that thrived in the late Second Temple period, and drew upon a Hellenistic intellectual educational model.

Theology: Torah as Abstract Ideal

Legends are not the only types of texts in which the rabbis produced their own origin stories, and the rabbis did not always connect their origins with the destruction of

Jerusalem. At times, the rabbis indeed told their story as an uninterrupted continuation of prior religious realities. *Ethics of the Fathers*, a *sui generis* tractate of the Mishnah that is a compilation of proverbs and ethical teachings, opens with a chain of transmission that connects rabbinic literature with God's revelation at Sinai:

> Moses received the Torah from Sinai and transmitted it
> to Joshua;
> and Joshua to the elders;
> and the elders to the prophets;
> and the prophets transmitted it to the men of the Great
> Assembly . . .
> Simeon the righteous one was one of the remaining
> members of the men of the Great Assembly . . .
> (*Mishnah Avot* 1:1–2)

Within a few words, the text moves from revelation on Mount Sinai to the late Second Temple period. The text's continuation is a bit more complicated, but a few additional generational links reach the period of the *tannaim*, the rabbis who were active before the oral publication of the Mishnah around the year 200 CE.

In the opening line of this chain, Torah is the entity that Moses receives and transmits to the rabbinic present. The chain of transmission is a genre employed in the Greek writings of near contemporary Stoic philosophers.[62] While the Stoics were interested in philosophical *truth*, the rabbis were interested in *Torah*. "Torah" literally means teaching, but the type of lesson implied by the word Torah led Egyptian Jews to translate the term into

Greek as "*nomos*" or law. "Torah" is the teaching of a religious way of being in the world.

The text describes Moses as receiving Torah "from" Sinai. The sentence makes Sinai (rather than God) the object of the preposition "from"—the *mountain* is the source of this teaching. This displacement of God is not incidental; it reflects a broader rabbinic substitution of the abstract value of Torah for the concrete God whose tangible home in Jerusalem no longer exists. [63]

The theology of the rabbis is often characterized as a doctrine of two Torahs: a written Torah produced with ink on parchment, and an oral Torah produced in an unwritten ether of transmission from teacher to student, that encapsulates ideas of Judaism not contained within the verses of the written Torah's text. This helpful characterization of rabbinic theology ends up producing the oral Torah as an analog to the written—one could imagine the oral Torah as a virtual text containing all the traditions missing from the written Torah. In the opening to *Ethics of the Fathers*, in contrast, Torah is not a text but an abstract concept. Moses is not receiving a second (oral) book.[64] Moses receives an idea of Torah more powerful than any tangible book.

Throughout their writings, the rabbis display a profound commitment to Torah that transcends its function as an educational book or a ritual object. Torah is the rabbinic *raison d'être*. Life derives meaning from its association with the exercise of learning and living Torah. Though the rabbis value biblical laws and understand the Bible's mandates as the specific commands of a divine

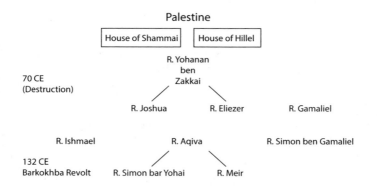

Palestine

| House of Shammai | House of Hillel |

R. Yohanan ben Zakkai

70 CE (Destruction)

R. Joshua — R. Eliezer — R. Gamaliel

R. Ishmael — R. Aqiva — R. Simon ben Gamaliel

132 CE Barkokhba Revolt

R. Simon bar Yohai — R. Meir

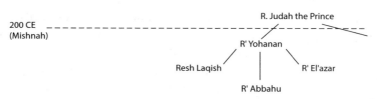

R. Judah the Prince

200 CE (Mishnah)

R' Yohanan

Resh Laqish — R' Abbahu — R' El'azar

300 CE

400 CE

FIGURE 1.1. Selective Genealogy of the Rabbis

commander, commitment to Torah study supersedes. While the rabbis do not advocate a monastic disappearance from the world, Torah study challenges material needs, and Torah relationships challenge those of flesh and blood.[65] Scholastic pursuit of Torah-as-ideal epitomizes religious commitment. Along the way, the

Babylonia

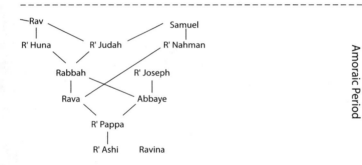

prioritization of Torah and the scholastic way of life that commits fully to its acquisition, threatens the religious primacy of God, ritual, liturgy, and all other cultic aspects of Judaism. And this prioritization is profoundly important to the biography of the Talmud for two reasons. First, because the Talmud is the result of this scholastic

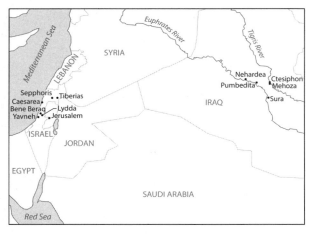

FIGURE I.2. Map of Palestine/Babylonia

prioritization—it was produced as part of this new cultural commitment to Torah above all. Second, because it is the cause of this increased prioritization—its discourse of reception made it into the central piece of a religion built around scholasticism as religious devotion. *Within a religious production that has rewritten its story and changed its lead from God to Torah, the part of Torah has been played for over a millennium by the Babylonian Talmud.*

How the Talmud Was Made

The early rabbis engaged in scholastic activity in small *ad hoc* disciple circles; each consisted of a charismatic rabbi surrounded by a handful of students.[66] In the period immediately surrounding the destruction of the Second Temple and for the next hundred years, the rabbis engaged in two pedagogical practices—one primarily interpretive and the other primarily a mode of organizing the interpreted material. The interpretive method of study was called midrash while the organizational articulation was called mishnah.[67]

Midrash

During the Second Temple period, the Hebrew Bible was becoming both increasingly central and more solidly fixed. The early rabbis studied their Bible in ways that contributed both to the nature of canonical authority (what it means for there to be a canon) and to the contours of the canon (what is included and what excluded).[68] They read their Bible in almost absurdly punctilious ways. In the hands of these rabbis, the Hebrew Bible became a cryptic code in need of deciphering. Every nonessential component of syntax (and even spelling) came to be understood as an opportunity for producing new meanings, whether legal, narrative, or theological. Biblical stories were expanded in plot, characterization, and drama; the nature of all things theological (God, heavens, Torah, angels, etc.) became richer; legal statutes were made both more specific and principled. At the same time, the rabbis developed a technique of resolving issues in one book of the Hebrew Bible through recourse to another passage of the Hebrew Bible.[69] This, even though the Hebrew Bible is an anthology of works in different genres written by different authors at different times. Whether self-consciously or not, the rabbis read verses in the book of Genesis, for example, in light of some in the Song of Songs and vice versa. This reading practice both reflected the rabbis' understanding of the boundaries of the biblical canon and solidified those boundaries by broadcasting which books were to be included as part of the hermeneutic corpus.

Mishnah

Even as the rabbis devoted significant backward glances at the Bible, they also engaged in a form of study that produced something new. This pedagogical process involved formulating their religious culture in statutory form as law. The ritual requirements of prayer, the calendrical requirements of the holidays, the particulars of sacraments and sacrifices; all of these were formulated as religious statutes. This procedure produced clarity within a cultural environment in which both inherited practices and interpretive polysemy could produce confusion about everything from basic requirements to smaller details. Organization was a major purpose of this form of pedagogy. The anthological makeup of the Hebrew Bible contributed a basic lack of substantive organization to the Hebrew Bible; the exegetical practice of reading across the corpus further undermined even local coverage of a religious subject. If the exegetical practices allowed the creative free work associated with the right side of the brain, the statutory formulation organized the material as might the left side of the brain.

Over the course of the post-Temple period, the two pedagogical practices of midrash and mishnah influenced each other but remained separate. During the second century CE, various rabbinic disciple circles developed their own approaches and produced varying versions of similar works. Within the world of midrash, Rabbi Aqiva and Rabbi Ishmael (both active in the first half of the second century) developed slightly different, consistent philosophies.[70] On a hermeneutic (rather than ideological) level, Ishmael was restrained and Aqiva creative.[71] What Aqiva interpreted as an extraneous feature (worthy of interpretation), Ishmael considered a regular feature of language. These philosophical differences led to the production of two midrashic oral traditions covering four Pentateuchal books (Exodus, Leviticus, Numbers, and Deuteronomy).[72]

Among the rabbis who constituted the Aqiva school of midrash, a standard practice developed to produce works of legal statutes covering all the topics of Judaism. This pedagogical process continued until the end of the second century, when a political figure and scholar, Rabbi Judah the Prince, gathered the different mishnah traditions, edited, and redacted them into the definitive Mishnah ("the Mishnah"). The Mishnah consists of sixty tractates that are organized into six orders. The Mishnah contains three levels of organization: there is a rationale for individual orders (e.g., Moed includes tractates related to holidays and the calendar), for individual tractates (e.g., Sukkot has its own tractate within Moed) and for individual chapters (e.g., the rules regarding the gathering of the four species on Sukkot are delineated in their own chapter in tractate Sukkah).[73]

Production of the Mishnah had a major effect on the rabbis. Over time, the Mishnah became so authoritative that it produced a chronological dividing line for the rabbis: those rabbis who lived early enough to be included in the Mishnah were called tannaim, and those rabbis active after the Mishnah's proliferation were called amoraim. It would eventually come to be understood within the rabbinic community that an *amora* could not directly contest the opinion of a *tanna*. The arrival of the Mishnah also affected the way in which the rabbis studied. Where tannaim bifurcated their study time into mishnah-style and midrash-style conversations, amoraim developed talmud-style conversations by formally structuring their study around the Mishnah but including midrash in those conversations.

Talmud

As midrash was a freestyle conversation surrounding Bible, talmud was a freestyle conversation surrounding the Mishnah. A mishnaic text is usually a statute which states a requirement or prohibition clearly without authoritative source or rationale. Talmudic discussions often begin by asking, "how do we know this?" about a mishnaic rule. The answer to the question is typically a midrashic explication of a biblical verse. In this way, the

Talmudic discussion opens the Mishnah to the rich lode of rationales and verse interpretations of midrash. Several generations of rabbis (Figure 1.1) in both Palestine and Babylonia conducted talmud conversations. Through these conversations, the Palestinian and Babylonian amoraim produced new midrashic interpretations of the Bible, new mishnah-style statements of law and new interpretations of the Mishnah's laws. The amoraim often disagreed with one another about these types of text. These distinct types of text (midrashic interpretations, mishnah statements, amoraic arguments about prior texts, etc.) are all captured within the two extant Talmuds, the Palestinian and Babylonian.

The Palestinian and Babylonian Talmuds are similar in form and content, but have significant differences. The Palestinian Talmud attributes ideas to rabbis who lived until the middle of the fourth century CE, while the Babylonian Talmud attributes ideas to rabbis who lived until the end of the fourth century CE. This additional gestation period is accompanied in the Babylonian Talmud by a comparatively richer layer of anonymous editorial text. These unattributed words function as signposts that alert the reader to turns within the text. A reader well-schooled in the Babylonian Talmud can have trouble reading the Palestinian because it comparatively lacks these internal textual aids.

Despite the nearly equivalent number of tractates (thirty-three for the Babylonian and thirty-six for the Palestinian) in the respective Talmuds, the Babylonian is considerably longer than its Palestinian counterpart in both length of individual conversations and the number of such conversations per mishnaic legal subject. [74] The Palestinian Talmud also often replicates identical passages in multiple tractates; when this phenomenon is taken into account, the Palestinian Talmud shrinks in size by a third.[75] The conversational style of the Talmud and its origins in a social educational practice led most traditional readers to the presumption that the Talmuds are a transcription of actual rabbinic conversations. This is not the case. The insufficiency of this paradigm is evident when one looks closely at the Talmud's multi-generational character. Since the Talmud's conversations span across centuries, the Talmud's literary conversations are evidently manufactured. The standard stylistic uniformity in the presentation of debates also indicates an editor's framing of controversy. In the past four decades, scholars have demonstrated that the anonymous editorial layer of the Bavli (Babylonian Talmud) routinely reflects a chronologically later voice that goes beyond framing the earlier debates and produces itself as the evolutionarily final approach to matters of law or theology.[76]

The final editors of the Talmud (sometimes referred to in the singular as the *Stam*—meaning anonymous, or in the plural as the *Stammaim*), are responsible for altering and framing the inherited traditions that are embedded in a Talmudic passage. The words of the Stam are the clearest site for identifying a conscious editing of the text.

The rabbis were active in two regions: Palestine and Babylonia (Figure 1.2). The rabbis of Palestine produced more than twenty works that survived the vagaries of oral, handwritten, and print transmission and are available for readers today.[77] *The rabbis of Babylonia produced only one surviving work, the Babylonian Talmud!* The Babylonians left no independent works of mishnah or midrash.[78] They used the Talmud to collect the opinions and interpretations of Babylonian rabbis from the second through the sixth centuries and perhaps even later. It is possible that the Babylonian rabbis produced many works, but none of them survived. It is also possible that the Babylonian rabbis produced only one *magnum opus*, the Babylonian Talmud, and used it as a repository for every scholastic idea. Either the Bavli overwhelmed all competition such that it did not survive or no other works were created. A single work produced over the longest duration of any rabbinic text, the Bavli encapsulates all rabbinic creativity and organization.

Multiplicity (the existence of more than one authorized statement on a topic) and polysemy (openness to multiple interpretations) are two hallmarks of rabbinic literature. Multiplicity emerged incidentally out of the editorial decision to incorporate multiple mishnaic traditions within a single definitive text.[79] The Mishnah registers differences by simple attribution (e.g., "Rabbi X said" or "these are the words of Rabbi Y"), without hand wringing or soul searching about the availability of multiple legal possibilities; frequently the Mishnah authorizes both one position and its binary opposite.

Polysemy is a byproduct of midrashic creativity.[80] The exercise of freely producing meaning out of material perceived to be extraneous is a creative process that invites multiple outcomes. Even as there are restrictions on midrashic creativity, midrash can be characterized as an exercise in producing fuller and more detailed understandings of texts in a mode that builds off the possibility of multiple interpretations. The Talmuds build on both multiplicity and polysemy by producing new generational layers of mishnah-style statutory rule and debate; this process involves registering several generations of rabbinic interpretation of scripture, Mishnah, or midrash, and allows such interpretation to grow with minimal restraint and with new and explicit justifications. Though neither multiplicity nor polysemy originated as determined ideological stances, later rabbinic texts came to understand these phenomena as such. A retrospective rabbinic judgment found in the Mishnah touts multiplicity as a boon to judicial fairness and the possibility of change.[81] The Talmud's late anonymous voice explicitly embraces both multiplicity and polysemy in theological terms as representing a divinely authorized pluralism.[82]

The Babylonian Talmud is the largest collection of rabbinic ideas, interpretations, or stories. Its lengthy period of gestation allowed it to evolve the most advanced explicit theorizations of pluralism and to develop the most sophisticated conceptualizations of abstract legal concepts. By combining the earlier rabbinic genres of mishnah and midrash into a meta-genre, and incorporating insights from seven centuries of rabbis in two distinct, robust regions of operation, the Babylonian Talmud was able to produce the most thorough and comprehensive version of rabbinic Judaism.

Anatomy
(ESSENTIAL TALMUD PART TWO)

CHAPTER 2

A biography of the Talmud would be incomplete without passages that communicate not only Talmudic content, but also the experience of studying the Talmud. The Talmud is extremely varied in both form and content. It is an anthology or compendium of the ideas of the rabbis. The prior chapter characterizes an important early rabbinic (pre-Mishnah) dichotomy that distinguishes between specific types of textual activity (midrashic study of the Bible v. mishnaic statute production). Another nascent distinction within the content of the curriculum also began to develop in which there was a compartmentalization of rabbinic ideas into buckets that would eventually, in the post-Talmudic era, come to have fixed identities as halakhah [law] and aggadah [non-law].[1] This dichotomy has been central to the study of the Talmud because it is useful for picking up on inherent variations within and among different Talmudic passages. This chapter opens with a Talmudic story that testifies to both the emergence of the dichotomization of halakhah and aggadah, and to the resistance to this division. Following the story, the chapter returns to treat the Talmudic passage on fire liability in greater depth and then shifts to a nonlegal example.

Halakhah and Aggadah: Bald on Both Sides

The sixth chapter of the Mishnah tractate Baba Qamma discusses individual liability for damage done by one's animals or objects. Citing Exodus 22:5, the fourth mishnah says that if one lights a fire that consumes wood or stone, the person who lit the fire is liable for the damage. This seemingly mundane topic becomes the setting for a sublime Talmudic passage that tells the story of an interaction between three third-century Palestinian scholars—a teacher and his two students—and introduces an important division in the rabbinic curriculum:

> Rav Ammi and Rav Assi were sitting before Rav Isaac Nappaha.[2]
>
> One said to [Rav Isaac], "let the master teach (something from)[3] the [halakhic legal][4] tradition," and the other said to [Rav Isaac], "let the master teach (something from)[5] the aggadah (nonlegal tradition)."
>
> [Rav Isaac] began to say something from the aggadah[6] and one [of the students] would not leave him be; [Rav Isaac] began to say something from the [halakhic legal] tradition and the other [of the students] would not leave him be.
>
> [Rav Isaac] said to them, "I will draw a parable for you; to what is this comparable? To a man who has

two wives, one a maiden and one a dowager. The maiden plucks his white [hairs] and the dowager plucks his black [hairs]; he ends up being bald from this [side] and that [side]."[7]

[Rav Isaac] said to them, "if so,[8] I will say something to you that will be worthwhile for both of you.

'When fire spreads and finds thorns—spreads: on its own—the person who lights the fire must pay (Exodus 22:5).'"

The Holy One Blessed Be He says, 'I spread the fire in Jerusalem'[9] as it says

'And He spread fire in Zion (and it consumed its foundations)[10] (Lamentations 4:11)'
and I will eventually rebuild her with fire as it says, 'And I will be for her[11] an encircling fire wall (and my glory will be inside her) (Zekhariah 2:9).'[12]
'*The person who lights the fire must pay* (Exodus 22:5):'

The Holy One Blessed Be He says, 'it is incumbent upon me to compensate for the fire that I kindled.'

[Halakhic Legal] tradition: the verse begins with a tort committed by property but concludes with a personal liability [kind of] tort to teach you that one's fire is like his arrow [i.e., an extension of his body and liability].

The disciple circle was the real world setting in which rabbinic literature was produced. A small group of rabbinical students attended a single charismatic teacher who would instruct them in the finer points of biblical exegesis and legal logic.[13] In this story, the students lobby aggressively for their favorite respective subjects. One of the students wants Rav Isaac to teach something in the spirit of the Mishnah's focus on legal cases and their interpretation. The other student prefers that Rav Isaac choose an inspirational homily from the nonlegal tradition. When Rav Isaac begins to speak, neither student concedes the point and allows the lecture to begin on their non-preferred subject matter. Rav Isaac analogizes this to the fable of a man with both a young and an old wife; each wife tries to produce the husband that matches her circumstance but the combined efforts create a husband less attractive to everyone.[14] Through the parable Rav Isaac communicates his need for space to begin the lecture; otherwise, neither of the students will have the benefits of his teaching. Having chastised the students with the fable, Rav Isaac unifies his students by sequentially offering homiletical and legal interpretations of a single biblical verse, the verse about liability for spreading fire.

Rav Isaac begins with a homily that employs the rabbinic technique of reading across sections of the Bible to transform the verse's notion of fire liability into a comforting divine promise. Rabbinic homilies were part of ancient synagogue practice and such homilies had a template.[15] Standard rabbinic homiletic technique initially wove a verse from the Torah [the Pentateuch that comprises the first third of the Hebrew Bible or *Tanakh*] with a verse from the *Kethubim* [the Writings section that comprises the last third of the *Tanakh*]. Rav Isaac's homily connects the notion of damaged property by fire to the burning of Jerusalem's first Temple as discussed in Lamentations. The connection allows God to take responsibility as the force that sent the Babylonians against Jerusalem—the agent who initiated the fire. Because God started the fire, God must pay for the damages. After the initial connection between the Torah and the *Kethubim*, a homilist would sometimes draw an additional connection to the *Nebi'im* [the Prophets section that comprises the middle third of the *Tanakh*]. Rav Isaac follows this template and finds a verse in Zekhariah in which God asserts a plan to function as Jerusalem's external wall of fire. In its biblical context, the wall of fire is a virtual wall that replaces the destroyed stone wall of Jerusalem and is flexible enough to allow for Jerusalem's expansion. Deftly, the homilist uses the fire imagery to link to the verses in both Exodus and Lamentations. Zekhariah 2:9 is read as a promise that the God who sent the fire of destruction will produce a fire of rehabilitation; and all of this is previewed in the basic tort lesson of Exodus 22 that the one who sends a damaging fire must pay for it. This reading is not only deft but extremely clever in its rendering of the precise meaning of Exodus 22:5. While the simplest grammatical understanding of the words of the verse is that the kindler pays for the fire, the word "fire" in the verse is an ambiguous direct object. Rav Isaac's homily reinterprets the word "fire" to be the object of the act of payment—to say that the kindler must *pay* with another fire.[16]

While the creativity inherent in Rav Isaac's homily is self-evident, the amora is equally creative in teaching Exodus 22:5 as a legal statement. The contextual meaning of the verse is that one who sets a fire is liable for the fire's damage. Rav Isaac, though, notes the tension between the opening verb of the verse, which imputes agency to the fire by making it the sentence's subject ("when a fire spreads . . ."), and the final clause, which renders the fire the liability of the kindler ("the kindler of the fire must pay"). This tension, Rav Isaac asserts, encodes the lesson that fire liability is *not* a function of the owner's responsibility for *property*, but *personal* liability for an act that extends the owner's body. Though fire, like a goring ox, possesses independent energy that makes it difficult to understand as an extension of the kindler's person, the tension between verbal subjects in the sentence highlights the message that fire is to be considered an extension of one's body—a spear or an arrow—rather than as an independent but owned entity such as a goring ox.

This passage introduces the concept that rabbinic learning is divided into two subjects—ones that would come to be more firmly labeled halakhah and aggadah in the post-Talmudic period. Even as the story encodes tension between these two subjects, it also evokes a fundamental unity of the two. The two rabbinic students wish to tease the subjects apart and specialize, but this energy is *resisted* by the figure of Rav Isaac, who is a master of *both* subjects. In his response to the students, Rav Isaac employs a fable that analogizes the two subjects to two wives; this analogy also produces a unified image of a single husband. When he finally lectures, Rav Isaac employs a *single verse* to teach both halakhah and aggadah, again communicating the idea that the subjects are intertwined.

Even though Rav Isaac presents them sequentially, seemingly conceding that the subjects cannot be handled together, he has produced overlapping interpretations that can be read not just sequentially, but together. The idea that God is responsible for destroying the Temple and that God will eventually rebuild it, is *magnified* by the legal interpretation that fire liability is the personal liability of an arrow and not the property liability of a goring ox. God accepts responsibility for the destruction of both Temples because the Babylonians and Romans are not God's property—they are extensions of the divine body or the divine will. An ambitious reader might read the *aggadah into the halakhah* and say that the aggadic interpretation of Zekhariah provides grounds for preferring restoration or restitution to compensation.

Following the paradigm of Rav Isaac, this chapter employs two paradigmatic Talmudic passages as an example. One of them is a continuation of the fire liability passage that was teased in the prior chapter. This kind of passage is typically classified as halakhah. The other is a much shorter text about the coerced giving of the Torah at Mount Sinai that is generally classified as part of the aggadah. Both passages will be the basis for further consideration of the Talmud's reception in subsequent chapters.

Halakhic Pericope: Fire Liability

One of the hallmarks of the Talmud is its internal variety. Even within legal sections, no two passages of the Talmud are identical in content or form. The dissimilarity in content is to be expected of a corpus whose base text (the Mishnah) ranges from agricultural law to the laws of purity, with ritual law, family law, criminal law, and civil law somewhere in between; the dissimilarity in form is less expected. If genre is a contract between writer and reader, the Talmud's genre is more of an informal agreement.[17] One could analogize the Talmud to jazz music; both are formal structures that mask their organization and provide opportunities for individualized creative expression.

The search for unified form in the Talmud is not entirely hopeless. The Talmud is consistent in its terminology. Some of the Talmud's language has a specific and recognizable patter that allows the reader to follow question-and-answer or to understand when there has been an abrupt shift in interest. Special phrases in the Talmud prepare the reader for a familiar set of logical operations—in some cases a term will predict the next two moves in the passage. This terminological density is aided by scribal stylizations that have transpired during the long history of the copying of the Talmud and have made the text easier to study. Consistent introductions have been inserted into the text to indicate the use of a citation from a mishnah or a *beraita* [a tannaitic text preserved outside of the Mishnah]. Other terminology evolved during textual transmission to signal when a source is being challenged from a local passage or a remote one, from a tannaitic source or from an amoraic one. The phraseology and terminology comprise a distinct language of the Talmud that allows someone who has been schooled in the reading of one chapter or tractate to have the confidence to read the next.[18]

Talmudic Fire Liability

On February 4, 2008, faulty wiring triggered a fire that set the 3,000-tire stock of Wyvern Tyres, a tire supplier in Hereford, England, ablaze. Tires are not particularly flammable, but are hard to extinguish once lit. Despite the efforts of firefighters, the fire spread from the premises of Wyvern Tyres and destroyed the neighboring property of Robert Gore. Gore sued Mark Stannard, owner of Wyvern Tyres; Worcester County Court ruled in Gore's favor because the unnatural method of storing tires made Stannard liable. At issue was a concept introduced by an 1868 House of Lords decision (Rylands v. Fletcher) that makes one responsible for storing something that is likely to do mischief if it escapes. A three-judge panel of England's Court of Appeals overturned the lower court's ruling and exempted Stannard from liability because it was the *fire* that was likely to do mischief and not the tires. The ruling in Stannard v. Gore has been characterized as a shift away from a view that one is always liable for fire that destroys a neighbor's property.[19] Though the modern conversation about fire liability includes notions of macroeconomics that are more modern than Talmudic debates about these matters, contemporary law is still contending with the challenge of fire. The law can have trouble handling fire. Civil law demands accountability according to strict rules, but fire is hard to predict or control. The texture of the legal complexity of fire liability makes such a case an ideal one for Talmudic discourse. And the Talmud does not disappoint. The Talmudic passage that follows (and that was briefly introduced in chapter 1) teases apart a functioning conceptual model for understanding liability for fire damage.

Mishnah Baba Qamma 2:3

The Mishnah is a code of laws that articulates most of its concepts through the presentation of cases rather than categorical principles. This case-based or casuistic style is the style of most ancient law codes; biblical legal material is also largely casuistic. Mishnah Baba Qamma 2:3b reads:

> A dog who took a cake [baking on top of a coal] and walked to a haystack: he ate the cake and ignited the haystack:
>
> [its owner] pays full liability for the cake, and half liability for the haystack.

A dog eats a cake attached to a coal (on which it had been baking) and causes the coal to ignite a destructive fire. The mishnah rules that the dog's owner is liable for the full amount of the eaten cake and for half of the value of the fire-damaged haystack.[20]

The Talmud's discussion of this mishnah consists of a prologue and three subsequent sections. The prologue outlines a conceptual debate about fire liability: the first section attempts to prove the matter for one side in the debate; the second section asserts a later rabbi's support for that same side in the debate; the final section supports the other side of the debate and undermines the terms of the debate itself. Traditional ways of thinking about the text will inform the initial presentation of this material. After this initial presentation, the chapter will return to the material while incorporating a critical lens.

Babyonian Talmud Tractate Baba Qamma 22a–23a

Prologue: The Debate between Third-Century Palestinian Rabbis

The Talmud has a well-deserved reputation for being loosely structured. Some passages, though, have clear structure.[21] The passage under consideration here begins with a prologue and first section that are well-structured before slipping into a loose structure that is perhaps more typical for the Talmud. For purposes of presentation, the passage is divided into a prologue and three sections; no such division exists in the original text. The prologue positions the discussion of fire liability as a conceptual categorical debate between two prominent third-century Palestinian rabbis, Resh Laqish and R' Yohanan:

> R' Yohanan says, "his fire because of his arrow."
> Resh Laqish says, "his fire because of his money."

R' Yohanan's position is even pithier in its three-word Hebrew original than in translation. An analogy is drawn between fire and an arrow. Both can produce

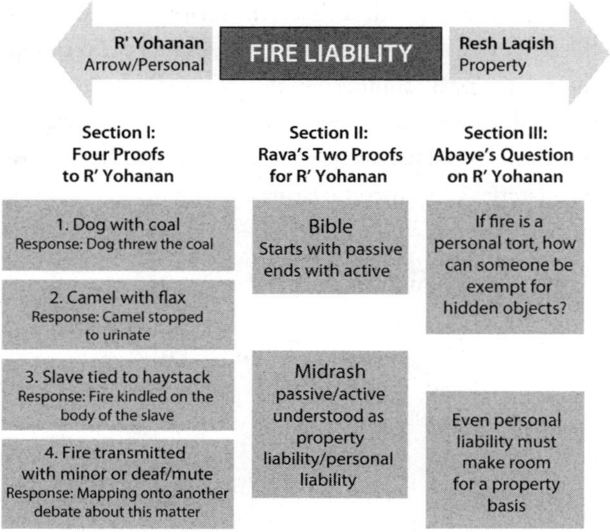
R' Yohanan
Arrow/Personal
FIRE LIABILITY
Resh Laqish
Property
Section I:
Four Proofs
to R' Yohanan
Section II:
Rava's Two Proofs
for R' Yohanan
Section III:
Abaye's Question
on R' Yohanan
1. Dog with coal
Response: Dog threw the coal
2. Camel with flax
Response: Camel stopped to urinate
3. Slave tied to haystack
Response: Fire kindled on the body of the slave
4. Fire transmitted with minor or deaf/mute
Response: Mapping onto another debate about this matter
Bible
Starts with passive ends with active
Midrash
passive/active understood as property liability/personal liability
If fire is a personal tort, how can someone be exempt for hidden objects?
Even personal liability must make room for a property basis

FIGURE 2.1. Overview of Fire Liability Passage, Baba Qamma 22a–23a.

damage at a distance. A kindler is responsible for a fire's damage just as a hunter is liable for the action of the arrow. Resh Laqish mirrors his mentor's three-word phrase with his own three-word phrase. In his view, responsibility for fire is likened to responsibility for damage done by anything owned. As an owner must guard an animal to ensure that it does not damage, one must similarly guard one's fire.

Both R' Yohanan and Resh Laqish make fire more sensible by drawing an analogy to an already established and clearer area of law. R' Yohanan thinks of fire as a weapon controlled by the person wielding it. Resh Laqish thinks of fire as an independent agent over which one exercises supervision and for which one takes responsibility. Both are sensible ways of understanding fire liability.

Before the Talmud gets to the business of trying to decide between these two positions, it offers rationales that justify why R' Yohanan and Resh Laqish do not opt for the other's approach. R' Yohanan does not like the analogy to property because property is tangible and fire intangible. Resh Laqish does not like the analogy to an arrow because fire has the capacity to travel on its own, while an arrow can only move when set in motion by a hunter.

SECTION ONE: FOUR ATTEMPTED PROOFS AND THEIR REJECTIONS

After introducing the debate, the Talmud attempts to prove that the law follows R' Yohanan that fire liability operates on an arrow paradigm in four ways. The Talmud does not succeed in proving that the law follows R' Yohanan; each of its proofs are rebutted on behalf of Resh Laqish.

Proof One: The Dog

The first attempt utilizes the specific mishnah (the dog eating the cake) as a prooftext. The choice of this text as a proof for R' Yohanan is a bit surprising. Since the mishnah is talking about a case of property liability (one is liable because of the owned dog) it hardly seems the ideal site for proving arrow-based personal liability for fire. Nevertheless, the Talmud focuses on the mishnah's assertion that the dog's owner is liable for half of the damages to the burnt haystack. The Talmud claims that this makes sense by analogy from a person to a dog—if fire is a person's arrow, then fire is the dog's arrow and the owner is responsible for the dog. But on a property-based notion of fire liability, the indirect connection between the fire-damaged haystack and the dog's owner calls liability into question. Why should the owner be liable for even half of the haystack?[22]

> The Talmud answers on Resh Laqish's behalf:
> Resh Laqish would have said that this is a case in which the dog threw the coal.
> The owner is liable for the full cost of the cake, half the cost of the spot on which the thrown coal landed, and exempt for the remainder of the haystack.

This is a classically confusing Talmudic answer. Instead of simply explaining *how* Resh Laqish could understand the half liability of the haystack, the Talmud's creates *three* sites of damage where the Mishnah had only had *two*. While the mishnah distinguished between the eating of the cake (s_1) and the burning of the haystack (s_2), this new version of the case has three sites: the cake (s_1), the moment of the ignition (s_2) and the rest of the haystack (s_3). Resh Laqish has answered the question by re-narrativizing the scenario to include the fact that the dog *threw* the coal. This additional factor creates a site at which Resh Laqish can assert partial liability (the site of the ignition) for burnt hay.

Let us unpack the logic slowly. The owner is responsible for the dog. The dog's actions generate liability. When the dog eats the cake, there is no question that the owner is fully liable. By introducing the throwing of the coal, the Talmud extends the physical action of the dog. The thrown coal suggested by the Talmud as an answer for Resh Laqish (who rejects arrow liability), ironically, is like a projected arrow. The owner is liable for the landing spot of the thrown coal because the dog is directly responsible for this damage. The owner is not liable for the remainder of the haystack because the spreading fire is not directly under ownership. The case of this mishnah is not an instantiation of the idea that fire liability is predicated on property liability, but it similarly does not prove that fire liability must be predicated on arrow liability. The thrust of the proof has been parried.

Proof Two: The Camel

The second of the Talmud's four attempted proofs utilizes a mishnah from elsewhere in the tractate (BQ 6:6) in which a different animal spreads fire. A laden camel walks through a public market with its owner, enters a storefront, and its flax load becomes enflamed, causing the transfer of fire from the shopkeeper's candle to the larger building, burning it to the ground. In its initial clause, the mishnah states unequivocally that the camel's owner is liable. In its second clause, though, the mishnah says that if the shopkeeper kept the candle outside the store in the public thoroughfare, the shopkeeper is liable. The lesson of the juxtaposed cases is that the camel's owner is liable for its fire damage unless the shopkeeper's negligence makes the shopkeeper the more liable party.

This mishnah is fundamentally predicated on property liability. The camel's owner is liable for damage created by the camel unless the shopkeeper's negligence changes the equation. Again, though, the Talmud asserts that the case works well for the *arrow liability* paradigm. If fire as an arrow is a direct extension of the camel, it is sensible that the owner of the camel should be liable for the damage done by this fire. But how can the property liability position make the camel's owner liable for damage done by the shopkeeper's fire? The Talmud again produces a hypothetical response for Resh Laqish:

[The case is one in which the camel] spreads [fire] all over the building.
    Since the animal is directly responsible for the fire damage, the animal's owner is responsible for the actions of the animal.
    (If so)[23], when the second clause says that the shopkeeper is liable, why is the shopkeeper liable?

If the animal actively spreads the fire, it should not matter whether the shopkeeper left the candle inside or outside the shop. The animal's owner should be liable.

In a case in which [the animal] stopped.[24]
    But if it stopped and spread the fire actively even more so (its owner should be liable)?[25]

Rabbi Huna bar Manoah said in the name of Rav Ikka,[26] "this is a scenario in which [the camel] stopped to urinate. In the first clause, the camel's owner is liable for not removing the animal's load.[27] In the second clause the shopkeeper is liable for leaving the candle outside the shop."

Rav Ikka modifies the mishnah so that the animal at the center of the action is immobile. Because the animal is immobile, attention is placed, instead, on the animal's load. The load transfers the fire, and the mishnah's two clauses diverge over the question of whether the camel's owner is liable (for not removing the load) or the shopkeeper is liable (for negligence in placement of the fire-lamp). Where the first prooftext (the dog) was rebutted by creating property liability out of the owner's liability for the animal, the second prooftext (the camel) is rebutted by creating property liability out of the owner's *negligence* regarding the camel's load. For Resh Laqish, this is not a case of fire liability but of property negligence regarding the load.

Proof Three: Things Tied to the Haystack

The third proof relies on the "doctrine of simultaneity,"[28] a concept that ensures that a criminal never suffers two punishments for a single crime. If, for example, a person commits a capital offense (murder) through an act that would ordinarily generate a financial penalty (e.g., theft), the person is only liable for the death penalty and is exempt from financial liability. The "doctrine of simultaneity" includes the word "simultaneity" because simultaneity is fundamental to this unique exemption. Only an act that *simultaneously* generates multiple punishments is eligible for this exemption. Two acts against one victim that are not simultaneous do not generate an exemption and the criminal is liable for both punishments. Mishnah Baba Qamma 6:5 says:

> If one set a haystack on fire ... [and] it had a goat tied to it and a slave standing next to it and [they were][29] burned, the kindler is liable [for the haystack and goat; the slave is presumed to run away].
>
> [If, however,] the slave was tied to the haystack and the goat was standing next to it, the kindler is not liable [for the haystack or goat].

The Mishnah often juxtaposes similar scenarios with different laws to communicate an underlying idea. The juxtaposed mishnaic clauses in the present example end up with opposite legal rulings that seem to more strongly punish a lesser offense. The basis for this paradox is the "doctrine of simultaneity." If one lights a slave on fire, the capital punishment exempts the criminal from financial liability.

At times, the Talmud presents moral challenges for contemporary readers. The Talmud is not of our era and some of its material assumes morally problematic positions on race and gender. The present example reflects the historical realities of the rabbinic world when it talks without self-consciousness about slaves. Because Talmudic discourse often engages deeply with hypothetical but engaging scenarios, readers can quickly find themselves thinking deeply within a set of categories that are, by modern standards, morally offensive. Immersion in the sea of Talmud can feel like time travel. It is advisable to explicitly label material that is problematic by today's standards and to create distance between ancient assumptions about patriarchy, hierarchy, or gender, and contemporary analogs. Slavery was an ancient reality but is universally recognized today as fundamentally evil. To understand the rabbis' ideas, one needs to engage the notion of owned persons, but that should be done with the recognition of the foreignness and moral problematics of this institution.

To understand fire as the source of capital punishment is to understand fire as a weapon with murder as its result. This works well with an arrow-based notion of fire liability. But if one thinks of fire as a form of property, it is hard to understand the invocation of the "doctrine of simultaneity." Is one ever subject to capital punishment for a crime committed by one's property? The Talmud, in the fire liability passage's continuation, phrases the question this way:

> According to the view that fire liability is property liability, if one's ox killed a servant would there similarly be an exemption from [financial] liability?

The question is a *reductio ad absurdum*—it is clear to all that one is not liable for capital punishment for the ox's murder of a servant.[30] Since the example of the "doctrine of simultaneity" statute does not seem to work within a property understanding of fire liability, the case represents a question on Resh Laqish. As in the previous cases, an answer is provided on Resh Laqish's behalf that rewrites the basic narrative of the scenario.

> Resh Laqish (would)[31] say to you that this is a case in which the kindler started the fire [directly] on the servant's body. [In such a case] one would invoke the doctrine of simultaneity [and the kindler would be exempt from financial liability].

If the case of the tied slave is one in which someone actively lights the slave's body on fire then it is clearly a capital case regardless of one's thoughts about the nature of fire liability. It is unlikely that this modification reflects the historical intent of the mishnah's authors when writing the case of the slave tied to the haystack. Nevertheless, Resh Laqish can successfully reject the proof by making the scenario a more explicit murder case in which the kindler literally lights the slave on fire.

Proof Four: Supplying Fire to a Minor

Throughout rabbinic literature there is a legal category of human actors who are considered less than full legal persons because they lack requisite intelligence. The category, another example of morally fraught material, includes deaf/mute people, intellectually disabled people, and minors. The fourth proof involves a scenario in which a fully able, legal person entrusted fire to one of these legal non-people. The Mishnah states that though the person who entrusted the fire is not legally liable in human court for the damage, divine justice holds the person accountable.

Rabbinic law has a striking ability to operate on multiple levels or registers. The present example distinguishes between two parallel judicial systems, the divine and the human (rabbinic). The rabbis employ the parallel divine judicial system as a legal safety net through which to catch unethical behavior that doesn't rise to actionability by human standards.[32] Similar examples include crimes that result in divine capital punishment, or financial transactions whose unethical behavior is punished through a curse invoking the divine. The more ubiquitous disparity of registers relates to rabbinic notions of the origin and authority of a law or a set of laws. The rabbis frequently distinguish between Torah law and rabbinic law with various respective stringencies and leniencies that emerge from these associations. Even as the rabbis are sensitive to a relative weighting of biblical or rabbinic law, the rabbis sometimes undermine the disparity by saying that anything the rabbis instituted, was instituted to be exactly analogous to biblical law.[33]

The existence of multiple registers gives the rabbis a powerful tool to deal with the relationship of morality and the law. The rabbis can accept the possibility that legal acts can be considered simultaneously odious and effective. An animal properly slaughtered on Yom Kippur is kosher even though the slaughterer is liable for the death penalty. Some prohibited marriages (e.g., a priestly male marrying a divorced female) are legally recognized despite their prohibition. It is not particularly surprising, then, when the rabbis should say that someone who transmits fire through a minor is not legally liable (by human rabbinic court) but will be held responsible by a higher authority.

The Talmudic passage focuses entirely on the human judicial situation. The dispatcher is not liable for sending fire with a child. This lack of liability stems from the fact that though the child is not a full legal person, she is enough of an independent agent that liability shifts from the dispatcher. The Talmud employs this example with the assumption that this idea works better if you have a personal (arrow) liability notion of fire liability. If fire liability is akin to shooting an arrow, here one has shot an arrow via a proxy which should not make one liable. It is harder to fit this case neatly into the lens of property liability. A hearing-impaired person is not the dispatcher's property to guard against. If the fire started by the dispatcher is itself considered property, though, then giving the fire to someone who is disabled *is* a form of negligence for which the giver should be liable. The Talmud makes this point by using analogies to clearer cases of property liability:

> If [an owner] gave one's ox to one's child and the ox damaged could one suggest that the owner of the ox is not liable?

Answers to the prior proofs all involved the introduction of a new narrative detail to create a working potential scenario of property liability. In this case, the resolution is a bit wordier, involving citation to a separate debate between Resh Laqish and R' Yohanan regarding the mishnah about sending fire with a legal non-person.

The two rabbis elsewhere debate the meaning of "giving fire" to one of these three categories of agents. In that other debate, Resh Laqish claims that the exemption from human justice only applies because the sender sent the child with a coal which the child stoked into a flame. If the sender sent an *actual* flame with the child, then the sender is responsible. It isn't necessary to articulate R' Yohanan's side in the debate or the mechanics of the debate. Suffice it to say that Resh Laqish can defend against the proof from the case of sending fire with a minor by saying that there is a case of liability within human justice that corresponds to his property paradigm for fire liability.

To review the Talmud's discussion of the Mishnah (see Figure 2.3): the Talmud introduced a conceptual debate between two rabbis about the nature of fire liability, offered four citations to earlier rabbinic legal precedent to prove that one of these positions (arrow liability) is correct, but was unable to do so.

As a literary unit, this opening section of four attempted proofs demonstrates remarkable coherence of purpose and structure. There is also internal cohesion within the rhetoric of this passage, even though the meaning of the equivalent rhetoric is at cross purposes. For example, the first two proofs involve fire damage helped along by animals—the dog and the camel. The Talmud in both cases initially posits that the Mishnah's statutory law works best with an arrow-based notion of personal liability since "they are the arrows of the dog" and "they are the arrows of the camel." That exact language recurs in the fourth proof, in the context of the

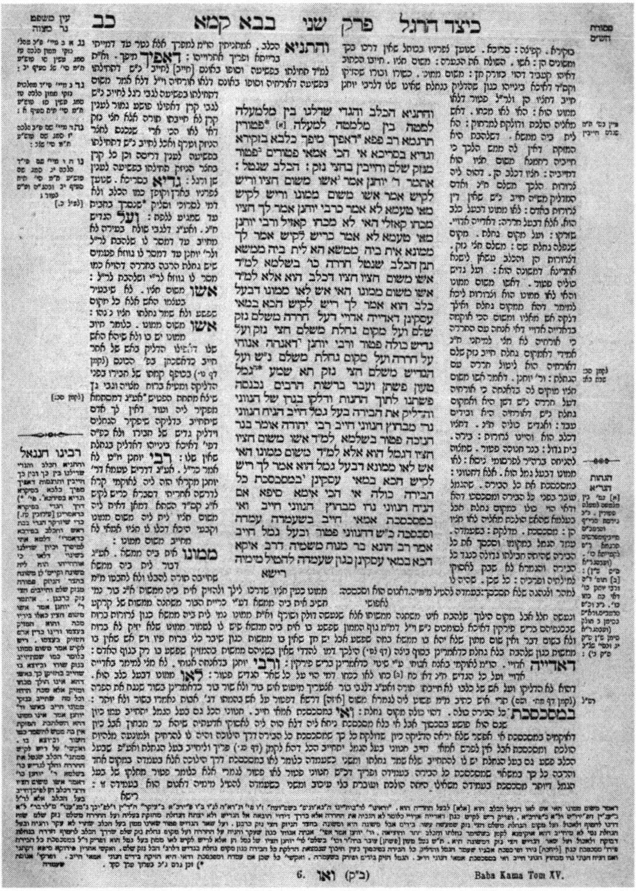
כיצד הרגל פרק שני בבא קמא כב

6. ואו (ב"ק) Baba Kama Tom XV.

FIGURE 2.2. Widow and Brothers Romm Edition of the Talmud, 1880–1886. Baba Qamma 22a. Image courtesy of Klau Library, Cincinnati, Hebrew Union College-Jewish Institute of Religion.

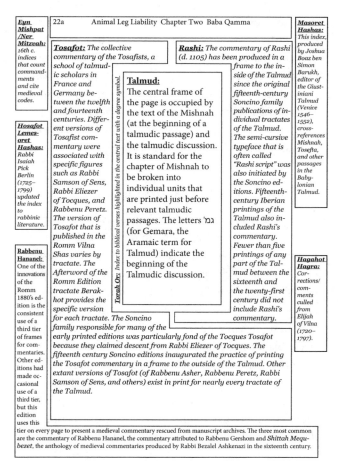

Eyn Mishpat /Ner Mitzvah: 16th c. indices that count commandments and cite medieval codes.

Hosafot Lemesoret Hashas: Rabbi Isaiah Pick Berlin (1725–1799) updated the index to rabbinic literature.

Rabbenu Hananel: One of the innovations of the Romm 1880's edition is the consistent use of a third tier of frames for commentaries. Other editions had made occasional use of a third tier, but this edition uses this

Tosafot: The collective commentary of the Tosafists, a school of talmudic scholars in France and Germany between the twelfth and fourteenth centuries. Different versions of Tosafist commentary were associated with specific figures such as Rabbi Samson of Sens, Rabbi Eliezer of Tocques, and Rabbenu Peretz. The version of Tosafot that is published in the Romm Vilna Shas varies by tractate. The Afterword of the Romm Edition tractate Berakhot provides the specific version for each tractate. The Soncino family responsible for many of the early printed editions was particularly fond of the Tocques Tosafot because they claimed descent from Rabbi Eliezer of Tocques. The fifteenth century Soncino editions inaugurated the practice of printing the Tosafot commentary in a frame to the outside of the Talmud. Other extant versions of Tosafot (of Rabbenu Asher, Rabbenu Peretz, Rabbi Samson of Sens, and others) exist in print for nearly every tractate of the Talmud.

Index to biblical verses highlighted in the central text with a degree symbol.

Torah Or: *Index to biblical verses highlighted in the central text with a degree symbol.*

Talmud: The central frame of the page is occupied by the text of the Mishnah (at the beginning of a talmudic passage) and the talmudic discussion. It is standard for the chapter of Mishnah to be broken into individual units that are printed just before relevant talmudic passages. The letters 'גמ (for Gemara, the Aramaic term for Talmud) indicate the beginning of the Talmudic discussion.

Rashi: The commentary of Rashi (d. 1105) has been produced in a frame to the inside of the Talmud since the original fifteenth-century Soncino family publications of individual tractates of the Talmud. The semi-cursive typeface that is often called "Rashi script" was also initiated by the Soncino editions. Fifteenth-century Iberian printings of the Talmud also included Rashi's commentary. Fewer than five printings of any part of the Talmud between the sixteenth and the twenty-first century did not include Rashi's commentary.

Masoret Hashas: This index, produced by Joshua Boaz ben Simon Barukh, editor of the Giustiniani Talmud (Venice 1546–1552), cross-references Mishnah, Tosefta, and other passages in the Babylonian Talmud.

Hagahot Hagra: Corrections/comments culled from Elijah of Vilna (1720–1797).

tier on every page to present a medieval commentary rescued from manuscript archives. The three most common are the commentary of Rabbenu Hananel, the commentary attributed to Rabbenu Gershom and *Shittah Mequbezet*, the anthology of medieval commentaries produced by Rabbi Bezalel Ashkenazi in the sixteenth century.

FIGURE 2.3. Explanatory Layout of Page of Vilna Talmud (Figure 2.2).

Anatomy

hearing-impaired person scenario, which says "they are the arrows of the deaf person." But while in the first two proofs the meaning of the passage is that the owner *should* be liable as the owner of the animal, in the fourth proof the meaning is the opposite. The dispatcher *should not* be liable since the deaf person is the human agent responsible for the fire. The rabbis are artful in employing rhetoric to smooth out differences among the cases and to lend greater coherence to the passage's structure.

Section Two: Rava's Proofs

Without any segue, the Talmud cites Rava, the most frequently cited Babylonian rabbi in the Talmud. Rava says there are both biblical and rabbinic supports for the view of R' Yohanan. Echoing the teaching of R' Isaac Nappaha to his two students, Rava notes the discrepancy in subjects within Exodus 22:5 which begins with a passive construction ("when a fire *is started*") and concludes by actively blaming the fire starter ("*he* who started the fire must make restitution"). The verse itself contains the very conceptual tension that the Talmud has been discussing. The passive construction treats fire as an independent agent (property paradigm). The active construction understands fire as a weapon marshalled by the one who kindled it (arrow paradigm). The Talmud cites Rava as inferring from the verse that fire liability is personal arrow-based liability. It is not clear how Rava draws this conclusion from the verse. Certainly the active verb of the second half of the verse can be understood using the metaphor of the arrow. But there is no reason to say that one who kindles fire could not be obligated based on a property based notion of liability.

The Talmud offers no defense for Resh Laqish. This section of Talmud does not follow the model of the previous section that explains Resh Laqish's position.

After citing the biblical verse, Rava adds a rabbinic precedent that also supports the view of R' Yohanan. This rabbinic midrash is so like Rava's own interpretation of the biblical verse that it is difficult to separate them. The rabbinic midrash says, "the verse opened with property liability and concluded with personal liability to teach you that fire has arrow-based liability." The midrash is a more explicit conceptual labeling of the verse's dynamics. It identifies the shift in verbs as a shift in conceptual categories from property liability to personal liability. This is a more evolved, conceptual way of reading the verse and plotting it onto the categories that have been active throughout this Talmudic passage. As with the direct reading of the biblical verse in the preceding paragraph, it is not clear why the existence of both designations within the verse *proves* that fire liability is personal liability.

Once again, though, the Talmud cites Rava as *proving* like R' Yohanan, and once again there is no attempt to explain the proof away on behalf of Resh Laqish. Does this imply a concession on Resh Laqish's part? After this second section, the reader has encountered tremendous energy marshalled against the view of Resh Laqish and for the view of R' Yohanan. The first section proofs were countered, but the second section proofs never receive a response. This makes the material in Section Three of the passage somewhat surprising.

Section Three: Abaye's Question

Having concluded his own proofs for R' Yohanan, Rava now cites his contemporary Abaye as challenging R' Yohanan. The source of the challenge is the idea, found in tannaitic statutes, that fire liability only covers visible objects and specifically excludes any items hidden within a burnt item. For example, if one stored one's fine china in a haystack and the haystack was burnt to a crisp, there is no liability for the fine china. Abaye observes that this exemption presents a challenge for arrow-based personal liability. If one shot an arrow and it punctured something and damaged something buried beneath, one would *not* be exempted from liability for the unseen item.

The Talmud attempts to defend R' Yohanan from this question by suggesting that the exemption for hidden objects happens only in a single unique scenario: A fire was lit in the kindler's property and would have been prevented from spreading by a protective wall that divided this property from the neighbor's; that wall, though, had fallen for an unrelated and unanticipated reason, and the fire then spread from the kindler's property to the neighbor's, where it damaged the haystack with its hidden trove of fine china. In such a scenario, the Talmud suggests, the fire is an arrow with no additional momentum— the momentum has dissipated. The combination of circumstances that contribute to this damage would render the kindler exempt for the hidden objects.

This re-narrativization, similar to the ones offered earlier in defense of Resh Laqish, does not satisfy the Talmud's anonymous narrator, who immediately questions it.

> if [the momentum of the arrow has dissipated], why is one liable for the visible haystack?

This question draws attention to the peculiar exemption of the invisible items. If one is liable for fire damage, why should it stop with invisible items? The text never explains how a property liability approach would explain the exemption, but property liability often presumes some notion of anticipation and negligence. One is liable for an animal's damages, for example, because they can be anticipated, and a failure to guard against them is tantamount to negligence. The case of the hidden china is not an anticipated damage, and the property liability view can explain it. The exemption makes little sense, though, within a personal liability model. Elsewhere, for example, the Mishnah says that a person is liable for damages caused even while sleeping.

Faced with this seemingly unavoidable challenge, the Talmud concedes that even those who consider fire liability based on an arrow paradigm, must occasionally also understand fire liability on the property model. This concession is strange. While the text has been, from the outset, attempting to prove the law according to one view or the other, it does not conclude simply that Resh Laqish was correct and that property liability is the paradigm for fire liability. It continues to express a preference for arrow liability by insisting on it with the caveat that sometimes even this approach must allow for property-based liability. Is it really an arrow-based approach if it adopts a property basis when under duress? Perhaps more profoundly, the deconstructive concession that a rabbi who has one model for liability can also adopt the other model, pulls the plug on the central structuring dynamic of the entire passage. The binary opposition of arrow liability and property liability, it turns out, is not diametrical—one can maintain both.

The Talmud draws attention to this disappointing conclusion by asking "what distinguishes" the two paradigms. This phrasing is ambiguous. It could be using this language to signal frustration with this entire change of strategy. It is as if to say, "after all this energy to prove one way or the other, does the choice of paradigm matter in the end?" The answer the Talmud provides clarifies the question. The answer implies that the question of "what distinguishes" the two paradigms is about finding practical concrete ramifications for liability determined by each of the paradigms. And the Talmud answers this question quite well. The difference between them is that if fire is understood on the arrow model, its liability includes not only restitution, but also medical, unemployment, pain, and humiliation payments.[34] This list of additional liabilities helps explain why there is a preference for the arrow model with its fuller personal notion of tort liability. The passage never provides a standard for transitioning between the arrow and property paradigms. It also never explains the exemption for hidden objects. Chapter 3 will return to some of these unresolved issues and see how later commentators dealt with these ambiguities.

"Traditional" students of the Talmud read this entire passage as if the text captures an actual historical conversation consisting of questions and answers and debate. Such readers expend interpretive energy trying to clarify the legal ambiguities or logical challenges of the text. These ambiguities and challenges have themselves generated a healthy set of commentaries, whose history will be documented in the next chapter with a return to this same Talmudic passage.

"Critical" students of the Talmud do not read the passage as the minutes of an historical conversation. Rather, they understand it to be a literary construct designed with the features of a conversation. When one approaches a Talmudic passage with this different assumption, several things change. Most significantly, the reader's focus shifts to include not only an understanding of the passage's self-presentation, but also an understanding of how the passage came to be composed. By focusing energies on the mechanics of a passage's composition—how it was assembled from prior parts and made to work as something like a live debate—one gains a new perspective on some of the exegetically challenging aspects of the Talmud. Beyond the exegetical benefits, though, the critical scholar also gains an opportunity for historiography. If every passage of the Talmud encodes a set of evolving ideological concepts, a careful reader can use passages of the Talmud to write the history of the development of Jewish ideas. Where a traditional reading prioritizes the study of the Talmud for its own sake, critical scholarship sometimes seeks to connect the evolution of concepts within the Talmud with the parallel development of such concepts in the larger (Greco-Roman or Persian) cultures in which the rabbis participated, and in sister communities, texts, or faiths.

Critical Analysis of the Talmud on Fire Liability

Something of a revolution in the study of the Talmud occurred in the late twentieth century.[35] The new consensus recognizes that while the debates of named amoraim are central to the Talmud, much of the strong conceptual argumentation of the Talmud occurs not in the debates between named amoraim, but in the unattributed framing comments of the Talmud's anonymous voice. Attention to historical details, such as the respective periods of activity of the amoraim, has compelled scholars to reevaluate the relationship between the Talmud as a work of literature and Talmud as a social and pedagogical practice. Critical scholars understand the Talmud to be a manufactured work of literature that is made to read as if it were a record of the conversations of the ancient study hall. This perspective has made the anonymous contributors to the Talmud who frame the attributed views of the amoraim the most compelling figures in the Talmud. A reader is often able to identify gaps (in legal positions, logical argumentation, cultural context) between the layer of the Talmud attributed to named rabbis, and the layer of the text that is unattributed and serves as the ether that structures and energizes the named rabbinic positions. Literary readers are increasingly aware of the possibility of gaps between the text's self-presentation and an historical understanding of the activity of the producers of the text. The Talmud self-presents as a record of historical conversations because it is manufactured to appear that way.

Source criticism (sensitivity to the different historical provenance of embedded sources) has revolutionized the study of Talmud over the past few decades. The tools at the source critic's disposal include: the use of parallel passages in other works of rabbinic literature, attention to shifts in language (Aramaic/Hebrew) or syntax, and an expanding understanding of the paradigm shifts that exist in the transitions from one rabbinic generation to the next. Applying this set of tools to the fire liability passage demonstrates that the history of the passage's composition does not precisely correspond to the sequence of the text's presentation. Historically, fire liability law evolved from an early case-based view that is best understood as a form of (categorically unarticulated) personal liability, to a conceptually categorical approach that creates a binary of property and personal liability. The Talmudic passage as we have it, encodes a historical story that can be teased apart with the proper interpretive tools.[36]

The prologue presents a conceptual debate between R' Yohanan and Resh Laqish, two historical figures who were active in the first half of the third century CE in Palestine. The debate is articulated as a clash of finely honed conceptual ideas: R' Yohanan thinks fire liability follows an arrow paradigm, while Resh Laqish thinks it follows a property paradigm. This kind of abstract explicit labeling was not the mode of scholarship in which the historical Resh Laqish and R' Yohanan engaged. A source critic who is aware of this immediately assumes that a historically later rabbi (active at least a century later in Babylonia) produced the actual text of the conceptual debate in the Talmud's opening lines. This happens frequently and much in the same manner as in this passage. The debate is not completely fabricated. Later rabbis routinely repurposed earlier materials and updated them to fit then-present ways of thinking. It is often impossible to determine whether such interpretive change happened consciously.

Suspicion of the historicity of the early Palestinian debate is confirmed by consulting the parallel passage in the Palestinian Talmud. The Palestinian Talmud is like the Babylonian since both are formally commentaries on the Mishnah and both capture debates and opinions of rabbis who lived after the Mishnah's composition. When the two overlap, parallel passages can be extremely valuable to the critical enterprise. In the Palestinian Talmud, there is a debate between R' Yohanan and Resh Laqish on similar material that could easily be the basis for the more conceptual version of the Babylonian Talmud.

R' Yohanan and Resh Laqish were active shortly after the oral publication of the Mishnah (in his youth

R' Yohanan studied with Rabbi Judah the Prince, the Mishnah's editor). Their typical mode of study and interpretation hews closely to the Mishnah's own casuistic style and to close exegesis of the Mishnah. Commenting on the case of the dog-and-coal in the Palestinian Talmud, Resh Laqish says that the dog actively spread the fire on each and every grain of the haystack. R' Yohanan disagrees and says that "it is as if [the dog] shot an arrow from one place to another." Resh Laqish is troubled by the owner's liability for the spreading fire. If the dog were not directly involved in spreading the fire, the owner should not be liable. R' Yohanan is not troubled by this matter since he views the fire as an extension of the dog just as an arrow is an extension of its hunter.

It is very easy to see how the Babylonian Talmud's conceptual debate emerged as an interpretation of this exegetical debate. R' Yohanan's idea of the dog's arrow became a general concept covering the entire topic of fire liability, not just in this specific and strange case. Resh Laqish's concern over the owner's liability was taken to derive from a property liability understanding of fire liability. While it is easy to see how this evolution transpired, it is vital to note that there is considerable space between the versions of the debate that appear in the respective Talmuds.

In the Palestinian Talmud, Resh Laqish is concerned about an owner's liability for a dog's actions; his statement might have intended no specific understanding of a person's relationship to fire. R' Yohanan's arrow metaphor is uttered in dismissal of Resh Laqish's idea; his statement need not have intended an entirely different liability paradigm.[37] A better way to understand the Palestinian Talmud's debate would be to situate it historically within contemporaneous rabbinic views of fire liability. The relevant texts of tannaitic midrash indicate that the tannaim [pre-Mishnah rabbis] understood fire liability on a case-based model with an as yet unconceptualized basis in personal liability.[38] Like a weapon or a tool, fire was understood to extend from the person who generated it. To be sure, fire has an additional factor of being able to spread beyond one's control, but it generally was considered a form of personal damage.

The problem with the Mishnah's case of the dog is that one cannot employ personal liability as a lens to view this case, since the dog's *owner* is not employing the fire personally. Liability for this fire stems entirely from ownership of the dog. This is what exercised the historical Resh Laqish and encouraged him to innovate the notion (as preserved in the Palestinian Talmud) that in this scenario the dog actively spreads the fire to every stalk. Resh Laqish is not saying that fire liability is like property liability. He is explaining how the owner of a dog who has property liability for that dog can be liable for the fire that dog employs.[39] R' Yohanan disagrees with the bizarre re-narrativization of a dog's actively spreading the fire because he thinks that the dog's owner *can* be liable for this damage if one considers the fire to be an arrow-like tool for the dog's damages. The historical R' Yohanan (as preserved in the Palestinian Talmud) works entirely within a property liability understanding of fire liability in this scenario.[40]

It is not impossible to read the Babylonian Talmud's conceptual re-articulation of this debate into the original debate in the Palestinian Talmud; this is what commentaries to the Palestinian Talmud commonly do, and how they read it in this case. But there is no evidence to suggest that the two early Palestinian rabbis conceived of these in conceptual terms ("arrow liability" vs. "property liability") or as universal ones (for the general category of fire rather than the specific case of the dog). The debate expressed in the Babylonian Talmud has been edited by later rabbis who were more conceptually oriented. These rabbis employed the conceptual ideas ("property liability" and "arrow liability") as a way of structuring their received material and absorbing it.

The Babylonian Talmud contains two types of material—texts that are cited in the name of one or more rabbis and texts that are stated anonymously. The major quantity of the material in Section One is anonymously stated. Looking even more closely at the original debate, we can notice both that R' Yohanan and Resh Laqish state their opposing positions using syntactically identical language ("his fire because of his arrow," "his fire because of his money"), and that the logical answers that comprise much of the initial presentation of their debate in the prologue do not quote them, but explicitly introduce ideas on their behalf ("R' Yohanan *would* say," "Resh Laqish *would* say").[41] The four proofs are composed almost entirely out of anonymously posited questions and answers produced on Resh Laqish's behalf. Once one is sensitive to the possibility that this material was composed later, confirmation is everywhere. Even more fundamentally, the four-proof section working off a binary conceptual debate is the type of structure that scholars have identified throughout the Talmud as one that reflects the work of the Talmud's latest editorial hands, a set of redactors sometimes referred to as the *Stam*. The Stam post-dates the final generation of named rabbis whose work appears in the Talmud. At the very least, this puts the Stam at the end of the fourth century. Hypothesized dates for the Stam range from the fourth to the seventh centuries.[42]

Where Section One is the product of the Stam, Sections Two and Three are comprised largely of material attributed to Rava and Abaye, two prominent fourth-generation amoraim who were active around the first half of the fourth century. Even in these sections, though, there are gaps between the original fourth-generation material and editorial modifications of this material. The most basic example of the influence of the editor is terminological. Both Rava and Abaye appear to utilize the conceptual framework of the arrow/property liability debate when they use terminology that references that debate. But sensitivity to syntax demonstrates that these terminological references have been added to the inherited material by editors. One cannot know if such additions were conscious. At the same time, there can be little doubt that the reuse of identical terminology lends the entire Talmudic passage a coherence it would otherwise lack.

Beyond the basic point about terminology, there are additional points to be made about the evolution of ideas in Section Two. Rava asserts that both the biblical verse and a midrash on that verse support the notion that fire liability is based on an arrow paradigm. The rhetoric of the midrash is particularly intriguing. Rava cites the idea that "the verse opens with property liability and ends with personal liability." This terminology—itself a more advanced conceptual categorization than one would find in the casuistic environment of tannaitic law—is Rava's innovation. These terms appear in this way only three times in the Talmud and always as statements of Rava's.[43] The ending of the midrash (to teach you his fire because of his arrow) does not correspond to the form of its beginning.[44] The format of Rava's original statement has been changed, and his original statement may have employed the verse to identify the conceptual categories which he was introducing. Furthermore, from a chronological perspective, Rava's categorical way of framing the subject (property liability v. personal liability) is the basis for the Stam's own categories of arrow and property liability (introduced in Section One). Historically, it was Rava who shifted discussion of fire to these more abstract categories; the Stam then read Resh Laqish and R' Yohanan in light of the categories and updated the debate accordingly.[45]

In its earliest period, rabbinic fire liability law reflected a case-based form of personal liability even if it was never articulated using that terminology. The historical Resh Laqish and R' Yohanan maintained this notion of personal liability and struggled to explain how a dog's owner would be liable for the dog's personal liability.

Half a century later in Babylonia, Rava began to reconceive of fire liability law in terms of personal liability and property liability, and named the categories as such. Influenced by Rava's sharply formulated categories, the Stam reinterpreted a minor exegetical debate between Resh Laqish and R' Yohanan about the dog case, to be a sharp conceptual binary.[46]

Another piece of this historical reconstruction emerges from Section Three of our passage. Rava cites Abaye about the exemption for items hidden in the haystack. Once again, there is a callback in this section to the rhetoric of Section One within the question ("according to the one who says his fire because of his arrow . . ."). Again, the syntax argues that this is not original to Abaye's formulation as cited by Rava. Abaye's question was originally a question about the mechanics of the exemption for hidden things, and not a question about arrow liability.

The casuistic quality of early rabbinic law left a great deal of space for unique circumstances or exceptions. Sometimes these were motivated by midrashic inferences, sometimes by common practices and sometimes by the limited context of the specific case. Within this context, we can understand an exemption for hidden items. The exemption may be justified by some midrashic inference (e.g., "haystack or a stalk" to exclude hidden things), some logic (it cannot have been anticipated), or as a precaution (so people won't invent things that were supposedly hidden).

As rabbinic law became more categorically conceptual, though, it became harder to explain the hidden objects exception. It is no coincidence that a contemporary of Rava's asks this question. Rava has just labeled the categories of personal and property liability. If one thinks of fire as a personal tort, as nearly all early rabbinic texts do, how can one explain this exemption for hidden things? A mishnah explicitly establishes that people are always responsible, whether awake or asleep, for the actions they do and the damage those actions cause.[47] If people are universally liable, how can they be exempt for hidden objects? Elsewhere in the Talmud, we find a minority view that blames the exemption on the threat of duplicity—such an approach understands this as a kind of meta-legal decree motivated by external forces.[48] For most of the rabbis, though, the solution to this challenge was to employ a property liability basis for understanding fire liability. Property liability has many case-based exemptions in rabbinic law and it is often limited by *a priori* expectations. The question Abaye asked regarding hidden objects is important both for the Talmudic passage's message *and* for the history of its composition. The precedent of hidden objects provoked a profound transformation within rabbinic understandings of fire liability, and pushed the rabbis towards a notion of fire liability as property liability.[49]

From a historical perspective, the contradiction between personal liability and the exception of hidden objects is well understood. The case-based early rabbinic legal presentation was not entirely conceptually coherent, and principles of equity in specific cases could undermine seemingly underlying conceptual categories. The inconsistency could explain both why there was a rabbinic statutory view that did not exempt hidden items, and why later post-Mishnah rabbis tried to view it as an evidentiary problem. But by the time of the fourth generation of amoraim, when conceptual categorical consistency was necessary, the exception proved a problem for the dominant notion of fire as personal liability.[50] It generated a historical trajectory that had much in common with our Talmudic passage: over time, the rabbis began to consider liability for fire on the model of property liability rather than personal liability.

Our reading of the Talmudic passage regarding fire liability has presented the materials in two orders. The first is the order in which the material appears in the Talmud—this is the order of sections one, two, and three, with which this chapter's discussion opened. The second is an historical one based on an evolution from case-based personal liability to an abstract conceptualization that prefers property liability. Two mishnaic statements—the dog/coal and hidden objects cases—presented challenges to new ways of thinking that were more conceptually consistent and explicit. Amoraim struggled with these difficult precedents and produced both case-specific interventions (Resh Laqish and R' Yohanan in the Palestinian Talmud) and new ways of conceptualizing (Rava's personal/property liability dichotomy and Abaye's fundamental critique of the hidden objects exemption). The anonymous Stammaim absorbed all of this and presented it within the framework of a binary dichotomy and an attempt to prove one way or the other. The structure breaks apart because its underlying history is more complicated than a simple binary debate and resolution.

Having produced both traditional and critical readings of the passage, let us contend with a different set of literary questions. Does the Talmud have an intended outcome for its reader? Is the process of reading a passage of the Talmud a journey that transports one from a beginning point to a destination? If one assumes the Talmud to be an almost accidental record of live meetings, one may not arrive at such a question. But the more one recognizes it as the work of a set of active redactors, the more one seeks to approach the Talmud as one would any work of literature.

If one takes the Talmud's presentation as intentional, one might agree with Section Three that even those who have a personal liability paradigm for understanding fire liability must also retain the possibility of rendering someone liable on the property model. But what about Section Two and its two proofs to the personal liability model that are never rebutted? In the post-Talmudic period, some readers would produce sets of rules for squeezing final decisions out of the Talmud when, as is often the case, it does not provide a clear opinion. These rules focus on sequence (e.g., prioritizing the final word) as well as quantity (e.g., the amount of text in one section of a passage relative to another). They also produce relative weightings of named rabbis with the idea that the views of certain rabbis outweigh those of others. For example, when Rava and Abaye (two figures who appear in our passage) debate, Rava takes priority in all but six cases.

As an historical matter, though, it is hard to accept that the Talmud's editors were strongly intentional in their design and arrangement of the material. Much of their work involved digesting materials inherited from prior generations and placing these in productive conversation with one another. The Talmud feels less goal oriented than other works because of this fact. As a matter of composition, then, the Talmud is more about process than about product. It is interested in exposing readers to nuance and depth in the consideration of an issue, without providing a final position.

This example highlights something on a local level that is true on a global level as well. The Talmud is a work that takes law very seriously; it often functions as a legal work. But the Talmud is a different sort of legal work. Where most works of legal literature attempt to produce law as a unified system or code, the Talmud does not produce such a rule or code. The Talmud is driven to produce law as a unified system, but there is at least as much energy expended producing a nuanced and complex way of thinking about legal matters.[51] In this sense, Talmudic legal passages stretch and pull legal scenarios, turning them over to examine and reexamine the various contexts and responses that law might allow.

Aggadic Pericope: God Overturned the Mountain upon Them Like a Barrel

Following the model of Rav Isaac Nappaha's instruction to his two students, the present chapter turns away from the Halakhic passage of fire liability and towards a fascinating aggadic passage of the Talmud. Aggadah has always been difficult to define, and some of the great minds of Jewish history have contented themselves with a negative description that aggadah includes everything that is *not* law. The passage below possesses several characteristics that could be understood as secondary descriptions of aggadah. The passage implies theological questions through a revisiting—indeed a re-narrativization—of biblical narratives. The Bible functions as the central mythology of rabbinic Judaism, and filling in gaps in biblical texts is one of the most important and frequent modes of rabbinic theologizing. The nonlegal passages of the Talmud, like their legal counterparts, are suffused with debate and intergenerational interpretation and commentary.

The first half of the ninth chapter of Mishnah tractate Shabbat contains a number of midrashic legal inferences from the Bible. The chapter's third mishnah infers from the three-day sexual separation period of the Israelites at Mount Sinai that a woman can become impure from intercourse for up to three days. This inference in the Mishnah forms the basis for a lengthy Talmudic conversation about the revelation at Sinai in the book of Exodus. This is the context for the following passage at Shabbat 88a:

"And they stood at the foot of the mountain."

R' Dimi[52] bar Hama[53] said, "[this] teaches that the Holy One Blessed Be He overturned the mountain like a barrel over them and said to them, 'It is good if you all accept the Torah, but if not . . . there will be your burial site.'"

R' Aha bar Yaaqob said, "[from this] there is a legal protest against the Torah."

Rava said, "they returned and accepted it again in the days of Ahasuerus, as it is written (Esther 9:27), 'the Judeans fulfilled and accepted . . . :' they fulfilled what they had already accepted."

The initial midrash in the passage is built around a single word—the Hebrew word *betahtit* (Exodus 19:17) meaning "at the foot of." The word includes a single letter prefix that is usually rendered in English as a preposition meaning "in" or "with." The prefix is unnecessary to the Exodus verse—one could have written the verse without the prefix and maintained the same lexical meaning.[54] By the rules of midrashic interpretation, an unnecessary feature in the text marks this feature as extraneous and open to interpretation. R' Dimi accepts the invitation of the marked text and imagines that the preposition teaches that the Israelites did not stand at the *base* of the mountain but literally *underneath* it. God severed the mountain, lifted it and held it above them like a barrel. God threatened the Israelites with the mountain until they accepted the Torah.

God's bullying Israel into accepting the Torah is significantly at odds with a basic contextual reading of the biblical story. In the biblical account, the Israelites are so eager to accept the Torah that they commit to following the strictures even before they know the particulars.

Elsewhere in the Bible, Israel's enthusiasm is a motif that explains God's singular love for the people, their specific chosen-ness.[55]

Not only is the midrash at odds with the basic biblical account, there is good evidence that the Talmudic midrash attributed to Rav Dimi is based on an earlier midrash that was specifically designed to *highlight* Israel's strength of commitment. The existence of multiple works of rabbinic literature allows one to identify parallels and to historicize rabbinic ideas. The earliest version of Rav Dimi's midrash is found in the tannaitic work Mekhilta of Rabbi Ishmael [rules of Rabbi Ishmael].[56] In that version, the mountain is severed by God and placed above the theater of revelation *before* the Israelites are underneath it. The Israelites *place* themselves under the mountain as a sign of their loyalty to God and commitment to the Torah.[57] The earlier tannaitic midrash draws upon a verse in Deuteronomy's version of the giving of the commandments that uses active verbs to describe the people's arrival "underneath" the mountain (Deut. 4:11). And then the homily continues with a connection to a verse in Song of Songs (2:14) that is understood metaphorically to celebrate Israel's coming close to God at Sinai.

In place of the original midrash about Israelite enthusiasm and commitment, the Babylonian Talmud cites a version in which God threatens the Israelites at barrel-point: "choose the Torah or die right here." The Talmud's dialogue format creates the possibility for an immediate intra-textual response. A third-generation Babylonian amora, R' Aha bar Jacob, responds to the midrash by pointing to a ramification of this kind of theological bullying: if the Israelites were forced to accept the law under duress, how can they be responsible for maintaining it? Every Jewish legal violation bears with it the defense that the law was forced upon Israelite ancestors. No sooner has Rav Aha asserted his defense of all Jewish illegality, when his near contemporary Rava reasserts the legal responsibility of Israel based on a midrashic reading of the book of Esther: the Jews of Shushan renewed their acceptance of the covenant without the duress of the mountain's hanging over their heads.

As quick as Rava's answer is at undermining the midrash of R' Dimi, the passage still unsettles. While Rava's answer renders the excuse of a forced acceptance of the Torah moot in a contemporary court, it does not undermine the mythical damage of imagining the giving of the Torah as a divine coercion. (The term used in rabbinic Hebrew for coercion is also the term for rape.) Furthermore, the passage's sequence opens two historical gaps. First, there is the historical period between the coerced commitment to the Torah and the renewal of that commitment in Persia some ten centuries or so later; during that time, any Israelite should have been able to claim duress. Second, there is also the historical gap between the second-generation rabbi Rav Dimi and his third/fourth-generation interlocutors R' Aha bar Yaaqov and Rava; for a generation or so, a rabbi familiar with Rav Dimi's midrash might have felt that any violation was justified by the coercion. The passage leads the reader to believe that the Israelites of the First Temple period operated under the fiction of a legally meaningless forced coercion. And for Rav Dimi (and his students), the rabbis themselves operated within a theology that imagines a divine bully's forcing Israel to receive the law.

The other problem with the solution posed by Rava is that it leaves the image of the coerced Sinai covenant intact. It responds to the legal *excuse* suggested by R' Aha bar Jacob, but it leaves in place the mythology that God forced a reluctant Israel to receive the Torah. This mythology is not consistent with the Bible itself, which often goes out of its way to paint Israel's willingness to follow God through the desert as one of its greatest strengths. And it is not consistent with many other rabbinic theological understandings of the Bible. The opening passage of Talmud tractate Avodah Zarah imagines an end-of-days scenario in which God is sitting with the Torah and seeks to reward all who engaged with this text (and implicitly its laws and practices).[58] This mythological scene imagines one nation after another coming before God and being rebuffed for not supporting and engaging Torah. Israel alone, according to this setup, is rewarded. In the middle of this elaborate scene, though, the other nations invoke R' Dimi's notion that the Torah was forced on Israel. How can God only reward Israel, they ask— "were we ever *compelled* to accept the Torah?" The question is sidestepped (did the nations keep the Noahide laws?) rather than directly answered. Both the question and the answer highlight the extent to which the new midrash of coerced acceptance of the Torah is now accepted and *problematic* Talmudic mythology.

It is possible that the three rabbinic positions (Rav Dimi's midrash, R' Aha's question, and Rava's answer) in the aggadic passage reflect historically uttered statements by three different rabbis. This poses a problem: the first rabbinic position is nearly identical to a tannaitic midrash in the Mekhilta (the major commentary on Exodus mentioned above), and the figure to whom it is attributed is difficult to determine. The instability around the name Dimi bar Hama, which becomes Abdimi bar Hama bar Hasa in many textual witnesses, testifies to the relative unknown nature of the name. This is a name that appears only five times in the Talmud, and many of those times it is only preserved in a single textual witness. It is possible that this midrash never existed independent of the responses of the two later rabbis. It is possible that the editor responsible for this text has made use of the form of the Talmud to present material not as it transpired historically, but as it works rhetorically. It is possible (even likely) that the person responsible for raising the stakes on the midrash about the overhanging mountain was fully aware of the violence this was perpetrating to the underlying biblical text and its foundational mythology. Nevertheless, the form of the Talmud (its multi-voiced conversation) allowed this editor to propose a radical mythological idea—that God threatened Israel into accepting the Torah—because the form allowed the editor to rein in that idea with the subsequent conversation of Rav Aha and Rava. Another way of putting this would be to say that Rava's midrash on Esther might be driving the entire reinterpretation of the midrash regarding Sinai.

Knowing Rava's claim that the Jews of the Book of Esther recommitted to God and Torah, the editor redirects the Mekhilta midrash to the more radical and potentially problematic idea that God forced the Israelites to accept the Torah at Sinai.

Rav Dimi's midrash borrows and upends an earlier midrash that saw Israel's willingness to come underneath the suspended mountain as a sign of Israel's passionate desire and commitment. The reinvention of this midrash was not developed entirely from scratch. A hint to its origins comes a few lines down in the Talmudic passage:

> Resh Laqish said, why did it say (Genesis 1:31), "and it was evening and it was morning *the* sixth day?"
>
> Why the extra letter "hey" (the definite article, when none of the other days of creation are articulated with a definite article)?
>
> This teaches that the Holy One Blessed be He hinged the Genesis creation on a condition: he said to [the things created], "if Israel accepts the Torah you will endure; if not, I will return you to being formless and void."

Resh Laqish's midrash echoes Rav Dimi's in God's presentation of a binary outcome. In the case of the Genesis creations, God's informing the creations is not an ultimatum; there is nothing the celestial bodies or sea animals, for example, can do to ensure that Israel accepts the Torah. There is no coercion that obliterates a partner's agency in the ways that make Rav Dimi's midrash so deeply problematic. It has long been noted that Genesis 1 lays out the process of creation in a way that clarifies the central purpose of man to the enterprise. The final creation is the human being; things and beings created before the final day are in man's service. Resh Laqish utilizes the extraneous letter to expand the passage's inherent framework that prioritizes human beings. For Resh Laqish, the letter teaches that it is not humanity per se but the Torah that is the *raison d'être* of creation. The story of creation does not end with the seventh day but with the giving of the Torah to Israel on Sinai.

If we consider Rav Dimi's midrash not as a historical utterance by a third-generation amora recorded verbatim in the text, but as a literary text, we can notice the role that the Resh Laqish midrash plays in the evolution of the motif of the suspended mountain. The Rav Dimi midrash combines the inherent framework of the Mekhilta (the severed mountain over Israel) with the purpose-driven God of the Resh Laqish midrash, to produce something of a monstrous bullying God who gives the people an offer they cannot refuse. The juxtaposition of the two midrashim at Shabbat 88a creates the further justification for God's behavior. Since the survival of the natural order itself rides on Israel's acceptance of the Torah, Israel must accept the Torah by any means necessary.

Halakhah in the Aggadah

The larger passage that includes the midrash attributed to Resh Laqish pushes this passage even further into the theological realm of aggadah by incorporating the rich theology of Genesis 1 within a thick mythological narrative that had previously been focused exclusively on the giving of the Torah at Sinai. This all seems comfortably aggadic. But halakhah makes an important appearance in the passage—within R' Aha bar Jacob's response to Rav Dimi's midrash.

To understand the import of the utilization of halakhah in this passage one must first understand the ordinary rules of aggadic discourse. The mythological and theological world of Talmudic aggadah permits a kind of pluralism that is not present in the Talmud's legal discussions. Part of this pluralism is an inclusion of the supernatural alongside the natural. The realm of aggadah is not confined by the limits of realism. This is not surprising for mythology, but it needs to be underlined as a positive characteristic of aggadah, especially because it is sometimes resisted even within passages that test its limitations. Consider a passage in which a number of early rabbis debate the meaning of the famous verses in the book of Ezekiel (37:1-14) in which a valley of dry bones is returned to vigorous life.[59] One early rabbi asserts that the bones were brought to life for a moment, they sang a song and they expired. This occasions a reaction from a colleague who thinks that this is too literal a rendering; the dry bones, in his view, are a hypothetical parable. A group of later rabbis disagrees with both ideas. The dry bones' corpses, says one rabbi, got married and had children and grandchildren in the land of Israel. Another rabbi adds to this claim by asserting that one of his ancestors was one of these dry bones people and the rabbi possesses his ancestor's phylacteries. Despite the passage's attempts to contain aggadah within a historically real frame, the evidence marshaled to demonstrate that the dry bones survivors were historical personages does not undermine either the interpretation that they were brought to life for just a moment or that it is just a parable. These (the realistic and the supernatural) are presented as viable understandings even if the specific views of the realists might have been trying to suppress the supernatural understandings.

R' Aha bar Jacob moves into the realm of halakhah to strongly object to Rav Dimi's midrash in a way that transcends any potential restriction from realism. Rav Aha says, "this represents a strong *moda'a* for the Torah." Use of the term "moda'a" (defined below) pitches the reader into the laws of coerced transactions that are covered in the third chapter of Talmud tractate Baba Batra.

Coerced sales are the Talmud's default example of coerced transactions; the Talmud imagines hypothetical scenarios in which the owners of chattel or land are bullied into a sale.[60] One of the fundamental questions the Talmud poses is whether a coerced sale is a valid transaction or whether it is retroactively null and void. The dominant Talmudic view is that coerced sales are inherently valid transactions. The justification for this position is logic: since a sale involves an exchange of value that maintains the formal appearance of volition, the receipt of the value (the money received as compensation for a forced land sale) by the coerced party renders that party legally willing.[61] The only recourse a coerced owner has in defending his or her property in such a case is the production of a legal document called a *moda'a*. This affidavit is signed by two witnesses and testifies to the duress that compelled the seller to sell something s/he does not wish to sell. The existence of a moda'a allows the seller to retroactively undermine the sale and retrieve the property. The Talmud extends its understanding of coerced transactions to three other transactions: gifts, divorces, and betrothals.

When Rav Aha uses the term "moda'a" he turns the giving of the Torah into a legal transaction. The term *"matan Torah"* [the giving of the Torah] is a common rabbinic term for revelation at Sinai. Rav Aha turns this giving into the formal, legal category of the gift. This would make sense but for the fact that it is God the giver who is forcing Israel the recipient to receive the gift. Perhaps it would be more appropriate to imagine that Rav Aha was not thinking of the coerced gift but the coerced betrothal. The Mekhilta that first introduced the notion of the severed mountain hovering over Israel utilized verses from the Song of Songs that are midrashically understood to mean that God and Israel are the book's lovers. God gives the Torah to Israel as an indication of commitment and Israel commits to God by receiving the Torah. But this suggests that Israel is like a coerced bride. While the Talmud frequently accepts the validity of coerced *sales*, it typically nullifies forced betrothals by arrogating power to the rabbis.[62] Rav Aha's use of the term *'moda'a rabbah'* [a great disclaimer] critiques the God of Rav Dimi's midrash as a coercing lover whose betrothal would be considered improper behavior. Rav Aha employs halakhic terminology to do something that is rarely done within an aggadic passage—to constrain a mythological position.

The case of the coerced bride returns us to the multiple registers of rabbinic law and the possibility of recognizing those different registers. Sometimes the rabbis are troubled by the possibility of simultaneous competing understandings of an act, such as a biblically valid marriage that is rabbinically invalid, or a slaughtered animal that is kosher but sends its slaughterer to death row. The coerced betrothal is one such troubling moment. The rabbis imagine a scenario in which the betrothal is sexually consummated (one of the options for implementing betrothal). Surprisingly, the rabbis do not skip a beat when they say that they can retroactively label the couple's sexual encounter, originally conducted as part of the holy ritual of sanctified betrothal, as a sinful act of extramarital sex.[63] This highlights the degree to which it is the legal lens rather than the lens of lived life that is the dominant one through which the rabbis choose to process the world in which they live.

Both Talmudic halakhah and Talmudic aggadah present rabbis who are remarkably free to make claims, interpret prior positions and rewrite mythological narratives. The positivism that allows them to separate law from morality, or from the authorizing agencies of God or the people, is surprising but ever-present in Talmudic halakhah. The rabbis are equally free as aggadists, when they challenge conventional notions such as the idea that

Israel willingly accepted the responsibilities of the Torah. In an age before Jews would invent systematic theologies committed to the respective banners of philosophy and mysticism (see chapter 3) rabbinic theologizing and mythologizing were relatively unconstrained. Rav Aha attempts (unsuccessfully, as the use of Rav Dimi's midrash in another Talmudic passage demonstrates) to restrain this freedom by transforming mythology into a legal scenario. Imagining a Jew brought before the law, Rav Aha says that such a Jew would have the ultimate defense—that there was no consent of the governed in the acceptance of the Torah as binding law. There is no way of restricting how Rav Aha's statement is interpreted. One can read it as a rhetorical argument against Rav Dimi's midrash based on halakhah: if one concedes Rav Dimi's midrash, then Jews are not legally bound in any case. Ergo, Rav Aha intends to say, Rav Dimi is incorrect. By this reading, the halakhic discourse functions as the grounds for rejecting Rav Dimi's midrash as beyond the pale. The fact that it isn't registered as such within the text, which chooses instead to concede Rav Aha's point (but sidestep it with the Purim story from the book of Esther), highlights the ability of an aggadic discourse to absorb the incursion of the legal into the mythological but remain within mythological territory. As in the case of the dry bones, halakhah may be no more powerful than reality to rein in aggadah.

Rava responds to Rav Aha from the story of the book of Esther. In an acontextual, close reading typical of midrash, Rava ignores the larger story of the persecution of the Jews, itself a form of coercion, and focuses on the words of one of the book's final verses. The final section of Esther explicitly articulates the legal requirements of the holiday generated by the events narrated within the book. Esther uses two roughly synonymous verbs—they upheld and they accepted—when only one such verb would have been necessary. Rava employs the extraneity to assert that the Jews of Shushan upheld volitionally what they had already accepted under coercion at Sinai. A critical reading of Rava's midrash suggests that it originally intended to make the claim that the Israelites of the Purim story did not just accept the rules of the holiday (as context would indicate). They also fulfilled the potential of their long ago Sinaitic acceptance of the Torah by recommitting to the Torah and God in Persia. An editor has combined Rav Dimi's midrash with Rava's via the question of Rav Aha to create a more provocative aggadic passage. While both Rav Dimi's and Rava's original midrashic statements were designed to highlight the great willingness of Israel to commit to God, the editor modifies the material to create an intermediate position in which Israel only accepts the Torah because God bullies them into doing so.

It would be futile to attempt to provide enough examples to demonstrate the Talmud as a whole. The work is vast and ranges broadly across all the topics that touched Jewish life in antiquity. The examples cited above should give the reader a sense of the variety of Talmudic texts both inherently and as read. Many of the Talmud's texts engage in analyses of fine points of legal statutes or hypothetical cases but there are also abstract articulations of legal concepts and logical justifications of legal values. At the same time, many of the Talmud's texts are not interested in law at all. Some of these embrace a tradition of re-narrativizing the Hebrew Bible that began during the period of biblical composition itself. These materials originated with the same rabbinic authorities and they sit cheek-by-jowl within a work that doesn't differentiate between them in any formal way. As helpful as it is to differentiate between different types of Talmudic passages, it is often equally helpful to reconnect aggadah with halakhah by putting the two discourses in conversation with each other.

Election: How the Talmud's Discourse Developed (Enhanced Talmud)

Medieval Jewish writers regularly employed the motif of ships' transporting Jews and Judaism from the old world of the Middle East to their new European locales.[1] In the twelfth century, writers in Germany, Spain, and Provence employed this motif to tell fantastic stories about their cultural origins. One common version collapses centuries of history and imagines Titus, sacker of Jerusalem, sending out three ships, each to settle a different new world Jewish community. A more dramatic account puts four distinguished rabbis on a ship overtaken by pirates who ransom the rabbis in different ports, distributing Jewish intellectual capital along the way. This motif proved very helpful to the writing of Jewish history, because it produced a continuous link with the ancestral past while simultaneously transferring some of the old-world authority to the new. There is a retrospective clarity to the myths created out of these motifs—they make the abrupt transition from the seemingly unified Jewish authority in the period of the Geonim in Babylonia to the diffuse authority of local European rabbis seem simple. But such stories are inevitably local, focusing on a variety of Jewish settlements in each European (or North African) locale. A more global version of such a story (which sadly doesn't exist) would imagine three travelers landing in the three major centers of Jewish ideological production between the eleventh and fifteenth centuries.

It is helpful to divide Jewish intellectual culture between the eleventh and fifteenth centuries into three geographic spaces because the intellectual products that emerged out of these environments were distinct (see map, Figure 3.1). The northernmost Jewish community, the French/German community is referred to as *Ashkenaz* in Jewish medieval sources. The Jews in this region lived among pious Christians who, like themselves, had little education in science or philosophy. The visceral bidirectional antipathy of Jews for Christians and Christians for Jews reached its apex in the two Crusades that wreaked havoc on this region's Jewish communities. The southernmost Jewish community, the Spanish/North African community, is referred to as *Sefarad* in Jewish medieval sources. While North Africa remained under majority Muslim control for the entire five-hundred-year period, Spain was a region perpetually contested by warring Muslim and Christian armies. During this period, Spain begins as a Muslim region and becomes a Christian one; even as a majority Christian region, though, Spain remained deeply affected by Muslim aesthetics and traditions. Spain's majority culture was philosophically and scientifically advanced, and Jews were

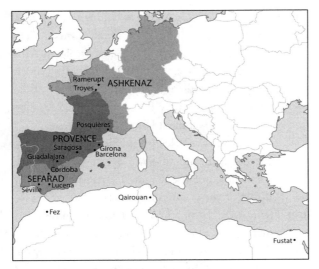

FIGURE 3.1. Three-Region Map

schooled in both philosophy and science. Between Ashkenaz to the North and Sefarad to the South was
Provence. This region includes the Northeast region of
Spain (including Barcelona and Girona) and the South-
ern cities of France (including Marseilles, Toulouse, and
Montpellier). As the buffer between the traditional Jews
of Ashkenaz and the intellectual Jews of Sefarad, the
Provençal Jewish intellectuals were mediators. Out of
this mediation emerged the reinvigorated Jewish mystical tradition known as Kabbalah.

At the end of the fifteenth century, Jews were expelled
from the Iberian Peninsula and most of the Jews of
Sefarad found themselves distributed throughout the

Ottoman Empire. Jews from further north had already been facing regular local expulsions and began to head further east into areas of Eastern Europe (present-day Poland, Lithuania, Ukraine, and Russia) where they were welcomed for economic reasons. By the time most Ashkenazic Jews found themselves in Eastern Europe and most Sefardic Jews had found themselves arrayed around the Mediterranean in the Ottoman Empire, the Talmud had become *the* central canonical text of Judaism.

It is provocative to assert the Talmud's primacy as the most important work of literature in the Jewish canon. To buttress this case, consider seven ways in which the Talmud was prominent at the dawn of modernity.

The Talmud:

1. was a sacred literature venerated alongside the Bible as a religiously significant work.
2. was the most sought-after font of collective cultural wisdom about theology, ecclesiology, historiography, and mythology.
3. was a guide to customary observance within a normatively dense traditional culture.
4. was the laboratory within which legal matters were tested, disputed, and decided.
5. was the central study text for the curriculum that produced intellectual and communal leaders.
6. was the primary study text for a culture that understood text study to be both an important vehicle for knowledge acquisition and transmission,

and the most important (even existentially necessary) ritual act.

7. was a form of capital that created its own form of
economic strata, elevating those who excelled in
this material above those with basic proficiency,
and those with proficiency above those with only
secondhand knowledge.

Though the above seven characteristics were present
throughout the sixteenth- and seventeenth-century Jewish world, a deeper analysis shows some significant distinctions in the ordering of the above list in, for example,
Eastern Europe and the Ottoman Empire. The final point
about the Talmud as capital, for example, was more profoundly expressed in Eastern Europe than in the Ottoman Empire. Nevertheless, the above list is helpful for
demonstrating the full authoritative power of the Talmud in early modernity. The remainder of this chapter
attempts to describe how the Talmud, a work produced
orally by a relatively small group of rabbis in Late Antique Babylonia, came to achieve the position it achieved
by early modernity. This is the story of the Talmud's medieval reception which is essentially the story of how the
Talmud, a work of literature, spawned a variety of other
literary genres of reception. It is the story of the enhanced
Talmud.

The division of the Talmud into two subjects—
halakhah (legal) and aggadah (nonlegal)—is so essential
to this story that this chapter also divides along these
lines. The first half of the chapter returns to the example

of fire liability to trace the story of the Talmud's legal reception in three genres of legal writing (responsa, codes, and commentaries) that differently produced the Talmud as legally authoritative. The second half of the chapter revisits the Talmudic aggadah of God's coercion of Israel at Sinai to show how the Talmud's aggadah forms a foundational source for three different discourses of Jewish thought: the homiletical tradition, Jewish philosophy, and Kabbalah.

Halakhic (Legal) Reception[2]

The Babylonian Talmud was a fully redacted work by the middle of the eighth century CE at the latest. By the dawn of modernity, this work had become thoroughly canonical. The Talmud had become central to the study habits of Jewish learning culture, its interpretation was dispositive in legal decision-making, and both its original and its derivative ideas and ideologies formed the bedrock of Jewish ideologies. It is hard to account for the rise of the Talmud and its centrality to medieval and post-medieval Jewish culture, but we can start with a description of the mechanics of this rise to authority.

Geonim

A very brief, and necessarily schematic, history of the centuries after the close of the Talmud begins in the Talmud's own backyard, Babylonia. The initial primary audience for the Talmud was a community of scholars in Babylonia (present day Baghdad) who played a fundamental role in the elevation and canonization of the Talmud. This community of scholars functioned roughly from 750–1000 CE, a period often referred to as the Geonic Era since the title Gaon (pl. Geonim) was used for the leader of a yeshiva.[3] Two prominent yeshivot, Sura and Pumbedita, were located there. Over the three centuries of their activity, the Geonim produced institutions and literatures that featured the Talmud while staking a claim to leadership of world Jewry.

When the Geonic academies waned in numbers and influence in the eleventh century, the energy of Talmudic learning was diffused in the direction of Sefarad, Ashkenaz, and Provence, that would each produce a robust academic conversation around the Talmud between the eleventh and fifteenth centuries. The regions corresponded with one another and influence was felt in all directions. Nevertheless, the regional differences were culturally and intellectually significant, and awareness of such differences helps us to understand the story of the Talmud's reception.

Three Genres of Reception

The Talmud is a single work of literature. But its legal reception is disrupted by an internal dualistic tension: the Talmud is often interested in law, but its legal discussions have a literary quality. A specific line of the Talmud can be absorbed by a reader as legally significant and become the basis for binding precedent, or it can be dismissed as a meaningless hypothetical or an initial position fated for replacement.

Three genres of literature represent the Talmud's legal reception history. Commentaries, codes, and responsa are distinct types of text that have mined the Talmud for its legal meaning since the Geonic Era. They implicate different relationships with the Talmud, particularly as the basis for their underlying law.

COMMENTARIES

Talmudic commentaries are works of literature that provide exegesis of the Talmud, resolving its many ambiguities or inconsistencies. As a group, commentaries stick closely to the Talmud's rhetoric and are more concerned with explaining the Talmud than with establishing legal precedent. As such, they are more closely aligned with the Talmud's literary features; they generally prefer explanations that account for unresolved Talmudic phrases and sentences over ones that are categorically consistent. Commentaries canonize a text by the very act of considering the text worthy of commentary. They are both the effect and the cause of serious scholastic engagement with a text.

CODES

Codes of law are works of literature that simplify legal precedent in the form of rules. Because of their interest in categorical understandings of law, codes are generally willing to prefer such understandings even when they come into conflict with specific clauses of the Talmud's text. Codes of law canonize in an ambivalent fashion. They rely heavily on the Talmud's legal content, but position themselves as substitutes and even improvements for the Talmud when a final legal ruling is required.

Responsa

Responsa are a genre of literature comprised of distant correspondences between authoritative scholars and letter-writing supplicants. Beginning in the Geonic Era, it became common for individuals throughout the Abbasid Empire to solicit religious counsel from the Geonim who headed the yeshivot in Babylonia. This practice played an important role in the construction of the Geonim and their institutions as international religious authorities. After the Geonic period, the practice of soliciting responsa continued. Individuals addressed queries to renowned rabbis. Scribes collected copies of these responsa in books that survived in manuscript form until their publication in the age of print. Even more than the law codes, the responsa (when they deal with law) represent actual legal decisions. Since the Geonic period, the Talmud has been the primary venue for a responsum-writer's deliberation about a pressing issue; respondents (down to the present) typically begin their responsum by connecting a new issue with an appropriate Talmudic passage, and process that issue through the lens of Talmudic analysis. Responsa canonize two things simultaneously: the act of writing and sending a responsum canonizes its author as a religious authority, and the content of the responsum canonizes the Talmud as the underlying textual source of that religious authority's power.

These three forms of literature were the dynamic engines that produced the Talmud as the central canonical work it is today. The Talmud did not have its authority as soon as it was produced. Rather, the literary conversations that transpired around the Talmud collectively elevated it, and continually emphasized and reemphasized its lofty perch.

Return to Fire Liability

The next section of this chapter returns to the passage of fire liability from Talmud tractate Baba Qamma, and uses the interpretation of that passage as a means of introducing the three different geographic cultures (Sefarad, Ashkenaz, and Provence) and the three genres of literature (codes, commentaries, and responsa) that are necessary to appreciate the mechanics of how the Talmud came to be enhanced with a centuries-long rabbinic conversation about its meaning.

THREE PARADIGMATIC NEAR CONTEMPORARIES

Maimonides

Maimonides (1135–1204), Rashi (1040–1105), and Rabad (1125–1198) are near contemporaries who played a foundational role in their respective cultures; the intersection of these three rabbis' work on the question of fire liability illustrates how the discourse of the enhanced Talmud of the medieval rabbis functions.

Maimonides was a systematic thinker famous for his philosophical writings and his pithy thirteen fundamentals of faith. Educated in the milieu of the Golden Age of Spain, Maimonides was a polymath who combined philosophical, medical, and rabbinic knowledge in one person; Maimonides also served as the formal political leader of the Jewish community in Fustat (Cairo). The work of literature to which he devoted the greatest quantity of his time is a code of law called *Mishneh Torah* [second Torah], a title that simultaneously calls to mind its antecedents in the biblical book of Deuteronomy (*Mishneh Torah* to the rabbis) and the rabbinic Mishnah.[4] *Mishneh Torah* contains a fresh taxonomy of Jewish law into fourteen books that are subdivided into smaller sections.

Before looking at *Mishneh Torah's* treatment of the dog-and-coal case of fire liability, let us review the original mishnah and attendant Talmud. The mishnah states that if a dog transports a cake with attached coal to a neighbor's haystack and sets it aflame, the owner of the dog is liable for the full value of the cake and half of the value of the haystack. The mishnah originally has two sites of liability—the cake and the haystack. The Talmud questions Resh Laqish, who believes that fire liability is predicated on property liability, by noting that the owner of the dog should be responsible for the dog, not the fire. In response to this question, the Talmud restates the case of the mishnah for Resh Laqish. In Resh Laqish's version,

the mishnah's scenario is one in which the dog threw the coal and there are three sites of liability. The dog's owner is liable in full for the cake (s_1), shoulders half liability for the spot on the haystack on which the coal landed when it was thrown (s_2), and is exempt for the rest of the haystack (s_3). By introducing a third site, the Talmud asserts that the mishnah's assertion of half damages was exclusively for the coal's landing spot. In general, the dog's owner is *not* liable for the neighbor's burnt haystack. After introducing this new understanding of the mishnah for Resh Laqish, the Talmud circles back to consider R' Yohanan's understanding of the mishnah. R' Yohanan, the Talmud states, understands the mishnah's scenario as one in which the dog *placed* the coal on the haystack. The dog's owner bears full liability for both the cake (s_1) and the site on which the coal was placed (s_2) and half liability for the rest of the haystack(s_3).

Maimonides' understanding of this law is reflected in *Mishneh Torah* at *Nizqe Mammon* [monetary torts] 2:17:

> A dog that took a cake and walked it to a haystack—if he placed it on the haystack, ate the cake and set fire to the haystack: [the owner] pays full damages for the cake and the place of the coal [on the haystack], but half damages for the rest of the haystack.
>
> But if [the dog] dragged the cake over the haystack and it was going and burning—[the owner] pays full damages for the coal, half damages for the place of the coal and is exempt for the remainder of the haystack.

The first paragraph is easily identified as the Talmud's articulation of R' Yohanan's understanding of the mishnah: full liability for the cake and the place of the coal, and half damages for the haystack. But what is one to make of the second paragraph? Maimonides seems to invent a case in which the dog does not place the coal but drags it over the haystack. In such a case, Maimonides insists, there would be three different sites of liability with one total exemption. This strange position echoes the mishnah as understood by Resh Laqish, a case in which there are three outcomes for three sites. Since Maimonides sides with R' Yohanan, why does he include a view reminiscent of Resh Laqish?

Consider the rationale for "half damages" in the mishnah. The idea behind half damages is logical, because it can sometimes be most just to split the cost of an event between two parties rather than making one shoulder exclusive responsibility. The Mishnah includes several cases in which half damages are assessed. These include cases in which an animal damaged in a manner that was not yet foreseeable, cases in which an animal damaged through secondary impact (like the damage of pebbles), and cases in which something was damaged in an unexpected or unusual way. All three rationales are possible explanations of the dog-and-coal mishnah. As a young man, Maimonides wrote his own commentary to the Mishnah. In his commentary on this passage, Maimonides writes that while the eating of the cake is usual and expected (and warrants full liability), the strangeness of the damage to the haystack justifies a reduction to half damages.

Maimonides does not offer a three-way breakdown of the Mishnah in the manner of the Talmud's explanation on behalf of Resh Laqish.

Maimonides was not the first post-Talmudic rabbi to produce a code of law. In the Geonic period there was an impulse to codification that led to the production of *Halakhot Pesuqot* [unqualified laws] in the eighth century, *Halakhot Gedolot* [great laws] in the ninth century, and R. Hai Gaon's several turn-of-the-eleventh-century subject-specific codes.[5] The most comprehensive code produced before Maimonides' *Mishneh Torah* is the *Halakhot* [laws] written by Rabbi Isaac Alfasi (d. 1103), an Algerian scholar with a direct intellectual connection to Maimonides; Alfasi's student R' Josef ibn Migash (d. 1141) was the teacher of Maimon, Maimonides' father. The only one of these codes that comments on the case of the dog-and-coal is Alfasi's *Halakhot*, which highlights the sections of the Talmud that resolve the law in favor of R' Yohanan while emphasizing the ending of the passage in which even R' Yohanan must at times accept a property-based notion of liability.

Three things strongly distinguish *Mishneh Torah* as a code from its predecessors. Previous codes employ the Talmud not only as a source of content but also as a default organizational framework. These codes are digests of the Talmud that follow its order and parrot its hybrid language and loose organization. *Mishneh Torah*, in contrast, completely reorders Jewish law; Maimonides did not just reject the Talmud's order, he rejected the framework of mishnaic orders and tractates for one completely of his own design. Instead of the Hebrew/Aramaic language of the Talmud and earlier codes, *Mishneh Torah* is written in pure Hebrew; laws are stated directly to avoid the ambiguities that are so common in the Talmud. Perhaps most provocatively, where the Talmud has the habit of citing its rabbinic authorities and tolerating disagreements among different rabbis, *Mishneh Torah* is unequivocal and does not divulge the names of the rabbis responsible for its content.

That the break with the Talmud and prior codes represented by the form of *Mishneh Torah* is not accidental can be confirmed by statements of Maimonides about his purpose in producing the work.[6] This code was produced to improve upon a Talmud that was ambiguous, disorganized, and a poor basis for final law. These features of the Talmud meant that only the greatest rabbinic exegetes could operate the Talmud as a legal guide. Maimonides imagined that *Mishneh Torah* could replace the Talmud as the central text of Jewish legal study. The possibility of such a replacement demonstrates that the Talmud was not yet as canonical as it would become.

Mishneh Torah epitomizes a phenomenological point made earlier: if one thinks of law as an organized system of precedent, the Talmud is a tough basic text. The Talmud's habits of citing multiple authorities, and meandering through collage-like passages with complicated rhetoric and discursive questioning, fly in the face of both organization and precedent. Maimonides attempted to produce a work of law that perfectly embodies the ideal of law as a categorized system. From this perspective, *Mishneh Torah* is an improvement upon the Talmud. Still, *it* relies for its content on the Talmud and has an exegetical relationship with it. Where Maimonides may have anticipated that subsequent readers would read this work independent of the Talmud, that was not *Mishneh Torah*'s historical fate. Rather, *Mishneh Torah*'s readers forced the work to remain connected to the Talmud by seeking to explain the underlying rationales and exegeses that drive the code.

The reason *Mishneh Torah* includes a second case in which the owner of the dog would be exempt for some of the liability is because Maimonides takes the Talmud and its rhetoric seriously. After the Talmud asserts on behalf of Resh Laqish that the mishnah's scenario is one in which the dog threw the coal, the Talmud circles back to assert that the mishnah's scenario for R' Yohanan is one in which the dog *placed* the coal on the haystack. In the process of this assertion on R' Yohanan's behalf, the Talmud borrows the three-site model it had used to describe Resh Laqish by again asserting a moment of eating (full liability), a moment of placing (full liability), and the burning of the rest of the haystack (half liability). Several medieval commentators suggest that this circling back to R' Yohanan is merely rhetorical—that R' Yohanan need not specifically require a case in which the dog placed the coal, and could explain the mishnah expansively to also govern in a case in which the animal threw the coal as Resh Laqish suggests.[7] Maimonides does not explain his logic, but the easiest way to understand his second clause in *Mishneh Torah* is to assume that he *did not* dismiss that line of the Talmud as mere rhetoric. If one takes the line seriously to mean that there are two outcomes for the three sites *only* in the case of placement, then there must be a different scenario in which the three sites are meaningful. Maimonides suggests a case in which the dog *dragged* the coal over a larger section of the haystack. In such a case, Maimonides says, there is full liability for the cake, half liability for the site of the dragged coal, and exemption for the rest of the haystack.

Rabad and Maimonides

The problem with Maimonides' exegesis of the passage is that while it takes the Talmud's line (which others dismiss as a form of literary parallelism) seriously as law, it creates a problem for systematic understandings of the law. The first and most fundamental critique of *Mishneh Torah*—and the one most responsible for bringing this work back into the rhetorical and exegetical shadow of the Talmud—was Rabad's critical gloss, referred to as *Hagahot* [comments]. A slightly older contemporary of Maimonides, Rabad— the established leading rabbi of Provence—is said to have written his terse and often sharp gloss to *Mishneh Torah* at death's door.[8] On this passage Rabad writes: "[this is] not right. For [the dog's owner] would not be exempt [at the least] from the quarter liability of unusual pebbles." Rabad takes issue with the notion that, according to R' Yohanan, one would be exempt from liability for the fire that consumed the remainder of the haystack. Drawing on a systemic way of thinking about liability derived from the entirety of the Talmud's passages regarding an owner's liability, Rabad cannot fathom how there would be no liability for the remainder of the haystack. Since R' Yohan-an's liability in this case is based on a notion that the fire is the dog's arrow and the owner is liable for the dog's torts, how could there be an exemption for *some* of the fire's damage?

Rabad was recognized in Provence as a founding figure whose original interpretations of the Talmud profoundly affected the scholars that followed. Many of Rabad's legal positions and exegetical insights reached modernity through their citation in the works of subsequent scholars in Provence; little of Rabad's commentary on the Talmud remains extant.[9] The surviving remnant demonstrates a mind that combined strong systematic legal thinking with sensitivity to rhetorical coherence.

Rabad's gloss to *Mishneh Torah* is his best-known work. It is sometimes characterized by a sharpness of tone that makes it appear that Rabad was critical of the work. But such a characterization fails to recognize the fact that the production of such a gloss was an homage that helped establish *Mishneh Torah* as a canonical work of literature. Rabad was the first of many who would elevate *Mishneh Torah* into a text that engendered its own rich reception discourse. The work was so valued that scholars would come to impute a form of legal omniscience to Maimonides that allows for a probing of even the slightest contradictions. Much of the work of Talmudic study in contemporary traditional yeshivot is comprised of interrogating the relationship between the Talmud and its commentaries on the one hand, and *Mishneh Torah* and its commentaries on the other.

Rabad's specific critique of *Mishneh Torah* in the present case is based on a systematic understanding of the entire legal topic of tort liability with all its attendant exemptions. The idea of insisting upon at least a quarter damages as a function of the pebble-like damage of the continuing fire, is based on explicit Talmudic passages found elsewhere in tractate Baba Qamma. As a systematic legal thinker, Rabad could not understand a way in which the dog's owner would be responsible for some of the dog's actions vis-à-vis fire (actively spreading the fire) and yet be fully exempt for the fire that resultantly spread to and consumed the haystack. To make that distinction would require positing that despite the analogy between fire and an arrow, it would be possible to understand that the arrow's energy had stopped, and the new kindled fire would be considered unrelated to the earlier kindling episode. In fact, just such an idea makes an appearance in another line found in the concluding section of the Talmud's fire liability passage that is also best understood as rejected rhetoric. We turn now to that ending.

Rashi

As we have observed repeatedly above, the Talmudic passage ends somewhat enigmatically with the idea that even R' Yohanan, who maintains the arrow paradigm of fire liability, must concede occasionally to a property liability paradigm. This enigmatic ending is a great opportunity to notice the work of Rashi, the Talmud commentator par excellence.

Rashi's commentary to the Bible is more famous than his commentary to the Talmud, but a strong argument could be made for the greater significance of the Talmud commentary. Rashi's Bible commentary enables a reader to quickly and easily understand the Bible through the lens of rabbinic literature; Rashi's Talmud commentary enables a reader to understand the Talmud at all. Both of Rashi's commentaries are remarkable for their combination of brevity and concision that was particularly valuable in a scholarly culture that relied on entirely handwritten texts.

Prior to Rashi, the scholarly community of Ashkenaz had produced a collectively authored paraphrastic commentary that is sometimes called (erroneously) the commentary of Rabbenu Gershom, after one of Ashkenaz's leading early rabbis. Rashi's own commentary significantly improves on that antecedent.[10] Rashi has a remarkable ability to develop a strongly coherent version of a textual passage by aligning skewed positions found in various parts of an extended Talmudic pericope.[11] A reader of his commentary will regularly note his habit of anticipating upcoming material and signaling that unresolved matters will be resolved later in the passage. In our passage, Rashi makes an unusual exegetical choice at the beginning that is best understood once one finishes the entire passage.

Recall that the fire liability passage had four units: a prologue and three separate sections. The prologue presented the debate between two rabbis who employ different paradigms for fire liability. The first and second sections advocated for R' Yohanan's arrow paradigm—that fire liability is like the liability of a hunter for an arrow. The third section questioned the arrow paradigm from the exemption for hidden objects, and established that

those who maintain the arrow paradigm must also maintain the property paradigm. We will now focus more care-
fully on that section. Because of its complexity and the
need to return to this passage repeatedly to understand
Rashi and other commentaries, the box contains a numbered outline of the seven sections of the passage. A reader
may wish to bookmark this page for future consultation:

1. *The Question:* How can R' Yohanan justify an exemption for hidden objects? Since personal liability knows
   of no limitations, what rationale could justify not being
   responsible for these items?

2. *An Attempted Resolution:* The exemption references a
   specific scenario in which the force of the fire-as-arrow
   is understood to have dissipated and the kindler is no
   longer liable. This scenario is one in which a fire-
   preventing barrier has fallen down for unrelated, non-
   negligent reasons and that there was insufficient time
   to rebuild.

3. *A Rejection of the Attempt:* The Talmud questions itself: if the fire kindler is not responsible for the hidden
   objects because the fire-as-arrow has dissipated, the
   kindler should also be exempt for the neighbor's haystack *in toto*.

4. *A Concession:* The Talmud concedes that R' Yohanan
   must also occasionally rely on the property model to explain fire liability.

5. *The Positive Assertion of a Property Basis:* After the
   concession, the Talmud provides an example within

R' Yohanan's view: "And for example, if he should have fenced it in and did not fence it in for there it is [analogous to] his ox and he did not close [the stable] before him."

6. ***Questioning the Debate:*** Having now conceded within the view of R' Yohanan, the Talmud now asks what distinguishes the two paradigms.

7. ***The Concrete Distinction:*** The distinguishing factor of the paradigms is their approach to the nonremunerative compensation (medical, suffering, unemployment, and shame) typical of personal torts but not of property torts.

Three implicit comprehension problems help to introduce and structure an understanding of the commentaries to this passage:

A) What relationship does this seven-part section have with the two sections of the talmudic passage that preceded it? This is particularly acute since the preceding sections prefer the arrow liability paradigm and this section prefers the property liability paradigm.

B) Does the elaborate scenario that is the basis of the attempted resolution (#2) retain value even after it is rejected (#3)? This question is complicated by the way in which the eventual assertion of a property basis for R' Yohanan (#5) echoes the resolution's language.

C) The final question (#6) seems to ask abstractly about the nature of the binary approach to paradigms of liability; the answer (#7), though, is a concrete set of differences

> between the two paradigms. A simple resolution would reinterpret the question (#6) considering the answer (#7) to be asking for concrete differences between the paradigms. The problem with this easy resolution is it makes the question somewhat unnecessary: section one's proofs contained several possible concrete cases of difference between the paradigms.

In his commentary to the prologue of the larger Talmudic passage Rashi lays the groundwork for an explanation of the final section on fire liability. Already in his comments on the opening lines of the passage, Rashi writes that the passage has an initial and eventually superseded understanding of the concrete stakes of the debate between R' Yohanan and Resh Laqish:

> And it is your initial supposition that the difference between them occurs in a case in which one lit a fire *with a coal that was not his own*; R' Yohanan renders liable because they are his arrows, but for Resh Laqish there is exemption because the coal is not his own.

Rashi's approach insightfully takes advantage of the fact that the term the Talmud uses to describe Resh Laqish's property paradigm is "his money." When the Talmud employs the respective cases of the dog and camel to challenge Resh Laqish, Rashi can easily persist in his explanation that the problem these cases pose for Resh Laqish is not because they are difficult to envision within a property liability paradigm, but because the coal did not belong to the dog's owner, and the candle did not belong to the camel's owner.

When Rashi arrives at the question (#6) of the final passage, he explains that the purpose of the question is to establish a concrete ramification for the argument, even in a case in which the animal's owner *does* own the item that causes the fire's ignition. As he puts it,

> And it is also true that concrete ramifications include all the earlier ones about the dog and the camel, since the person who adopts an arrow-based view would render him liable . . . and the one who does not have the arrow paradigm would only render liable if [the camel] was wagging [across the whole building] as we established earlier.

In one fell swoop, Rashi resolves questions A and C, and he does so by using C—the question about the disconnect between the abstract question (#6) and the concrete answer (#7)—as the key to unlocking the passage as a whole. Rashi assumes from the answer (#7) that the question is about the concrete ramifications of the debate. Since such a question is hard to fathom considering the earlier parts of the passage, Rashi takes this opportunity to reimagine the relationship between the sections of the larger passage. The first two sections presume an initial understanding that places a lot of stock in the ownership of the coal or candle. The third section (in its final question (#6) and answer (#7)) circles back to consider whether there would be any concrete ramification for the debate if the person responsible for spreading the fire also owned the original source of the fire.

Rashi is not unaware of the second question (marked B above)—the question about the rejected, attempted resolution and its later echo. In his comments on that part of the passage, Rashi reads the rejection (#3) and concession (#4) very creatively. In his understanding, the concession does not *replace* the original attempted resolution, but responds to and furthers the goals of the initial attempted resolution (#2). The concession (#4) that R' Yohanan must also have a property paradigm, works to explain the liability gap between the hidden objects and the haystack that obscures them (the basis for #3). The kindler is exempt from liability for the hidden objects because *these* are evaluated based on an arrow paradigm and within a notion that the arrow energy has dissipated (#2). But the kindler is liable for the haystack itself in the same scenario because of a property paradigm. By refusing to read the rejection (#3) as definitive, and the concession (#4) as providing a different pathway to a resolution, Rashi maintains the value of the attempted resolution, and deftly explains its seeming echo in the positive assertion of the property basis (#5) later in the passage. The positive assertion (#5) restates a view that has been modified, not rejected.

Notice how much work was necessary to explain Rashi's motivations. He does not operate with a format of question and answer that signals the things that drive him to specific interpretations. A common pedagogical approach to Rashi's biblical commentary promotes a hermeneutic in which the reader must repeatedly ask after Rashi's motivations—to see the commentary as a set of answers to unasked questions. A similar approach is necessary for Rashi's Talmud commentary if one is to appreciate the impressive achievement of this work. One of the limitations of studying the Talmud in translation is that translators often presume Rashi's commentary within their translation, and the reader is not able to appreciate the work that Rashi does to produce the text as a completely consistent logical work.

Rabbenu Hananel

Rashi's interpretation of the larger passage is not without its drawbacks. One of the biggest limitations is its supposition that the earlier sections presume that ownership of the flame is the central matter of debate and not the property paradigm itself. This may explain a cryptic line in an earlier commentary. Rabbenu Hananel ben Hushiel (d. 1053) of Qairouan (present day Tunisia in Sefarad), wrote a paraphrastic commentary that predates Rashi's and relies heavily on prior Geonic readings.[12] Within his comments on the question posed on Resh Laqish from the dog-and-coal case, Rabbenu Hananel reads the challenge on Resh Laqish—as Rashi does—as predicated on the fact that the dog's owner does not own the coal. Following this comment Rabbenu Hananel says,

> And we have seen a comment along these lines by the Geonic rabbis, and it appears to us that there is a fundamental question with the basic underlying law, and we therefore have refused to speak both about the comment and about the question.

Since Rabbenu Hananel does not articulate the problem with the Geonic interpretation shared by Rashi, we must turn elsewhere.

Tosafists

Rashi's success as an exegete made the Talmud accessible to a wider audience and also enabled the marshalling of interpretive energies in new directions. Now that a student of Talmud could access a basic understanding of the text simply, new hermeneutic approaches developed. Rashi famously had several daughters and no sons; some medieval customary texts remember these daughters as protofeminist figures whose ritual and scholastic performance violated the period's gender norms. These daughters were also the wives and mothers of male rabbis. Several of Rashi's grandsons were influential in producing the Tosafist school, a group of scholars whose approach came to dominate the Northern European landscape for a couple of centuries. Rabbenu Jacob Tam (d. 1171) is considered the intellectual father of an approach that sought to make the Talmud coherent not simply on a local level (as Rashi had done) but on a Talmud-wide basis.[13] The Tosafists systematically hunted for discrepancies in the laws and ideas presented in one passage and those presented in another passage found anywhere in the Talmud. By positing such findings as contradictions, they created opportunities for distinguishing between the contradictory passages. This dialectical approach carved out space for the canonicity of all the Talmud's passages by using conceptual nuance to assert that competing passages did not govern the same cases.

The Tosafists reject Rashi's interpretation of the fire liability passage out of hand because, even as an initial idea, the notion that one would only have fire liability for owned fire is unworkable. There is a passage later in the tractate about pushing someone into fire and a mishnah about the fire caused by a blacksmith's hammer spark that are clearly unowned fire.[14] The Tosafists also note a logical flaw to the notion of unowned fire; if one is not liable for unowned fire, an intelligent kindler will simply declare the initial fire ownerless as a form of legal protection and no one would ever have fire liability. It is perhaps this flaw that so bothered Rabbenu Hananel. This example vividly demonstrates the ways in which the new Tosafist hermeneutic comes into conflict with Rashi's. Rashi is largely driven by the need to render the local passage coherent, and while his reading of the ownerless fire is a bit forced, it masterfully holds the local passage together. The Tosafists, in contrast, are unwilling to tolerate (even as an initial position) a legal idea that is contradicted by other passages found elsewhere in the Talmud.[15]

Rabad and Rashi

One of the only tractates for which the commentary of Rabad is still extant is tractate Baba Qamma.[16] A close reading of his commentary on the final question (#6) and answer (#7) provides an opportunity for recognizing Rabad's skills as a subtle reader. The major problem with the question and answer (C) is that the question seems abstract and the answer concrete. One can read the answer back into the question and assume the question to be asking for a concrete answer easily, but doing that weakens the question since the preceding passages have several concrete differences between the paradigms. Rabad explains:

In other words, your initial position was that there was no distinction either for stringency or leniency [between the two paradigms].

If so, the Talmud asks, "what separates them?" (#6) And I teach you [that that is] not [the case].

Rather, they apply to him the stringencies of [both] the arrow paradigm and the property paradigm: and what are they—to render liable for four payments. (#7)

And also, there are hidden objects in that courtyard and all of the distinctions taught on behalf of Resh Laqish earlier; but it comes to add to what has already been said.[17]

Rabad addresses the fundamental gap (Question C) between the abstract question (#6) and the concrete answer (#7) by doubling the answer such that it responds both concretely and abstractly. Rabad opens space between question and answer by imagining an implicit abstract answer that is communicated by the concrete one. The original viewpoint and basis for the abstract question is the idea that now that we have heard the concession (#4) there is nothing separating the paradigms. When the answer (#7) responds to the question, it both provides a concrete case and *through that case* rejects an original assumption of indistinct paradigms. The first thing the concrete answer does is undermine the original assumption and teach that the concession (#4) does not mean that there is no difference between the paradigms. Rather, it means that a single rabbi, R' Yohanan, employs a hybrid paradigm that absorbs the stringencies of both. This creatively allows a concrete answer to respond effectively to an abstract question. Rabad then adds that there were other concrete differences between the two paradigms as articulated earlier in the first two sections of the passage.

Rabad's solution is not as elegant as Rashi's because he is forced to state that the concrete ramification (#7) is not unique; rather, it adds to others (hidden objects, etc.) that have come earlier in the Talmudic passage. But if we focus on the concrete aspect of Rabad's final question and answer, we can see that there was originally a binary either/or character to the debate between the paradigms. We also see that the combination of the concession (#4) and final answer (#7) have destroyed that binary in favor of a notion that the paradigms are a set of non-dichotomous lenses which can be adopted even together by legal authorities. This is a more explicit and self-conscious (almost critical) rendering of the Talmudic passage than one finds in any of the other commentaries (though we will see something similar in a Sefardic responsum below).

Though Rabad's Talmud commentary is mostly lost to posterity, many of his ideas and legal positions echo into the present through their citation in the works of subsequent scholars, some of whom also resided in Provence.[18] Rabad's thoughts are merged with a Tosafist style hermeneutics in the *novellae* of four prominent figures (Nahmanides and Solomon ibn Aderet of Barcelona, Yom Tov ben Avraham of Seville, and Rabbenu Nissim of Girona). Two unique and novel positions emerged in the context of fire liability within this school of scholars. Rabbenu Nissim (d. 1380) provocatively asserts that the arrow paradigm of fire liability is a civil rather than a criminal idea, and one would not receive capital punishment for death by fire unless the murderer physically held the victim in the fire or pushed the victim into inescapable fire. Rabbenu Nissim's student Josef ibn Habib wonders about the effect of the arrow paradigm on the lighting of Shabbat candles every Friday night in Jewish homes, and concludes that while the lighting of a fire has the ongoing liability effect of an arrow, the act of kindling is not equal to its liability and is understood to be over once the fire is lit.

As a Provençal, Rabad was geographically situated between the North African culture of codes and the Northern European culture of Talmud commentaries. He was well positioned, then, to offer something of a corrective for both. His commentaries evidence a more legally systematic form of thinking than those of Rashi, who was most concerned in the readability of the local Talmudic passage as a piece of literature. Meanwhile, Rabad's gloss to *Mishneh Torah* corrects a disconnect with exegesis by forcing a justification of Maimonides' positions based on the Talmud, and a return to the Talmud's concepts and a system of thinking within its confines.

Ri Migash

Another explicit comment on the final section of the fire liability passage is found in a responsum written by Rabbi Joseph ibn Migash, the Spanish scholar and student of Alfasi who taught Maimonides' father, Maimon. Responsa began to flourish in the period of the Geonim, when individuals from across the Mediterranean and occasionally beyond would send questions by letter to the yeshivot in Babylonia. Responding to these queries was an important part of the yeshiva curriculum. We think of responsa as a legal genre, and some scholars of the history of Jewish law compare responsa to legal opinions both in form and in function, but they were not originally limited to questions of practical law.[19] During the Geonic period, the responsum addressed philosophical, theological, or very often, exegetical questions. One of the most important extant responsa is a letter written by Rav Sherira Gaon (d. 1006) in response to a theological question, and is the earliest attempt at Talmudic historiography.

The Letter of Rav Sherira Gaon is a responsum penned around 987 to a rabbi in Qairouan (Tunisia). The questioner seeks the history of the composition of rabbinic literature, and Rav Sherira Gaon obliges with a history of the rabbis from Temple times to his day focusing on institutions and works of literature. Much of this is historically imprecise by modern critical standards, but the work remains valuable, particularly for its description of the Geonic period.

Responsa largely traveled via trade routes. Scribes at nodes on these trade routes would sometimes copy the responsa in transit. Some rabbis retained handwritten copies of their own responsa. Medieval responsa usually come to us from such collections. Occasionally, they were preserved through other avenues. A sixteenth-century rabbi, Bezalel Ashkenazi, who lived in Ottoman

Palestine, is the source of an important anthology of medieval Talmud commentary to several tractates. *Shittah Mequbezet* [gathered opinion] collects the full citations of various commentaries from the eleventh through the fifteenth centuries including several that are no longer extant. *Shittah Mequbezet* cites a responsum of Rabbi Joseph (Ri) ibn Migash on our Talmudic passage.

The responsum opens with a repetition of the petitioner's question. The unnamed questioner has written Ri Migash asking an exegetical question: why does the Talmud ask the question (#6) "what is between the [paradigms]?" when the earlier sections of the passage provide several concrete answers to this problem—the debate about hidden objects, the matter of the slave tied to the haystack, and the other things that were said in the context of the dog and the camel? Ri Migash's answer begins with a protocritical comment about the nature of Talmudic rhetoric:

> We have seen that this thing is not worthy of question, for there are many similar instances in the Talmud where we say, "what is between them" even though we have seen that there is *much* between them. And the reason for this is since there are also other aspects that differ between them in addition to the ones we already know, we have seen in the Talmud that they identify the existence of such differences in the form of a question—"what is between them"—in order that it will return an answer of 'such and such differentiates

them.' This means, in other words, there are *also* such and such differences.

The initial answer that Ri Migash offers points to an aspect of the rhetorical nature of the Talmud and a problem that emerges from a conflict between this rhetorical character and the attentive reading practices that developed around it. Ri Migash tells his questioner that one can take a Talmudic question *too* seriously—there needs to be room to say that a phrase is just there to lead to the next line and should not be examined too rigorously. Like his peer commentators, Ri Migash struggles with one of the core exegetical problems (a ramification of Question C above)—if the question (#6) is understood concretely, it becomes a rather easy question since there are many available answers earlier in the passage. By discounting the *import* of the question, Ri Migash ensures that the answer can be read for its best contextual meaning without the modifications suggested by Rashi or Rabad above. In effect, Ri Migash says that the question should be understood concretely, and the fact that it is not a good question should just be ignored.

The questioner might have been disappointed with this answer if it had arrived without its continuation. Fortunately, Ri Migash continues with something more intellectually satisfying:

Additionally, when one probes the differences [between paradigms already] found in the Talmud, it turns out *that all of them are not about the fundamentals of fire liability but are specific cases* of fire damage that have differences only when the cases happen in a certain way. And if the cases do not happen in this specific way, then we would not find differences between the arrow [paradigm] and the property [paradigm]. Therefore, [*the Talmud*] *needed to look for a matter in which there is a difference in the fundamental basic law* of fire liability that is found in all types of fire damage cases.

This second answer is insightful. Ri Migash notes that while there are other concrete ramifications that differentiate the paradigms earlier in the passage, all of those are specific to cases with very particular circumstances. The final concrete ramification (four payments) is fundamental to every fire liability tort, because an arrow paradigm would render one liable for those four payments while a property paradigm would exempt. It is worth unpacking the work that this accomplishes. On the simplest level, this interpretation responds to the secondary question of why the question (#6), understood concretely, is necessary when there are various other concrete differences. But one can also understand this interpretation more profoundly to be saying that the difference of four payments (#7), while appearing to be a mere ramification, can also be understood abstractly, because it is a fundamental and comprehensive difference that affects all cases of fire liability. Ri Migash essentially understands the answer (#7), in light of the question (#6), as a more important fundamental conceptual distinction than the others. And in doing so, Ri Migash differentiates his interpretation from that of Rashi, Rabad, Tosafot, and all other commentators on this material.

Three Genres in Early Modernity

The three genres of reception (codes, commentaries, and responsa) continued to be produced as the fifteenth century gave way to the sixteenth, and ushered in Jewish early modernity with the Iberian expulsion and the dawn of print.

Codes and Commentaries

The production of law codes increased in the sixteenth century. The most significant code is *Shulhan Arukh* [set table] written by Joseph Karo, a Spanish native who moved to Ottoman Palestine in the wake of expulsion from Portugal as a nine-year old in 1497.

Shulhan Arukh's organization is borrowed from a fourteenth-century code produced by Jacob ben Asher (d. 1343) called *Arba'ah Turim* [four columns]. Jacob ben Asher had been trained by his father Rabbenu Asher (d. 1327), a German scholar who was trained as a Tosafist before migrating to work as a rabbi in Toledo, Spain. This cultural heritage allowed Jacob ben Asher to produce a code that draws in nearly equal degrees from Northern Europe, Spain/North Africa and Provence. Jacob ben Asher's code *Arba'ah Turim* has a simpler organizational structure than *Mishneh Torah*. The law is divided into four sections: daily ritual, non-daily ritual, criminal/civil, and family laws. Each section has numbered topical units.

Arba'ah Turim reverses course from *Mishneh Torah*; though it has its own organizational apparatus, it reintroduces a discursive style that includes both multiple opinions and citations to the names of the authorities responsible for those views. Because the citations in *Arba'ah Turim* are largely to medieval authors, this work stands as something of an updated Talmud that considers and explicitly labels the legal positions and related exegetical stances that had emerged in the three major medieval cultures. If *Mishneh Torah* is a Talmud 2.0, *Arba'ah Turim* is a Talmud 3.0. Karo wrote commentaries on both codes that relate back to their Talmudic and medieval antecedents.

In the context of fire liability, *Mishneh Torah* takes a split approach to its use of the scenario in the attempted resolution (#2) in which a barrier fell for unrelated reasons. While Maimonides embraces the scenario as the standard for establishing the transition from the arrow paradigm to the property paradigm of fire liability, he does not make use of it in his discussion of the laws of hidden objects.[20] This is a bit surprising because the scenario was utilized as part of an attempted resolution (#2) which was responding specifically to the question of hidden objects. Vidal of Toulouse, a fourteenth-century Provençal scholar who wrote a prominent commentary to *Mishneh Torah*, questions Maimonides on this exclusion in the context of hidden objects.[21]

Arba'ah Turim deviates from *Mishneh Torah* and applies the fallen fence scenario as the standard both in the context of the shift in paradigm (from arrow to property) and in the context of hidden objects.[22] In his *Beit Yosef* [house of Joseph] commentary to *Arba'ah Turim,* Karo notes *Mishneh Torah*'s deviation and Vidal's question; *Shulhan Arukh* follows the approach of *Arba'ah Turim* in retaining the meaning of the Talmud's falling fence scenario as a standard for both the shifting paradigm and the exemption for hidden objects.

As a law code in general, *Shulhan Arukh* splits the differences between *Mishneh Torah* and *Arba'ah Turim.* Like *Mishneh Torah, Shulhan Arukh* articulates its laws in rule form and does not attribute to named sources; Karo frequently lifts the initial elegant Hebrew presentation of his text from *Mishneh Torah.* Like *Arba'ah Turim, Shulhan Arukh* allows for a multiplicity of approaches; this pluralism increased significantly when printers began, almost instantly, to include the gloss of the Polish scholar R' Moshe Isserles (d. 1572) called *Hamapa* [the tablecloth], which provides the missing positions— particularly the customs—of an Ashkenazic community that was now centered in Eastern Europe.

The emphasis on codes in the sixteenth century shifted the central learning focus of traditional Jews from the Talmud to the codes.[23] Though the codes rely on a Talmudic basis, much of the energy of scholars in the seventeenth and eighteenth centuries was focused on understanding the codes as coherent presentations of Jewish law. Printed editions of the codes would borrow the printing format of Talmud and publish all three prominent codes (*Mishneh Torah, Arba'ah Turim,* and *Shulhan Arukh*) as central texts with framing commentaries. An impressive number of code commentaries were written during this period. The shift to the primacy of codes lasted until the turn of the nineteenth century, and was reversed largely through the agency of the Vilna Gaon (d. 1797), the most celebrated scholar in Eastern European Jewish history.[24]

Vilna Gaon's vast literary legacy was largely compiled out of personal notes or the notes of students, and his writing is often preserved in a shorthand that is hard to decipher. The Gaon's learning is characterized by his return to the original canonical sources of rabbinic literature, including the Babylonian Talmud, and his habit of resisting the interpretations of prior readers in favor of fresh close readings of the original sources.

Biur Hagra [clarification of the Gaon Rabbi Elijah], the Gaon's commentary to *Shulhan Arukh*, critiques the way in which both *Arba'ah Turim* and *Shulhan Arukh* employ the fallen fire barrier scenario as a standard for liability or exemption of hidden objects. In his typically forceful and cryptic rhetoric, he returns to the Talmudic passage and points out that: a) the gist of the passage is that there is no limit to the hidden objects exemption, b) the very verse that establishes an arrow paradigm for fire liability also establishes the hidden objects exemption, and c) the rhetoric of the question (#6) "now that the arrow paradigm has a property paradigm what is the difference . . . ," is a poor fit if one still maintains that the arrow paradigm has a different standard for the hidden objects exemption than the property paradigm. Considering these observations, the Gaon asserts that the rejection (#3) denies the attempted resolution (#2) and the concession (#4) represents *an entirely new approach to dealing with the problem of hidden objects*—by abandoning the arrow paradigm for a property one. Unhappy with the reassertion of the property basis (#5), Vilna Gaon attempts to modify its text slightly so that it cannot be read as reaffirming the original attempted resolution (#2). As proof of his reading of the passage, Vilna Gaon points to *Mishneh Torah*'s omission of the scenario of the fallen barrier in the context of hidden objects as an indication that Maimonides read the passage along these lines. This is an insightful original reading, and it creates additional possibilities for understanding how Maimonides' understanding of the passage differs from Rabad's, and justifies the position that Rabad had attacked.

Recall that Maimonides had written that if the dog *drags* the fiery coal over the haystack this produces three liability sites: full liability for the cake, half liability for the places the dog directly lit aflame, and no liability for the rest of the haystack. Rabad criticizes the full exemption for the rest of the haystack because that requires some notion that the force of the fire-as-arrow had dissipated. Now that we have delved into the morass of the final section of the Talmudic passage, it has become clear that the notion of dissipated fire is intricately intertwined with one's reading of the final passage. *Mishneh Torah* uses the fallen fence scenario as the standard for defining the paradigm shift from arrow to property liability. This means that Maimonides *retains* a notion of dissipated arrow energy, originally stated in the attempted resolution (#2) *because it is resuscitated* by the restatement of the property basis (#5). In the case of the dog's dragging the coal, Maimonides (as was mentioned above) takes the Talmud's restatement of the mishnah on R' Yohanan's behalf seriously, and infers from it that there must be a case in which R' Yohanan would also have a full exemption. Maimonides then uses the notion of dissipated energy found in the final section of the passage to justify such an exemption within a systematic understanding of R' Yohanan. By connecting a "throwaway" line at the beginning of the passage with a "throwaway" line at the end, Maimonides can take both seriously for legal precedent.

It turns out that Maimonides, the most systematic of the code writers, can also be hypersensitive to lines in the Talmud that other legal readers dismiss as mere rhetoric produced out of a literary sense of parallelism. And a reading of the passage first explicitly articulated in eighteenth-century Lithuania by Vilna Gaon helps resolve a question first posed by a Provençal rabbi on the work of a North African rabbi in the twelfth century. While the nuances of these debates in exegesis and law are complicated, they allow one to appreciate the way in which the Talmud's multigenerational and geographically diverse conversation paved the way for an enhanced Talmud that has a wider generational span and a much higher degree of geographic and cultural diversity than the essential Talmud.

Vilna Gaon's student Hayim of Volozhin (d. 1821) incorporated the Gaon's idea of a return to the Talmud in the curriculum of the first large institutional yeshiva of Eastern Europe, the Volozhiner Yeshiva, founded in 1803.[25] One of the most prominent alumni of Volozhin was Chaim Soloveitchik (1853–1918), whose father had been a lecturer in the yeshiva. Chaim Soloveitchik would himself teach in Volozhin but would later take a position as a rabbi of Brest (Brisk in Yiddish) in Belarus near the Polish border. Soloveitchik reinvigorated Talmudic dialectic in the wake of the return from a focus on *Shulḥan Arukh*. One of the innovations behind Soloveitchik's methodology, sometimes referred to as "The Brisker Method," is its frequent juxtapositions of legal rulings of Maimonides with incongruent positions in the works of other medieval authorities like the Tosafists or the authors of the novellae. These contradictions can be resolved historically by attending to the different cultural contexts and reading assumptions. By ignoring this historical explanation, the Brisker method opens the entire enhanced Talmud to the kinds of questions that the Tosafists produced when they decided that all passages of the Talmud must agree with all other passages of the Talmud. These questions provide tremendous opportunities for sharp dialectic, which Soloveitchik and his creative followers can produce. Today the Brisker Method is the dominant way in which the Talmud is taught at the highest levels of traditional yeshivot.[26]

Responsa
The shift of emphasis towards codes in early modernity does not imply that rabbis stopped writing responsa. To the contrary, responsa were written and published all over the world in the age of print. These were now almost exclusively legal in nature and generally involved some

degree of pressing and practical legislation or adjudication. An overview of this literature reveals that the Talmudic passage on fire liability turns up as a canonical basis for very different modern conversations. Rabbi Shlomo Kluger (1783–1869) turns to this material when considering the ritual viability of matzah made by a machine.[27] Rabbi David Zvi Hoffman (1843–1921) considers the ramifications of fire causality when discussing the possibility of cooking on the Sabbath with a timer.[28] Rabbi Moshe Feinstein (1895–1986) weighs this material when analyzing the social status of a man who has had prostate removal surgery, considering biblical injunctions against castration.[29]

Today, responsa have become a popular genre for digital distribution. One of the earliest textual digitization projects was the Responsa Project, produced by Bar Ilan University, which digitized all extant printed responsa and made them searchable; this has moved responsa more centrally into the study curriculum of those who study the enhanced Talmud.[30] One of the most popular modern forms of responsa is an Israeli program called ShutSMS that allows people—regardless of their observance—to pose religious questions via text message to Rav Shlomo Aviner, a leading religious Zionist rabbi. The Central Conference of American Rabbis, the rabbinic arm of American Reform Judaism, hosts a website on which one can consult Reform responsa that have been penned over the last half century on a wide range of issues; the topical index to this collection runs to seventy-six pages.[31]

Aggadic (Nonlegal) Reception

Thus far, this chapter has outlined the way that the Talmud came to be canonized as the sacred book of law, studied as the primary curricular work of law, and displaced and expanded into the discursive space of Jewish law *par excellence*. But Jewish ideology is not limited to law and neither is the Talmud entirely a work of law. Nonlegal matters—of theology, folklore, biblical exegesis, wisdom, and mysticism—comprise roughly half of the Babylonian Talmud. These materials were also received within post-Talmudic intellectual culture, and came to function as the bedrock of conversations of this type within Jewish ideology and culture. There is a crucial difference between the function of the Talmud in its respective reception in legal and nonlegal discourses: while the legal discourse canonizes the Talmud as a repository of information and a framework of processing materials, it also elevates positions found within it above parallels found elsewhere in the rabbinic canon. The Talmud's nonlegal materials are not granted the same stature in post-Talmudic nonlegal discourse. While the Talmud crowds out other works of rabbinic law within its legal reception, the Talmud is read *alongside* other aggadic materials from elsewhere in rabbinic literature, with little pride of place for those ideas that reside in the Talmud rather than other works of rabbinic literature. On a related note, the new nonlegal discourses that emerged in the postrabbinic period did not emerge out of the Talmud and orbit around it. Rather, they developed a conceptual coherence into which Talmudic materials could be inserted.

One could easily divide aggadic reception into ten or fifteen movements. But three is a more manageable number, and the three movements described in this chapter map loosely onto the three medieval cultures: Ashkenaz, Sefarad, and Provence. The intellectual culture of Ashkenaz digested aggadah as part of a comprehensive traditional mythological and theological program that led to the extensive production of synagogue sermons and liturgical prayers. Since the most analytic aspect of this traditional engagement with aggadah was in the form of didactic homilies, we will call this form of aggadic reception "homiletical instruction." The Jews of Sefarad, who were well versed in contemporaneous intellectual conversations based upon Greek philosophy and metaphysics, inaugurated "Jewish philosophy," a synthesis of Greek metaphysics and traditional Jewish mythology and theology. Caught between the traditionalist aggadah of Northern Europe and the philosophy of Spain/North Africa, Jewish intellectuals in Provence invented "Kabbalah", which developed a nascent Jewish mystical tradition into something with enough space for both traditionalist and philosophical metaphysics, theology, and mythology.

Homiletical Instruction

Recall from the preceding chapter that the midrash at Shabbat 88a asserted that God held Mount Sinai above the Israelites like a barrel and threatened their survival to make them accept the Torah. This midrash is resisted by a rabbi within the Talmud who claims that Jews could invoke this coercion as the ultimate legal trump card. Another rabbi concedes both preceding points, but claims that the Jews of the Purim story in the book of Esther later reaffirmed their previously coerced decision willfully. This passage is theologically provocative. It characterizes God as a bully and Israel (at least initially) as a passive and unwilling partner in revelation. The passage's described action (God holding a barrel over the people) is vivid and easy to visualize. On the other hand, the outrageous violation of the laws of nature in this account lead a reader to think that the entire description may be a metaphor or allegory rather than the description of a transpired historical event.

The midrashic expansion of biblical narrative is easy to describe but hard to evaluate. Beginning within the Bible and continuing in the literature of the Second Temple and rabbinic periods, there was a tendency to expand prior narratives by providing gap-filling details and full-blown backstories.[32] Some of the more famous of these narratives are the story of young Abraham's destruction of his father Terah's pagan icons, the story of Jacob's sojourn in a yeshiva for fourteen years before arriving at Laban's home, and baby Moses' selection of a hot coal instead of a gleaming diamond before Pharaoh. While such stories are easily enough understood as expansions of biblical stories, they force one to confront questions about the cultural reception of biblical stories and their expansions. It might be that Second Temple or rabbinic readers accepted the historicity of biblical tales but presumed the midrashic expansions to be fictive embellishments. Alternatively, cultural insiders may have treated the expansions with the same historic credulity as the originals. When one reads a midrash about God's turning the mountain over as a barrel on top of the people, it is not clear how a rabbinic reader would have understood it. Would such a reader have accepted that the miraculous events of revelation happened but that this embellishment is a fictive fantasy, or would such a reader incorporate this account into the accepted biblical story? A still further, but far less likely, possibility would be that the ancient reader would have treated the entire account of the Bible as fictive fantasy.

The above set of questions feed into a traditional framework for receiving Talmudic aggadah. A traditional reader is faced with the above set of choices about how to think of the historical truth of such texts. In addition to this set of reading choices, though, the traditional reader of aggadic mythology and theology is also trying to produce theology, mythology, and ethics for his or her contemporaneous audience. Already in the rabbinic period, much of the literature of aggadah was produced as part of a social practice of sermonizing.[33] Sermons were part of the synagogue service and, as with sermons today, their intent was inspiration. A sermon can be either uplifting or upbraiding, but it is generally designed to be impactful. This practice continued in the post-Talmudic, medieval era, and works written in this form constitute some of the best examples of a traditional reception of rabbinic aggadah.

Two of the earliest works of homiletical literature, *Sheiltot* [propositions] of R. Ahai Gaon (eighth century) and *Midrash Tanhuma* [Tanhum's midrash] (redacted in Geonic Babylonia), incorporate the midrash of the mountain-cum-barrel into their homilies. The *Sheiltot* version expands the original midrash to incorporate several other biblical verses from different tiers of the Hebrew Bible to support the concept.[34] *Tanhuma*'s version builds on the original midrash while confining some of its potential damage.[35] *Tanhuma* recognizes explicitly that the midrash conflicts with the biblical phrase "we will do and we will listen" that is generally understood to display Israel's unbridled yearning for the law's yoke. Therefore, *Tanhuma* explains the story of the threatened barrel to refer only to the oral Torah—that secondary supplemental tradition so important to rabbinic theology. Because of both the comprehensive coverage of the oral law and its harsh judgment, the Israelites are pressured into receiving it; they willingly accept the written Torah. This text is a perfect example of the overdetermined nature of exegetical texts and of aggadah. The writer accepts the expansion of the story, but needs to ensure that it doesn't contradict another explicit text. The distinction introduced to resolve the contradiction becomes an opportunity to say something about the religious meaning of the oral law—to recognize the awesome nature of the thing. Turning this midrash inspirational, the writer concludes: "The only one who learns [the oral law] is one who loves God with all his soul, with all his heart and with all his resources." This reference to Deuteronomy 6 turns the midrash about en-forced acceptance into a paean to the love that Israel has for God.

As much as *Tanhuma*'s interpretation builds on the original midrash, it also has a limiting function. By redi-recting the myth of God's forcing Israel from the written Torah to the oral Torah, the midrash reduces some of the damage of a coerced covenant. *Tanhuma*'s expansion can be understood as a form of traditional apologetics—a form of discourse in which religious insiders can use the internal logic of their religious system to defend against seeming problems. *Tanhuma*'s is not the only traditional apologetics that attempts to handle this provocative text. The thirteenth-century Provençal *novellae* provide two such explanations. One asserts that R' Aha bar Jacob's question (that this was a strong legal argument against the binding nature of the covenant) was never a genuine challenge, but merely the hypothetical question of a her-etic.[36] This assertion undermines the provocation by re-fusing to accept the Talmud at face value that the lack of consent is a problem; for nonheretics, apparently, this is not an issue. The second commentary asserts that the dra-matic coercive act of the barrel over the head is over-dramatized for effect.[37] By its logic, the Israelites merit the reward of the Holy Land by their acceptance of the Torah. If they had refused to accept the Torah, they would not have entered Israel and would have died (of old age) in the desert. This explanation downplays the threat as descriptive rather than exhortatory. God wasn't threatening to *kill* with the barrel but indicating that nonacceptance would lead to death in the desert. These kinds of apologetics did not end in the fourteenth century. A nineteenth-century Torah commentator asserts that the story of the barrel only happened to a specific segment of the Israelites: the "mixed multitude" of non-Israelites that Exodus 12 describes as attaching itself to Israel upon its exodus from Egypt.[38] This interpretive move salvages the reputations of the proper Israelites who would never have needed coercion to accept the Torah.

Because of the vivid supernatural event described in the midrashic expansion (God's holding a mountain over the people), one traditional response to the event was to think of the entire episode as an allegory. Most of those who interpret this midrash allegorically do not similarly allegorize the supernatural biblical story. They continue to understand that God descended from heaven with pyrotechnics and spoke to the people and then to Moses. But the midrash of the barrel is allegorized. Isaac Arama, a fifteenth-century Spanish sermonizer, writes that the barrel is a metaphor for the kind of overwhelming divine supernatural proof they had encountered.[39] After the Exodus and revelation, the offering of the Torah was a choice they could not but accept—*like* a barrel held over one's head. At Purim, when God was absent (the name of God does not appear in the book of Esther), Israel could make a noncoerced choice. The nineteenth-century Iraqi rabbi Yosef Chaim unpacks the allegorical meaning of the metaphor—just as a barrel contains many drops of wine, so the oral Torah contains many interpretations of the written Torah.[40] This move makes the barrel equivalent to the oral Torah rather than to the miracles of Egypt and revelation. These allegorical understandings of the midrash simultaneously build upon the midrash, clarifying its inspirational meaning, and undermine the provocation of a concrete nonallegorical understanding.

As the above examples attest, a traditional mode of studying aggadah has persisted from Late Antiquity until the present. Alongside traditional readings, though, two new systems of Jewish thought emerged in the medieval period that had a tremendous impact on theology, mythology, and metaphysics. The two thought systems are Jewish philosophy and Kabbalah. They affected both their staunchest advocates and those who were affected either by the reaction to these movements, or through their subtle infiltration into traditional practices like homiletics and commentary on biblical and rabbinic texts.

Jewish Philosophy

It can be difficult to properly apprehend the long-ago impact of Greek philosophy on theories of nature, the function of the world, and the roles of human beings and divinities, respectively, within the world. Not only did the thought of Plato and Aristotle stake out essential positions on these issues, the existence of the framework of philosophy threw down the gauntlet to those who would, as Abrahamic religions did, frame the questions differently.

The tension between philosophy and monotheism did not bear its first literary fruits in the medieval period. The first-century Egyptian Jew, Philo, penned an entire corpus that fuses Platonic ways of thinking with the Hebrew Bible. But this Greek corpus was not preserved by Jews and was unavailable to medieval Jews as a model for the fusion of Talmudic aggadah and Greek philosophy. Though Greek culture profoundly influenced the rabbis who produced rabbinic literature, these rabbis had no awareness of Philo and took little interest in Greek philosophy.

Despite the rabbis' noninterest, by the time of the rabbis there were two dominant strains within Greek philosophy. Aristotle's strain promotes the deistic idea that no divine entity affects the daily operation of the natural world. Neoplatonism opposes some of the deism of this strain, and posits the existence of an original fundamental source out of which all things emanate, and towards which they should be productively oriented. Jewish philosophy derives primarily from the Aristotelian strain and Kabbalah from the Neoplatonic.

By the end of the period of the Geonim, Greek thought had become intellectually unavoidable. Within cosmopolitan Babylonia, clerics of Judaism, Christianity, and Islam joined forces to strategize about how their respective traditions would accommodate the truths that had been philosophically established. The *Kalam* dialogues of Abbasid-era Babylonia produced various theological responses to the clash between Greek thought and scriptural monotheism.[41] Most prominent among these was the *Mutazilite* school of Islamic theology, whose platform insisted that the divine was singular and unified, that free will was possible despite divine omniscience, and that scriptural knowledge was valuable because of its confirmation through reason.[42] The first Jewish work of systematic theology, Saadiah Gaon's (d. 942) *Sefer Emunot V'Deot* [book of beliefs and opinions], is a work that plays Mutazilite theology in a Jewish key.[43]

Maimonides' philosophical work, *Guide of the Perplexed*, builds on Saadiah's precedent. This original philosophical work adopts a fusion of Neoplatonism and Aristotelianism while critiquing the Mutazilite notion of reason.[44] It is evident from the *Guide* that Maimonides had full command of the Talmud's aggadah. In the introduction to his commentary on the *Guide*, Maimonides indicates an intention to eventually produce a full-blown commentary on the aggadah; no such commentary survives.

The *Guide* produces truly radical innovations regarding basic Jewish beliefs. Maimonides characterizes the biblical religious mode of sacrifices as a divine concession to human weakness, understands the divine on a deistic model that does not allow for personal relationships with people, and considers only philosophers to have the capacity for achieving religious ideals such as the afterlife and love of God. Though Maimonides' work would stand the test of time as the most elegantly composed and theoretically sophisticated work of Jewish theology/philosophy, it generated opposition. One of the strongest philosophical opponents was the Catalan rabbi Hasdai Crescas (1340–1411), who was instrumental in representing the Jewish community during the Iberian persecutions of the late fourteenth and early fifteenth centuries.

Where Maimonides asserts thirteen principles of Jewish faith, Hasdai Crescas posits a single notion—that God the commander willingly gave the Torah to Israel—as a basic principle out of which emerge six fundaments. One of these fundaments is the idea that human beings as commanded entities can choose whether or not to accept the Torah. The midrash of the coercion of Israel with a barrel over their heads is a problem for Hasdai Crescas. Splitting hairs as only philosophers and Talmudists can, Hasdai distinguishes between the act of accepting the law and the emotions that accompany the action.[45] The Israelites, in his understanding of the myth, were compelled as though with a barrel (he follows the allegorical understanding) and had no choice but to accept the Torah; this is in keeping with his deterministic philosophy that says that external factors can force action against one's will. But the notion of reward and punishment, he continues, is directly connected to the emotional response. Only when the Israelites of the Purim story emotionally embraced the Torah, could they be made responsible in the sense of being rewarded and punished for their actions. Absorbing the entirety of the Talmudic passage, Hasdai Crescas sees an evolution from the problematic philosophical position of coerced acceptance to the benighted idea of making an emotional commitment during the time of Esther; that second commitment is the basis for philosophical understandings of reward and punishment.

Kabbalah

While the discipline of Jewish philosophy would continue to engage Maimonides' thought until the present, there was significant contemporaneous resistance to Maimonides' philosophy. Maimonides' reception was culturally specific. The noncosmopolitan climate of France and Germany had little interest in philosophy and ignored the *Guide*. The loudest resistance originated in Provence.[46] That this region played a significant role in mediating the flow of intellectual innovation can be seen in its projects of translating Greek ideas from Arabic to both Latin and Hebrew. But this middle position brought Provençal Jewish intellectuals under the influence of both the high intellectualism of Spain/North Africa and the traditionalism of France/Germany. Negotiating these tensions helped produce Kabbalah, which remained in dialogue with the Talmud.

Kabbalah, the mysticism developed in medieval Provence, combines earlier Jewish mystical traditions (chariot and throne mysticism from the Second Temple period and the later mysticism of the medieval pietists of Ashkenaz) with Neoplatonist philosophical forms of mysticism that also absorb some Aristotelian notions. Kabbalah produces a notion of an ineffable and inaccessible God (*Ein Sof*) alongside a series of divine emanations (*Sefirot*) that take on the traditional functions of God. The kabbalist absorbs Aristotelian notions of an indescribable deistic God while also producing divine entities that can be thought of as Neoplatonist sources and goals. Kabbalistic writers drew upon nonphilosophical traditional sources such as those of the Bible and rabbinic literature. They also drew upon the philosophical writings of Saadiah and Maimonides. Thirteenth-century

Kabbalistic authors interpreted the *Guide* as an encoded work of mysticism whose true meaning can only be unearthed esoterically.[47]

The earliest Kabbalists were a group headed by Isaac the Blind (d. 1235), the son of the legal scholar Rabad. Many of the initial Kabbalists focused primarily on biblical and earlier mystical literatures rather than the Talmud. But these Kabbalists were aware of the occasional Talmudic passages that are explicitly mystical and those that could easily be interpreted in a mystical manner.[48] A later developing node of Kabbalah was in Girona, where its most famous practitioner was Nahmanides (1194–1270), a reputed legal scholar in addition to being a mystic. Some of the literature produced in Girona took the form of Kabbalistic interpretations of Talmudic aggadah.[49]

The most impactful work of Kabbalah produced in Provence was the *Zohar* [splendor], penned by Moses de Leon in Guadalajara in the 1280s. This elaborate pseudepigraphy was written in an archaic form of Aramaic to support the claim that R. Simeon bar Yohai, a famous charismatic early rabbi, authored the book. Though the Zohar is written in the style of a mystical midrash, it contains features that demonstrate the Talmud's influence. The Zohar's ten main characters include a combination of tannaim and amoraim, and some of the latter are chosen based on Talmudic stories in which they feature. The Zohar shares with the Talmud the tendency to free associate to new topics, and includes small inserts referred to as *Matnitin* and *Tosefta* that look like the

Talmud's own tannaitic introduction markers. In its content, the Zohar leans heavily on rabbinic literature both to seriously engage the protomystical material found within rabbinic texts and to further the performance of the pseudepigraphy. Two centuries after its appearance, the Zohar came to be considered the third great canonical work of Jewish literature, alongside the Bible and the Talmud.[50]

Among the profound transformations wrought by Kabbalah on Jewish aggadic thinking was the production of a radical hermeneutic for interpreting earlier, particularly biblical, texts. The ten Sefirot, or divine emanations, form the basis for an incredibly dense and self-referential semiotic system in which the Sefirot are understood to have relationships with one another that form mystical explanations for things that happen in the human earthly realm. Kabbalists commonly map the Sefirot onto the biblical ancestors and understand biblical stories as encoded descriptions of Sefirotic relationships. Another common mapping understands each one as a section of the human body. These mappings provide the basis for extreme allegorizations of the content of biblical and midrashic narrative. Some of the most significant Kabbalistic textual interpretations were produced by Hasidic thinkers in the nineteenth and twentieth centuries.

Rabbi Kalonymous Kalman Shapira, a Hasidic rabbi who died in the Warsaw Ghetto in 1943, draws on established mystical mappings from the Zohar to assert that the mountain held over Israel like a barrel represents the forefather Jacob.[51] The visual of the barrel refers to the barrel's specific physical properties—it has a cavity that permits a person inside it to touch its sides. When the text says that God overturned the mountain like a barrel, it means that God created a possibility in Torah that allows Israelites to reach for their ancestors. Israel should comport itself in a manner that would make the ancestors proud. The Purim scenario of joyous acceptance is the fulfillment of the potential of Sinai. It was in Shushan during the episode of Esther that the Israelites finally "reached the sides" and could connect to their predecessors. Shapira's interpretation employs a Zoharic mapping to produce an extreme allegorization that has moved quite far from the original text.

Rabbi Yehuda Ashlag (d. 1954), a Polish rabbi who migrated to Palestine, was a prominent traditional kabbalist who authored a comprehensive and widely distributed commentary on the Zohar. Yehuda Ashlag's son, Rabbi Barukh Ashlag (1907–1991), comments on the barrel mountain midrash.[52] Taking the liberty that Kabbalistic interpretation allows, Ashlag makes an interpretive choice that is as violent to the original midrash as uplifting a mountain. Undermining the basic premise of the midrash's notion of coercion, Ashlag says that while there exists coercion by torture there also exists *coercion by pleasure*. The overturning of the mountain as a barrel to bury the Israelites is a metaphor for such coercion. This interpretation makes the text oppose its plain meaning and completely dulls the text's provocation. The text that paints Israel as unwilling, mistakes Israel's joy for pain.

The passage that seemed to show Israel's reluctance and lack of agency, expresses Israel's joyful enthusiasm.

As the examples of the barrel midrash attest, traditional interpreters of the aggadah have venerated Talmudic nonlegal materials and productively engaged with them for over a millennium. Much of this engagement has been unsystematic, characterized by the search for inspiration and religious meaning. The development of systems of Jewish nonlegal thought (philosophy and mysticism) provided new frameworks for digesting this material and new techniques and strategies for producing interactions with the text. The result is a broad array of techniques and ideas that make an already plural original even more variegated over time.

Aggadic Talmuds

The above examples of aggadic reception are culled from works of biblical commentary, Talmudic commentary, and collections of sermons. In addition to these sources, though, a small industry of aggadic reception of the Talmud developed that did not emerge as a byproduct of biblical commentary or primarily legal commentary to the Talmud. A recently discovered thirteenth-century commentary on rabbinic aggadah implies the existence of other such commentaries by contemporary Jewish philosophers; recall Maimonides' pledge to write such a work.[53] Two fourteenth-century works look to the Talmud specifically for the type of nonlegal moral and ethical guidance that is the specialty of Talmudic aggadah. Bahya ben Asher's (d. 1340) alphabetically arranged topical essays entitled *Kad Haqemah* [jug of the flour], and Isaac Abohab's similar fourteenth-century (ca.) *Menorat Hamaor* [lamp of the light], produce essays on spiritual/ethical topics and draw heavily on Talmudic aggadah.[54] In these works, the Talmud does not have pride of place but stands as an important repository of rabbinic teachings. The authors of these works make a deliberate and self-conscious attempt to rescue Talmudic aggadah from the discursive framework that had developed in predominantly legal directions.

The rise of print in the sixteenth century enabled the publication of two aggadic digests of the Talmud. Jacob ibn Habib (d. 1516), who had been exiled from Iberia and made his way to a leadership position in Salonika, published *Ein Yaaqov* [spring of Jacob], an aggadic digest of the Talmud that included ibn Habib's own commentary to this material, in 1516.[55] This work had been preceded by a similar work (sans commentary) entitled *Haggadot Hatalmud* [the aggadot of the Talmud] which had been printed in Constantinople in 1511. *Haggadot Hatalmud* was not reprinted. *Ein Yaaqov*, by contrast, went on to be published many times. In Eastern Europe, it was common for synagogue rabbis to offer classes for the laity using *Ein Yaaqov* as the curricular text. Such editions of the Talmud's aggadah helped canonize the Talmud as an inspirational guide for laypersons.

The Talmud was not born with the canonical authority that it was later to achieve. This authority is largely a product of the robust discourse of interpretation that arose around the work—the expanded Talmud. The richest part of this discourse is the Talmud's legal subdiscourse, the literature of halakhah. Commentaries, codes, and responsa produced the Talmud as both the laboratory of legal investigation and the raw materials for the experiments that transpired within it. A tremendous amount of cultural work went into understanding every sentence of Talmudic law and determining how those sentences would, in turn, have meaning in scholastic study halls and in the lived lives of Jews. A second nonlegal subdiscourse, the literature of aggadah, was far less unified but no less affected by the importance of the Talmud as a repository of the basic mythological, theological, and ethical ideas of Judaism. By the dawn of the print era, the Talmud was the most important canonical work of Judaism, the source of law and ideology, and the object of the most important devotional activity—study.

Rivals, Naysayers, Imitators, and Critics (Emblematic Talmud)

Talya Fishman's award-winning *Becoming the People of the Talmud* argues that the Talmud did not emerge from Late Antiquity with the authority and cultural centrality it was to have by the fourteenth century.[1] Fishman observes that both the theory and practice of jurisprudence and its relationship with the Talmud changed significantly from the ninth through the twelfth centuries. At the same time, the Talmud was undergoing a major technological shift from its existence as an oral literature to its re-creation as a written one. The story of the Talmud's cultural position is further complicated because the cultural authority of the Talmud and its role in education and jurisprudence were not identical in the different geographic regions of the period.

Fishman's 2011 book was the target of a review written by Haym Soloveitchik, a scholar with a long history of sharp reviews, in *The Jewish Review of Books*.[2] The review engendered a response from Fishman and the two scholars went back and forth with online missives. The strongest arguments in Soloveitchik's critique are predicated on spotting Fishman's mistakes of translation, interpretation, or emphasis. Rhetorically, Soloveitchik relies on these factual blunders to undermine Fishman's larger theses about the changing canonicity and social role of the Talmud. Fishman's book might be factually flawed, but it is also extremely consequential. Fishman has rung a bell about the Talmud's changing cultural position that cannot be unheard.[3]

Fishman's insight about the changing authority and canonicity of the Talmud connects with critical changes in the way academicians think of authority. It was once common to think of authority on an institutional model as a fixed quantity of power possessed by a certain group. Books were considered canonical, which was similarly considered a static essential quality. Michel Foucault's scholarship has transformed academic thinking about authority.[4] It is now more common to think of authority as a dynamic quality that is regularly being negotiated in relationships. Even in the context of institutional authority, such authority is regularly being constituted and reconstituted by all parties in the relationship. Applying this insight to works of literature, the canonical position of a book is also subject to the ebbs and flows of its reception. Even a work as profoundly canonical as the Bible has been transformed in modernity by the way its content no longer possesses the unequivocal authority it once did. It is undeniable that the Talmud's position as a canonical text has changed with time and place, and it is incumbent upon scholars to attempt to sensitize themselves to this fact and its ramifications.

The prior chapter introduced the enhanced Talmud through a description (and performance) of the mechanics of that discourse—how the various literatures of reception absorb the Talmud and interpret it in new ways. This insider picture of the Talmud's reception assumes the older historiographic paradigm in which the Talmud was an established work promulgated by the Geonim and spread in roughly the same form and with the same meaning throughout the Jewish world. The present chapter steps outside the insider discourse and provides a set of antagonist literature and movements that attempted to resist the Talmud as a source of cultural and legal authority. In some cases, ironically, this resistance helped buttress the cultural position that was being cultivated by the insider discourse.

One of the remarkable aspects of the Talmud's reception history has been its continued endurance and vitality despite the roadblocks it has encountered. One way of explaining these features might be to chalk them up to the Talmud's unique qualities, and to suppose that the Talmud would have endured under any historical conditions because of its inherent quality. The material in this chapter allows for a different explanation. It is not an inherent quality of the Talmud, but a specific set of events that allowed the Talmud to survive its antagonists. The emblematic Talmud—the register of the Talmud that is disconnected with its internal content and reflects its position as a cultural token—may be the key to understanding the Talmud's surprising persistence.

Much of the positive reception of the Talmud chronicled in the preceding chapter took place within larger cultural environments that were less than receptive to this eventuality. Embracing the conceit of a biography more fully, this chapter focuses on the Talmud's hostile relationships, producing four categories of people who opposed the Talmud: rivals, naysayers, imitators, and critics. From the rival Palestinian Talmud to the various historical movements, both Jewish and non-Jewish, that were antagonistic to the Talmud, there have been threats to the Talmud's survival, its canonization, and its election. Many of the Talmud's opponents are best understood as engaging the emblematic register rather than the essential or enhanced registers. Some of the fiercest opposition came from people with little familiarity with the book or its discourse, but strong interest in the cultural meaning of the Talmud—what the Talmud symbolizes. This negative symbolic attention at times augmented the reputation of the Talmud that emerged from its insider discourse. Ironically, some of the Talmud's most virulent opponents may have helped it become more culturally significant.

Rivals

The Babylonian Talmud (the Talmud) has a sibling in the Palestinian Talmud, its rival from the outset. As a term, "talmud" refers to a method of study that evolved into a genre of literature. During the period after the Mishnah was redacted around 200 CE, rabbis in both Palestine and Babylonia studied in an unusual style we now call

Talmudic, combining the definitive Mishnah with mi-drashic texts and other mishnah-style texts that were floating around in the rabbinic ether.

Both the Palestinian Talmud and the Babylonian Tal-mud are incomplete commentaries to the Mishnah. Where the Mishnah has sixty tractates, the Babylonian Talmud has only thirty-six and the Palestinian Talmud a different thirty-six.[5] The two Talmuds overlap on twenty-five tractates; the Palestinian has a nearly complete treat-ment of the mishnaic order Agriculture, while the Baby-lonian has several tractates on the mishnaic order Sanctities. The most fruitful comparison of the two works takes place within their overlapping tractates. This comparison demonstrates the strong relationship be-tween the two works despite their seeming geographic distance. Passages of the Palestinian often represent an earlier draft of the parallel treatment in the Babylonian.[6]

Nearly every page of the Talmud demonstrates that the Babylonian is more developed than its sibling. The named authorities in the Babylonian span six generations from the production of the Mishnah. In contrast, the Palestin-ian's named authorities span only four generations. The Palestinian had a gestation period that was around two generations shorter. The shorter gestation period affects the conceptual sophistication of the two works. There is a direct correlation between later named authorities and abstract conceptual articulation of ideas; the fourth gen-eration of Babylonian amoraim made astounding strides in legal conceptual thinking, and much of this work was furthered by the anonymous contributors who post-date the sixth generation of named amoraim in the Babylonian Talmud.[7] The Palestinian Talmud has only a small quantity of fourth-generation material and relatively little from Babylonia; not surprisingly, it is less conceptually sophisticated.

The anonymous authorities (known as the Stam) who are responsible for redacting the final versions of Talmudic *sugyot* [topical sections] in the Babylonian Talmud also play an important role in the distinction between the two siblings. The Babylonian is a highly stylized text, with clear delineation of questions and answers. Some of this stylization is the direct result of the editorial interventions of the Stam, who clarified the material they had received from their forebears by providing it with a loose but still recognizable structure. The Palestinian is far less stylized and its organization feels comparatively haphazard and opaque.

During the post-Talmudic period, the Geonim of Baghdad and their institutional yeshivot chose the Babylonian Talmud as their central curricular text. There was a yeshiva in Palestine that may have preferred the Palestinian Talmud.[8] No literary record survives from this institution, though, and there is no reliable evidence of it before the ninth century. The literary remains from elsewhere in Palestine during the second half of the first millennium CE suggest a diversity of interests from mysticism and philosophy to grammar, poetry, and biblical commentary. One reason for the elevation of the Babylonian Geonim as the world's *legal* experts was their single-minded devotion to the study of Talmudic law above all else. The attention paid to the Babylonian Talmud in their curriculum led to stylizations that were never performed on the Palestinian.

The rise of the Babylonian Talmud in Babylonia and later in France/Germany, Provence, and Spain/North Africa contributed to the inherent imbalance between the two Talmuds. While the Babylonian Talmud was copied repeatedly and generated various forms of commentary attending to all manners of textual confusion, the Palestinian Talmud languished unstudied. It did not develop a discourse like the ones detailed in the previous chapter. The continued study of the Bavli (Babylonian Talmud) led to even further stylization of its text in ways that allow the reader to quickly determine what the textual discussion intends. Rashi's commentary provides accessible explanations for the thorny issues; no similar work of commentary survives for the Palestinian Talmud. When critical scholars began to attend to the Palestinian Talmud in the modern era, they recognized a uniquely daunting set of technical problems that often make even basic comprehension of the text unattainable.[9]

The earliest printed edition of the Palestinian Talmud was published in two columns of text with no commentary.[10] Seventeenth- and eighteenth-century rabbis produced commentaries and enabled the production of print editions with surrounding commentaries that give the Palestinian Talmud the look and feel of its imposing sibling. These commentaries generally rely heavily on the Babylonian Talmud and often insert its ideas and interpretations into the Palestinian to explain the latter's ambiguously terse passages. English translations of the Palestinian Talmud have furthered this approach by leaning heavily on these Bavli-based commentaries.[11] The rivalry has become entirely unthreatening for the Bavli. Today, only a small subset of well-trained critical readers consistently works to tease out the rivalrous meanings of the original text.

Naysayers

The Karaites are a sect of Judaism that became demographically significant in the late ninth century. Karaism would remain an important sub-ideology for Jews within medieval Babylonia, Palestine, and North Africa for several centuries; remnants of the sect survive to the present but are less significant demographically and intellectually than they were at the height of their influence at the end of the eleventh century.[12] Early Karaites and their Rabbanite opponents considered Anan ben David, an eighth-century figure, to be the founder of Karaism, but this is an historical retrojection.[13] The Karaism that emerged in the late ninth century consolidated various sectarian groups deriving from Persia and Babylonia.[14] Anan ben David was employed as a shared origin figure because his literary work offered something of a unifying tome for the underlying core disagreements the Karaites had with their Rabbanite opponents.[15]

As in most schisms, the production of a formidable schismatic group in the Karaites produced a reactionary identity for the Rabbanites. While it would be simple to equate the Rabbanites with the Geonim and those earlier Babylonian rabbis who produced the Talmud, it is important to recognize that some of the positions espoused by the Rabbanites were direct polemical products of the Karaite opposition and were not long-held rabbinic positions. With this caveat, there is a fundamental feature that unified the Karaites behind Anan ben David: the rejection of the Talmud as a canonical work. Karaism draws its name from a renewed commitment to biblical scripture; the Karaite is a Biblicist. Ironically, to make the Bible work, the Karaite often must license radical strategies of reading. This was considered superior, however, to reliance on the Talmud, which represented (at least in part) someone else's radical strategies for reading the Bible.

Much of the struggle between the Karaites and Rabbanites was about matters of communal authority and control.[16] The smaller sects were critical of the coalescing authority of the Geonim and exilarchs. But the struggle was perceived by intellectuals in intellectual terms, and Anan ben David became a figure associated with this critique, probably because of the survival of his work, *Sefer Mizvot* [book of commandments]. Though the work, portions of which remain extant today, is thoroughly familiar with the Talmud and its hermeneutics, it honors this familiarity by consistently disagreeing with the Talmud and its rabbis.[17] Its insistence upon dogmatic rather than debated formulations and distinctions demonstrates a deliberate break with the Talmud.

Over the years, Anan's historical memory was associated with anti-Talmudism. The ninth-century figure Natronai Gaon describes Anan as having told his followers, "Forsake the word of the Mishnah and Talmud, and I will compose for you a Talmud of my own," and further describes Anan as having "composed a Talmud of wickedness and injustice for himself."[18] The rhetoric employed here echoes God's biblical threat/promise to Moses to destroy all of Israel and produce a new nation out of him.[19] The Talmud has come to embody the Jewish people and the threat of producing a new Talmud is analogized to doing nothing less than embodying a new religious culture. This kind of embodiment is the first rumbling of the Talmud's emblematic register. The original context for Natronai's comment is an alternative tradition in the Passover Haggadah, the liturgical guide to the ritual of the Passover Seder. Natronai believes that the Karaites have embraced this alternative formulation and rejected the standard Rabbanite formulation not for any substantive reason, but simply because the text in question emerges directly out of a Talmudic passage—for the symbolism of rejecting the Talmud. The Talmud's canonical position and liturgical role came to mark the boundary between the Karaites and the Rabbanites: as much as the former defined themselves in opposition to the Talmud, the latter defined themselves through insistence upon its canonical centrality. This is an important addition to the story outlined in the previous chapter of how the Talmud came to be canonized as the central work of Judaism. The more the Karaites insisted upon a

CHAPTER 4

Bible free of the Talmud, the more the Rabbanites and those who followed them would insist upon the Talmud as the exclusive filter through which the Bible is consumed. The Talmud's canonical authority grew as it became a symbol contested by two sides of the polemic.

Imitators

The previous chapter's discussion of codes explored the ambivalent relationship they have with the Talmud. Fully reliant on the Talmud for their content, such codes in a sense sought to supplant it and become the new central legal text. Some early codes are imitative of the Talmud both in form and in content because the early codifiers paraphrased the Talmud's content into code form. The most successful of these imitators, Alfasi's *Halakhot* [laws], came to somewhat replace the Talmud as a curricular text in twelfth-century Provence. In modernity, this work has seen something similar happen in terms of print format. Beginning in the late eighteenth century, it became standard practice to produce Alfasi's *Halakhot* in a layout that is associated with, and standard for, the Talmud itself.

Another imitator of the Talmud was the Zohar, the central canonical work of Kabbalah written by Moses de Leon in the thirteenth century as a pseudepigraphic second-century work. Though the Zohar is generally understood as a work of mystical midrash, it has features that are reminiscent of the Talmud. While the Zohar is an exegetical midrash (a work of midrash that tracks the order of the biblical text), it is frequently distracted or loses the train of argument in favor of something only loosely connected by association. Part of the author's pseudepigraphic strategy was to write the work in Aramaic. This connects the Zohar not only with Palestinian midrashim, but also with both Talmuds. The Palestinian (Western) form of Aramaic employed in the Zohar caused some contemporaries and near contemporaries to regularly cite the Zohar as the Palestinian Talmud.[20]

Though the Zohar's primary organization is exegetical, it is secondarily organized as the narrative (or narratives) of a set of ten mystical rabbis. The prevalence of stories about this inner circle of rabbis gives the Zohar the feel of Talmudic aggadah. It has been suggested that the rabbinic protagonists may be ciphers for Castilian mystics who, as a school, produced the material recorded in the Zohar.[21] Such a theory would make the Zohar a form of learning before it was a book—something like the genres (mishnah, midrash, and talmud) of rabbinic literature.

Scholars have noted a chronological depth to the Zohar's text whereby later texts comment and expand upon earlier texts. This has led to debates about authorship of the Zohar. Irrespective of those debates, this literary effect imitates the Talmud.[22]

Like *Halakhot*, the Zohar became a rival to the Talmud for certain groups at certain times. Most particularly, it reached iconic status in the Ottoman Empire with the dawn of the print age.[23] Among the Jews in

Ottoman lands, the desire for the Zohar was only loosely connected to its actual study. The number of printings suggests that many who purchased the work were not capable mystics but wanted to connect with this text by owning it. This chapter will go into more detail below about Shabtai Zevi and the Sabbateans; note, though, that Sabbatean loyalists routinely claimed devotion to the Zohar as opposed to the Talmud.[24] In these formulations, the Zohar is the Talmud's rival and successor as well as its imitator. Though this claim is unlikely to have been the historical intent of the Zohar's producers, its reception history produced it as a Talmudic imitator and occasional rival.

Critics

The Talmud has had vocal critics in its history both from outside the Jewish community and from within. Christian authorities at different points in time have been critical of the Talmud as an anti-Christian book.[25] For these critics, the Talmud symbolized Judaism and the Jews, embodying Jewish ideology for Christian religious thinkers who were inclined towards a concretization of ideology. Jewish factions and splinter groups have also been regular critics of the Talmud. When the criticism has come from within the Jewish community, it has generally not focused on a subset of content (as in the case with Christian criticism in light of anti-Christian content), but on the Talmud's discourse of reception (the enhanced Talmud) and its centrality to the production and sustenance of traditional life. Though the gap between each respective Jewish faction and a "traditional center" is both varied and fluid, for all of them the Talmud and its discourse were perceived as an anchor against which they could to push to liberate from tradition.

Christian Criticism

Christianity emerged from a bedrock of biblical and Second Temple Judaism and in competition with rabbinic Judaism that emerged similarly from those origins.[26] Religious ideologues from each of these religious groups were cognizant of the other's existence and, to some extent, of the differing choices the other represented with respect to their shared patrimony. Christian and Jew are important hermeneutic others for one another. Proximity forced ideologues to define the boundary by this specific exclusion—to be Jewish is not to be Christian and vice versa.

Early Christian intellectuals were curious about Jews and Judaism. Several such intellectuals produced a genre of literature that articulated the differences between Jews and Christians in a polemical attempt to celebrate the latter at the expense of the former.[27] Tertullian (d. 240) wrote his work *Adversus Judaeos* [against the Jews] asserting the replacement of Jews by Christians as people of God just as the rabbinic movement was hitting its stride with the publication of the Mishnah. One of the most influential works in this genre is John Chrysostom's

(d. 407) *Adversus Iudaeos*, a series of eight sermons intending to prevent Christians from enjoying the aesthetic experience of the synagogue and Jewish ritual that is contemporaneous with the later Talmudic materials. This genre of literature would continue to generate exemplars into the medieval period. During the twelfth century, there was an uptick in literary dialogues that imagined an encounter between Jewish and Christian interlocutors.[28]

The rise of Christianity as a state religion, beginning in the fourth century CE, forced Jews to react to their sister religion more guardedly. The hidden transcript of Jewish culture included a genre of literature, *Toldot Yeshu* [lineages of Jesus], which deals with its rival religion by producing an irreverent take on the gospel story of Jesus' life.[29] The quantity and variance of extant manuscripts of *Toldot Yeshu* suggest that this was more of a folk genre of writing rather than a scholastic project, but examples appear in the Talmud. The genre communicates a strident and satirically expressed animosity towards Christians.

Palestinian rabbinic literature is replete with passages that describe encounters between Jews and Christians or between Judaism and Christianity as ideologies. Since Palestine in the fourth century was a Byzantine (Eastern Roman) province in a newly Christian empire, the rabbinic writers had little choice but to engage the majority culture. Recall, though, that the Babylonian Talmud was produced within a Sasanian Zoroastrian culture in which Christians were a parallel minority to Jews.[30] Typical encounters between Jew and "other" in the Babylonian Talmud presume "others" who are either pagan or

Zoroastrian; there are comparatively few references to Christians or Christianity. Nevertheless, as a voluminous anthology with tremendous range, the Babylonian Talmud occasionally references Jesus and Christianity.[31]

The Talmud contains eight passages that reference Jesus by name. The form of some of these passages suggests that they originated as oral *Toldot Yeshu* genre stories. The story of their inclusion in the Talmud is like the story of the inclusion of all kinds of texts in the Talmud, which serves as a grab bag of Jewish Babylonian cultural production. To characterize the Talmud as an anti-Christian work based on these texts is as accurate as characterizing the Talmud as a work of throne mysticism or folk medicine. The Talmud has nearly two million words; fewer than two thousand discuss Jesus or Christianity.

The twelfth-century genre of imagined dialogues between Jew and Christian produced the first examples of Christian criticism of the Talmud.[32] Jewish converts to Christianity (Apostates) who could read the Talmud and understood its significance were the first critics. In a dialogue that imagines a conversation between his preconversion self (Moses) and his present self (Peter), Petrus Alfonsi (d. 1140) considers several Talmudic aggadot in order to demonstrate the irrational and silly nature of Jewish beliefs.[33] Another common issue raised by early Christian critics was the Talmud's mitigation or reinterpretation of the Old Testament; since Christians were invested in Jews as Old Testament people, they understood the Talmud to threaten the New Testament as a supplement that abrogates the Old Testament.

Several trends in the beginning of the thirteenth century brought the Jewish-Christian theological and literary tension off the pages and into reality in the form of live debates. The increasing power of the papacy combined with the new and strident mendicant orders (Dominicans and Franciscans) to reconsider the presence of the Jew as the medieval Christian "other".[34] Some of the latent interreligious hostility between the faiths had been expressed in the events of the Crusades (1096 and 1145), and also in cultural and religious reflections on those events by both traditions. The new orders applied some of their energies in the direction of proselytizing to the Jews, which led to an increase in the number of Jewish converts to Christianity in Northern Europe.[35]

THE PARIS DISPUTATION

Nicholas Donin is the major anti-Talmudic figure in the Paris Disputation of 1240. Though officially a disputation, a term that reflects the two-way dialogue of a debate, the encounter has long been characterized as a trial in which the Talmud was the defendant.[36] Donin had been a student of Rabbi Yehiel of Paris, one of the prominent Tosafists of this period. In 1238, Donin approached Pope Gregory IX with an indictment listing thirty-five accusations against the Talmud; these pointed to Talmudic passages that are theologically problematic for Christians as well as those that derive from the *Toldot Yeshu* genre and deride Jesus, Mary, and other figures of early Christianity. In separate letters, Gregory IX addressed the church authorities of Western Christendom, the mendicant orders (Franciscans and Dominicans), and the political rulers of Western Europe demanding that Talmuds be seized and delivered to the orders.

Louis IX (d. 1270) of France was the only figure to respond affirmatively to the request. At his behest, French Jews were arrested in their synagogues, and their books seized and turned over to the Franciscans and Dominicans. A trial was conducted in the presence of Blanche of Castile (d. 1252), Louis IX's mother. On June 25–26, 1240 Friar Nicholas Donin and Rabbi Yehiel of Paris debated the merits of the Talmud. The Talmud was convicted of the charges and sentenced to burning; after some delay, more than twenty cartloads of handwritten Talmudic codices were burned in the Place de Grève, the site of high profile Parisian executions.

Donin's accusations included claims: that the Talmud is an autonomous body of literature that undermines the connection between Jews and the Bible; that the Talmud is anti-Christian; and that some of its truth claims conflict with fundamental matters of Christian theology.[37] Aware of official theological understandings of the role of the Jews in Christendom as connected with the Old Testament, Donin specifically highlighted the ways in which the rabbis of the Talmud produced a work that licenses itself to overrule and ignore the Bible.[38] This argument was eye-opening within a Christian intellectual milieu that was invested in Jewish biblicism and had little exposure to or appreciation for the Talmud and its hermeneutic strategies. Through his accusations, Donin undermined the image of the Bible-loyal Jew and replaced it with the self-authorizing Jew who can ignore the Bible.

While Gregory IX had been most affected by this "new Jew," other clerical listeners, including Queen Blanche, were more taken with the *Toldot Yeshu* materials that were markedly anti-Christian. Donin also included other Talmudic materials that can be characterized as antisocial because of the ways in which they elevate Jewish insiders over non-Jewish outsiders (e.g., different liability protections for Jews v. non-Jews). Donin utilized materials from the larger Jewish canon, including liturgy and other works of rabbinic literature. The disputation was a trial of the Talmud (rather than of Judaism writ large) because that was how Donin and Gregory IX framed the matter. They constructed the Talmud as the repository of Jewish cultural knowledge. The Talmud was an excellent choice for such a construction since it is an anthology of rabbinic culture. By constructing the Talmud in this way, Donin could attack the core canonical text of the tradition from the meager set of texts in the *Toldot Yeshu* style that entered the corpus.

The Paris Disputation personified the Talmud. It indicted the book as though it were a person, put it on trial, and executed it at the site of public, high-profile executions. Donin was intimately aware, as a cultural insider, of the significance the Talmud held for the Jews. Personification of the Talmud made its body a substitute for the body of Israel.

Donin was not the only one to personify the Talmud. When defending it from attack, Rabbi Yehiel of Paris employs metaphors that incorporate the Talmud into the national body of the Jews: "he who touches [the Talmud], touches our very eye."[39] And then, understanding that the physical destruction of copies of the Talmud in Paris is at stake, he notes that copies of the Talmud exist outside of France and in the non-Christian world: "our bodies are in your power but not our souls."[40] In this line of thought, the Talmud becomes synonymous with Judaism or Jews, and the physical destruction can only destroy the body, for the content will survive in copies elsewhere. This is a particularly damning response within a theological understanding of the Jews as *Carnal Israel,* Israel of the body. R' Yehiel, in effect, responds that the Jews will not be embodied in the Talmud, for the Talmud is its soul (content) which inhabits other bodies elsewhere and will survive this execution.

The thirteenth century was a visceral time in Northern European Christendom. Disputes over relics in the twelfth century had demonstrated a shift in religious rituals towards embodied and physical artifacts. There was an increase in devotional practices related to Christ's body, and to a more profound commitment to notions of incarnation present in the Eucharist and other practices. The shift is also evident in the ways in which imitation of Christ, once a question of personality traits and ethics, became, in the hands of Francis and his followers, a physical pietistic practice of receiving the stigmata.[41]

These transformations in Christian theology and perception had an effect on the Jewish population. The 1215 Fourth Lateran Council instituted the notion of marking the Jewish body with a sign of Jewishness. Consider also the typical anti-Semitic accusations that began in the late twelfth century and flourished in the thirteenth and fourteenth. The blood libel, ritual murder, and host desecration charges all imagined Jews as invested in the visceral religiosity prevalent within Christianity. These represented a form of counter-ritual in which the Christians imagined Jewish rituals as analogs of Christian embodied practices. Within this cultural mindset, it was entirely expected that a Jew would need to physically embody Christ and reenact the Passion to fulfill his or her ritual. If wafer and wine could be the body and blood, then matzah and blood could work in similar ways. The rise of these kinds of accusations against Jews, even in the absence of supporting evidence, pointed to the cultural necessity of the charges—the cultural work that the charges were doing. The first time a ritual murder charge provoked anti-Jewish violence was in 1235.

The absence of Jewish iconography is another factor in explaining the prevalence of the host desecration charges within Christendom. It is as if the lack of Jewish religious symbols required the Jews (who are being constructed on a Christian analog) to engage in negative rituals—rituals that employed and destroyed Christian religious bodies. Along the same lines, the physical embodying of the Talmud as Jews or Judaism provided another avenue for making Judaism analogously visceral. The burning of the Talmud became a form of ritual murder in its own right. The Talmud functioned as the scapegoat for Judaism and the Jews by embodying their perceived perfidies and receiving their punishment.

The burning of Talmuds was witnessed by Meir of Rothenburg, who had come to study with Rabbi Yehiel of Paris as a young man, and who would later achieve rabbinic literary renown as Maharam of Rothenburg (d. 1293). Struck by the intensity of what he witnessed, Meir penned a lament that remains part of the Jewish liturgy of the Ninth of Av, a summer fast day commemorating all Jewish tragedies since the destruction of the Temple. Meir's lament addresses the burnt Talmuds in the second person:

> "Ask, oh you consumed by flame, how your mourners fare; Those who long to reside in the courtyard of your palace; those who pant to inhale the dust of the land, and those in pain. Those confounded by the scorching of your scrolls. . . ."[42]

The poem is modeled on prior Hebrew poetry and is most influenced by "Zion whom I will not ask," a poem written by the Andalusian poet Judah Halevi.[43] Halevi's poem follows traditional biblical and liturgical models to understand Israel as the embodied feminine love interest of the masculine Jewish people. Maharam substitutes the Talmud for Jerusalem, producing the Talmud as the new Zion, the new emblem of erotic attraction. The word Talmud has grammatical male gender, so Maharam takes considerable license to alter the book's gender. The switch highlights the extent to which Jewish erotic attraction to the Talmud is essential to the poem. Within the Talmud itself there are moments in which the rabbis constitute the discourse of learning, sometimes referred to as the talmud, as a rival to their female spouses.[44] The most famous example of such is Ben Azzai's response to the normative requirement that he wed and have children: "what shall I do, my soul yearns for Torah."[45] Wedding this rabbinic attraction for Talmud-as-Torah with the need to replace Zion in a post-destruction world yields Maharam's unique lament. He communicates in unequivocal terms the canonical place of the Talmud in the thirteenth century: this once oral piece of literature had become the embodiment of Jewish ideology and Jews, and its study had become the driving metanarrative of an elite learning culture.

FROM BURNING TO CENSORSHIP

Other disputations followed the precedent of 1240. A 1263 disputation in Barcelona featured a single Jewish disputant, Nahmanides. A twenty-month disputation was later conducted in Tortosa during 1413–1414, in the context of attempts to generate mass Jewish conversions. The Talmud played a central role in both disputations as the source of Jewish dogma. The Christian side employed the Talmud differently in these disputations than it had in 1240 Paris. In Paris, the Talmud was tried and executed. In Barcelona and Tortosa, the Christian side raised the charges of Talmudic blasphemy, alongside an attempt to employ the Talmud and other works of rabbinic literature to prove the truth of Christianity.[46] One of the participants in the Barcelona affair was the Dominican

Raymundi Martini, who wrote a book, *Pugio Fidei* [identification of faith], which references many rabbinic passages that dovetail with Christian ideology. This utilitarian use of the Talmud suppressed some of the anti-Talmudic hostility. Rather than oppose the Talmud as blasphemy, Christians were now reading the Talmud and using it to entice Jewish apostasy.[47]

Pope Gregory IX died in 1241 and was succeeded, briefly, by Pope Celestine IV. Celestine IV was succeeded in 1243 by Pope Innocent IV, who wrote a letter in 1244 to King Louis IX ratifying Gregory's actions vis-à-vis the Talmud, and asking that the Talmud again be collected and burned. In 1247, though, Innocent IV backtracked from this strident position based on the plea of French rabbis that the Talmud is essential to Jewish life. This is somewhat surprising since the centrality of the Talmud motivated the original trial. Innocent decided to allow the Talmud to survive in censored form. This, in effect, allowed the Talmud to continue if it could be excised of its anti-Christian bits. Innocent's change of heart was not embraced by all his underlings. Odo of Chateauroux, the chancellor of the University of Paris who had been involved in the Donin disputation and burning, wrote a long letter objecting to the reversal.[48] Odo would later head a commission that reexamined the Talmud and, using the new findings, refused to follow papal instructions to return the Talmud to the Jews of Paris.[49]

This policy of censorship would continue under subsequent popes, but the technological context of handwritten codices made censorship impractical. In 1320,

Pope John XXII asserted that Christians who studied the Talmud were guilty of Judaization and, under his orders, the Talmud was again burned in Burgos, Toulouse, Paris, and elsewhere.[50] The rise in surveillance and censorship was made possible by the rise of the mendicant orders and the nascent universities that produced intellectuals who could read the Hebrew/Aramaic text and edit it.

A final episode of Talmudic persecution during the twilight of handwritten codices (in 1509–1510 Germany) found the Talmud defended by Johannes Reuchlin, a noted Christian Hebraist, on the grounds of intellectual curiosity. Johannes Pfefferkorn, a Jewish convert to Christianity, issued a pamphlet recommending the seizure and burning of the Talmud. Emperor Maximilian was persuaded and licensed Pfefferkorn to seize books in Frankfurt. The Archbishop of Mainz, Uriel von Gemmingen, opposed Pfefferkorn's actions, and Maximilian appointed him to lead a panel to investigate the Talmud. Reuchlin was one of the panelists and decided in the Talmud's favor. Reuchlin felt that only polemical works such as *Toldot Yeshu* should be prohibited, but that the Talmud itself should not be banned, particularly by people who did not know it. [51] Reuchlin was more interested in Kabbalah, but could not countenance banning a book he did not know. Reuchlin interrupted an action against the emblematic Talmud through a call to its essential content.

The true impact of censorship began to be manifest in the sixteenth century when the dawn of print and the Reformation led to a programmatic insistence on surveillance and censorship of Hebrew texts. In September

1553, Pope Julius III issued an edict to gather and burn all copies of the Talmud in the Campo die Fiori in Rome.[52] Similar burnings took place throughout Italy (in Venice, Milan, and Cremona) as well as in Spain and France. The seizures and burnings were part of a Counter-Reformation war waged against heresy of all types, and primarily targeted a Christian rather than a Jewish public. Despite Jewish entreaties to the Pope, the ban on the Talmud remained in place even as permission was granted for the printing and studying of codes of Jewish law. In the sixteenth century, this factor contributed to the rising prestige and curricular centrality of these codes at the Talmud's expense (as discussed in the prior chapter).[53] Eventually, the internal deliberations within the church led to a new policy of expurgation that allowed works to be printed so long as they were cleaned of their blasphemies.

In 1564, the Council of Trent permitted the publication of the Talmud, with restrictions. One of these restrictions was the word "Talmud," which was now routinely replaced by its Aramaic equivalent, "Gemara"; this term appears ubiquitously in the text and came to be a common Jewish term for the Talmud. The seizures and restrictions in Italy made the Talmud scarce in Western Europe and led to the printing of the Basel edition of 1578–1581.[54] Proximity to controversy marks this edition as the most damaged by censorship. An entire tractate, Avodah Zarah (dealing with Jewish relationships with pagan non-Jews) was omitted. In other places, passages are either omitted, modified, or printed with an accompanying marginal interpretation. Many of these changes remained uncorrected in subsequent print editions until the present. Some subsequent editions were printed with disclaimers to inform the reader that the Talmud's use of the term "others" does not refer to contemporary Christians.

ENLIGHTENMENT CRITIQUE

While the anti-Christian *Toldot Yeshu* passages functioned metonymically to define the Talmud in the High Middle Ages, it was the antisocial Talmudic passages that came to define this corpus in the Renaissance and Enlightenment. The issues of rights and citizenship spotlighted consideration of the position of the Jew in society. The microscopic attention to Jewish difference that ensued from consideration of these issues led to a new non-Jewish encounter with the Talmud. The Talmud was a concrete and tangible object to reference when suggesting that Jewish ideology was antithetical to modernity, and held the Jews back from participation in the modern state. As Western thought was becoming more explicitly philosophical rather than religious, the Talmud's support for ethnic difference in commercial law and in theology became a justification for anti-Semitism and philosophical resistance to Jewish emancipation. Johann Eisenmenger's *Endecktes Judenthum* [Judaism unmasked] sought to paint Judaism in a negative light by producing a specific selection of primary text and translation, the bulk of which was taken from the enhanced Talmud.[55] This work generated considerable controversy when it was first published in 1700, which only increased as it was later translated widely and influenced many nineteenth-century anti-Semitic writings. A subsequent scandal erupted over the publication of Alexander Mc-Caul's *The Old Path*, a work that did not target the Jews as such, but the specific character of Judaism communicated by the Talmud.[56] McCaul addressed himself to Western political rulers and asked them to require Jews to renounce their Talmudism and embrace Christian brotherly love as a prerequisite for rights. The same idea motivated the Russian Minister of Education, Sergei Uvarov, to attempt a state-imposed educational system that would de-emphasize the Talmud within the Jewish curriculum in the Pale of Settlement.[57]

Criticism from Jewish Factions and Splinter Groups

The Talmud was not just criticized by Christian non-Jews. Rather, various new Jewish movements used distance from the Talmud as a defining feature. By the early modern period, the Talmud was entrenched as a canonical work whose authority was essential to the traditional community and its ritual, family, and commercial life. In different ways, Sabbateanism, Hasidism, Frankism, Reform, and Zionism all established themselves by separating from the traditional community. The Talmud served as a finite stand-in for that community.

External factors played as important a role as internal ones in maintaining the unity of the Jewish community before modernity. Tax burdens placed on the Jewish community and anti-Jewish violence exerted external pressure on Jews to remain within their communities. Anti-Jewish economic and social policies made it virtually impossible to survive as an individual outside the Jewish community. All this contributed to the collective authority of the insider establishment. Rabbis and other communal leaders gained power not only through their scholarly merit, but also through family connections, socioeconomic position, and personal charisma.

SABBATEANISM

No drama of modern Jewish history can match the story of the man from Smyrna (present-day Turkey) who was the most successful aspirant to the title "Messiah" in modern history. From humble origins as a migrant aspiring mystic, Shabtai Zevi (d. 1676) became internationally renowned and developed a strong following both in the Sefardic Ottoman Empire and in Ashkenazic Europe. Zevi's candidacy was promoted by Nathan of Gaza (d. 1680), a learned Palestinian mystic who believed Zevi to be the fulfillment of the latent messianic aspirations in the mystical teachings of Isaac Luria (d. 1572). Luria had produced a new metanarrative for Jewish mysticism. The original Kabbalistic metanarrative is the story of the arrangement of the Sefirot into different patterns. Luria inserted both linearity and purpose into this understanding. The Sefirot were broken by God's act of creation and could be likened to shattered glass receptacles; the present-day kabbalist works ritually to repair these receptacles and make God whole again. The linearity in Luria's metanarrative had clear messianic ramifications: when enough good deeds had been done to repair the world, a messiah would materialize and usher in an idyllic period. Shabtai Zevi was born a half century after Luria's ideas began to be propagated.

Shabtai Zevi's charisma sometimes took the form of public violations of traditional law or grand theatrical performances that highlighted his messianic claims. At the height of Zevi's fame and popularity, tensions rose between the camp of the "believers" and the camp of the "infidels." Nathan of Gaza recommended that followers of Zevi abandon the study of rabbinic halakhah (law) for the study of aggadah and Kabbalah. This was identified by two of the leading polemicists for the infidels, Judah Halevi and Jacob Sasportas, as undermining the authority of the Talmud and potentially leading to a schism that would produce two different religions.[58] Note how the Talmud has been identified entirely with its legal content through this reaction. One could say that Nathan of Gaza was merely shifting emphasis from the legal to the nonlegal, but that is not how Halevi and Sasportas understood it. The threat to tradition was articulated as a challenge to the Talmud, and that challenge inherently represented the threat of a religious schism.

In its explicit embrace of mystical and mythological traditions, Sabbateanism often pushed for antinomian transformations to traditional communal life. This led to declarations to transform fast days to feast days, ritualized enactments of mythological relationships between

Zevi-as-God and Torah-as-bride and even to Zevi's marrying a former prostitute. This antinomian energy connected with mysticism and mythology gave the Sabbateans the strength to resist the moral policing of the rabbinic authorities who would claim that such events violated Talmudic law. This clash between the law and mystical understandings of the world would continue with the Hasidim.

HASIDISM

It has been some time since Gershom Scholem invited controversy by connecting the rise of Hasidism in the eighteenth and nineteenth centuries with the success of Sabbateanism.[59] While there is understandable resistance to the connection, there is important overlap for these movements' respective attitudes towards the Talmud. Like Sabbateanism, Hasidism was a popular religious movement that combined charismatic leadership, a form of messianic thinking (albeit in localized form), and Lurianic mysticism to completely reimagine the metanarrative of Jewish life. Both movements appealed to an ignored populace that was not being spiritually nourished by the elitist forms of traditional Judaism and its Talmudic discourse. And both movements occasioned explicit comments, primarily among detractors, that they set out to depose the Talmud and its authority.

The founding of Hasidism is attributed to Israel Ben Eliezer (1700–1760), also known as the "Ba'al Shem Tov" [master of the good name] or by its acronym, *Besht*, though it is more accurate to say that his spiritual ministerings—folk religiosity characterized by amulets, spells, and healing—lay at the heart of a popular shaman-based religiosity that in retrospect came to be understood as the beginning of Hasidism. As the movement coalesced into a demographically significant one, it came to be characterized by: an emphasis on mystical access to God, embrace of emotions, wordless music, inspirational storytelling, and the personal charisma of individual *tzaddikim/rebbes* [righteous ones/masters]. Its take on Lurianic mysticism involved the radical extension of Lurianic notions of repairing the world to all life activities, whether sacred or profane.

The charismatic shamans who founded the earliest Hasidic movements drew their authority from personal charisma and mystical achievement rather than scholarly achievement or reputation. According to a statement attributed to *Besht,* "The *neshama* [soul] told the Rav (Besht) that the reason why the supernal matters were revealed to him was not because he had studied many Talmudic tractates and codes of law, but because he recited his prayers with great concentration."[60] The Besht and other Hasidic authorities often had little training in Talmud.[61] And this cannot be discounted as part of these leaders' popular appeal.

Beyond the popular appeal of an anti-Talmud platform, early Hasidic writers registered a strong critique of Talmud study as an intellectual activity.[62] As part of their focus on prayerful intention as a mystical avenue, Hasidic writers mocked rote Talmud study as mechanical and devoid of devotional intention. Some even explicitly encouraged devotees not to adopt these practices. As a result, there emerged a charged opposition, collectively known as the *Misnagdim* [opponents], who opposed the Hasidim. The Misnagdim in Lithuania were particularly animated by the ramifications of Hasidism for Talmud study and Talmudism. In their polemical writings, the early Misnagdim drew attention to rumors of episodes in which Hasidim disrespected Talmudic authorities or the Talmud itself.

Hasidism was less radical than Sabbateanism in its antinomian move. The initial push away from the Talmud and Talmudism, nevertheless, was intentional and strident. Over time, though, Misnagdic criticism, the needs of traditional life, and the decline of mystical charisma led to a return of Talmudo-centrism within Hasidism. Some groups already emphasized Talmud study in the late nineteenth century and others only in the twentieth. Once Hasidism had been established as its own viable traditional community, it did not need the anti-Talmudic energy that had been essential to producing its escape velocity. An established Hasidic community needed the benefits of continuity and institutionalization afforded by Talmud study and the Talmud's discourse.

FRANKISTS

The Frankists were far less demographically significant than either the Sabbateans or the Hasidim. Jacob Frank spent his childhood in many areas of the Jewish world. Born in Podolia (Ukraine), Frank moved to several places in the Ottoman Empire and Central Europe where he was exposed to Sabbateanism.[63] Returning to Podolia in the 1750s, Frank unified the Sabbateans around himself until 1756, when he was caught leading a group of them in antinomian rituals. Though Frank fled to the Ottoman Empire, those who remained behind were presented by the Jewish Council of the Four Lands to Mikolas Dembowski, bishop of Podolia, for violating norms (like adultery) that would offend both Christians and Jews. Dembowski gave the Frankists the opportunity to defend themselves, and they defined themselves out of the Jewish community by labeling themselves "Contra-Talmudists" and claiming to find Trinitarian theology within their study of Kabbalah.[64] On August 2, 1756, several Frankists submitted a document to the Lvov consistory renouncing the Talmud as a work of blasphemy that is contrary to both reason and the word of God.[65] On June 20–28, 1757, a disputation was held between forty rabbis and nineteen Contra-Talmudists in Podolia. Dembowski ruled for the Contra-Talmudists, the Talmud was ordered burned, and Sabbateanism became an officially recognized form of Judaism. Dembowski's death shortly thereafter brought a halt to his support, and many Frankists fled to Turkey to join Frank there. When a successor of Dembowski got into trouble over blood libel issues, he revived the "Contra-Talmudists" to extract from them a "confession" that the Talmud requires the use of Christian blood in the production of matzah. A new disputation was held over the summer of 1759 that explicitly discussed the Talmudic requirement on all Jews to use Christian blood. This disputation was a turning point in Frankist ethnic definition. After this disputation, the Frankists were seen not as deviant Jews but as candidates for Christianization. Most of them were baptized shortly thereafter and the Frankists came to be a form of Christianity.[66]

What is striking about the Frankist example, is the way in which the Talmud comes to explicitly mark the boundary for ethnic inclusion such that one can claim to the authorities, "I am not Jewish because I do not abide by the Talmud." The Frankists were aware of the Karaites and in some ways modeled themselves on the Karaite example of an anti-Talmudic Jewish community. But the Frankists seem far more opportunistic, taking advantage of the Talmud's curricular centrality to employ it as an anchor from which to push away and achieve escape. The combination of the Sabbateans, Hasidim, and Frankists makes the symbolic centrality of the Talmud to traditional premodern Jewish identity quite explicit.

Anti-Talmud in Modernity: Haskalah, Reform, Zionism

For three modern Jewish movements, Haskalah, Reform, and Zionism, the Talmud came to embody tradition and resistance to modernity. As with the three mystical charismatic groups charted above, these movements distanced themselves from the Talmud in order to establish the new group as modern and nontraditional.

Haskalah

The *Haskalah* [Jewish Enlightenment] is strongly associated with one figure, Moses Mendelssohn (1729–1786). Mendelssohn achieved renown as a friend of Gotthold Lessing, who would base a character in his play *Nathan the Wise* on him. Though Mendelssohn was an intellectual powerhouse, his person was as historically significant as his scholarly output. He embodied the enlightened Jew whom enlightened Western European Christians could imagine as possessing equal rights. Mendelssohn's scholarly works consisted of philosophical essays and his translation/commentary to the Bible. Inherent in his choice of translating the Bible into High German was a form of Jewish Protestantism that sought to turn to the Bible and away from the Talmud and rabbinic literature. Heinrich Heine (1797–1856) once said that Moses Mendelssohn overthrew the Talmud in the same way that Luther overthrew the papacy: both turned to the Bible to overturn later authority.[67] This quote equates Talmud with pope, demonstrating the way in which the Talmud personifies rabbinic authority.

Toward the end of his life Mendelssohn addressed himself to "The Jewish Question": the issue of whether Jews should receive human and civil rights in post-monarchic representative governments and their respective civil societies. This issue animated much of the *Haskalah*'s intellectual project, which was largely tendentious, motivated by the need to project an image of Judaism as ecumenical rather than particularistic. The Talmud contains many texts that reflect ethnic exceptionalism. Whether dealing with metaphysical questions of the afterlife, or legal questions regarding torts, the Talmud regularly differentiates between Jewish self and non-Jewish other. As a massive anthology, though, the Talmud also contains passages that do not differentiate between ethnic insiders and outsiders. The reputation of the Talmud as an exclusivist document was compounded by the dominant social context of Talmud study, which was insular, exclusive, and occurred within a Jewish cultural bubble sealed off from engagement with external philosophies and sciences.

But the Talmud was not only studied in such bubbles. Christian interest in the Talmud increased in the seventeenth century, and several leading Christian intellectuals engaged Jewish study partners to properly immerse themselves in study of the text for several years. This engagement led to far more sophisticated Christian understandings of the text, which yielded both Aramaic-Latin lexicons and the occasional Christian defense of the Talmud as far more than a repository of anti-Christian sayings. It also produced a larger number of Christians conversant with the Talmud on a basic level and able to focus on the Talmud's exclusivist positions. Haskalah inherited this intellectual reality.

Mendelssohn's choice to focus on the Bible was one solution to the problem. By shifting the curriculum from the Talmud to the Bible, *Maskilim* [enlightened ones] would be able to somewhat abandon the reputational issues of the Talmud.[68] Other Maskilim were less inclined towards amputation and more inclined towards rehabilitation.[69] Recognizing that the problem of the Talmud was largely its curricular role and context, some Maskilim began to reconceive of Talmudic education and reimagine what the Talmud represents. They objected to the exclusive study of the Talmud, the study of the Talmud in a vacuum, and the pilpulistic style of Talmud study that favored intellectual gymnastics over knowledge acquisition and development.[70]

In 1782, Naphtali Herz Wessely published *Divre Shalom Ve'emet* [words of peace and truth], an open letter to the Jews of Austria asking them to comply with the edict of tolerance and capitulate to the demand that Jewish schools teach more than exclusively Jewish content. The Free School, founded in 1778 on this basis, did not include Talmud in its curriculum. Wessely writes, "We were not all created to become Talmudists."[71] The curricular efforts of the Maskilim were aided by government authorities who also accepted the theory that insularity was keeping the Jews separate, and sought to make them more useful to the state by educating them into the broader culture. Under the influence of the Russian Haskalah, Russian authorities compelled the yeshivot in the late nineteenth century to teach several daily hours of a non-Jewish curriculum.

Some of the earliest Maskilim, though, set out to reclaim the Talmud as a work that can and should be studied alongside science and other disciplines.[72] *Measef*, [gatherer] an early journal of the Haskalah, committed itself at the outset to regularly publish articles on the

Talmud. Isaac Euchel (1756–1804), one of the editors of the journal, asserts in the premier issue that with the proper scientific context, hitherto disrespected passages of the Talmud will glow like the purity of heaven.[73] In the hands of various early Maskilim, the rabbis of the Talmud become Maskilim themselves, possessed of rationality, engagement with other disciplines, and reflective of humanistic values and talents.

The Maskilim had grown frustrated with the tendency for the Talmud to become more important as cultural capital, and its manipulation more important for establishing the bona fides of a practitioner, rather than as an end. Thus, they sought to move the study of the Talmud away from fine casuistry and its heaps of distinctions and towards a substantive engagement with this text from the past. By severing the Talmud from the pedagogical and cultural discourse that had risen around it, they attempted to reclaim the Talmud as a sacred and inspirational work possessed of rigorous, rational, and even scientific knowledge. The Maskilim wished to represent the Talmud as a modern text. In this sense, they prefigured the Jewish Studies movement that began in the 1820s and employed the new tools of university classics to treat rabbinic literature as classical literature.

REFORM

As Jewish emancipation came to be a strong possibility, and civil life was possible outside of the Jewish community, westernized Jews bristled at the contours of conventional traditional life. For many, the solution to this friction was conversion to Protestantism. Others remained within the Jewish fold but found outlets for their identity primarily outside of that community, and increasingly schooled their children according to non-Jewish post-Enlightenment standards. Histories of Reform Judaism focus on the ideologues and institutions that broke away from the traditional community, but in a larger sense, these communal individuals and structures were catching up to a trend of de-Judaization that had already begun and was demographically significant.

In 1837, an anonymous German Jewish author penned an article entitled "Jews and Judaism" and subheaded "Reflections of a Layman" that laid out a strong critique of traditional Judaism, and recognized that the rabbis who must cater to broad interests in the community cannot be expected to do what is necessary to transform Judaism.[74] This is a generous way of stating what must have been obvious—that one could not count on a rabbinate comprised of people who had been trained in a certain way, to suddenly deny their own credentials by reforming the faith. Among the article's declarations is the statement that today's laity

> do not feel in conscience bound to invest the prescriptions of the Talmud, to say nothing of the later rabbis, in as far as these cannot be proven by scientific exegesis to have been derived directly from the Bible or to have been handed down by Moses, with any greater authority that is accorded all other temporary

religious institutions whose reasonableness and whose agreement with the spirit of Judaism must first be established.[75]

This quotation connects the overthrow of the Talmud with the role of science in producing knowledge, the elevation of the Bible as the exclusive religiously authoritative canonical text, and the strategy of treating the rabbinic period as deliberately nonspecial. The man on the street had little use for the Talmud. As Benjamin Disraeli's father, Isaac, had put it in the British context of 1833, "let their Talmud be removed to an elevated shelf, to be consulted as a curiosity of antiquity, and not as a manual of education."[76]

A few years after the anonymous article's appearance, a group of laypeople banded together, calling themselves *Reformfreunde* [friends of Reform] and espousing three fundamental principles. The second principle was that "[t]he collection called the Talmud, as well as the rabbinic writings and statutes which rest upon it, possess no binding force for us in either dogma or in practice."[77]

Intellectuals pining for reform emerged from two related intellectual movements, the Haskalah (with its preference for Bible and critique of Talmudism) and *Wissenschaft des Judenthums*, [science of Judaism] the academic Jewish Studies movement whose founding coincides with the earliest Reform intellectuals and which had some personnel overlap with early Reform. Prior to becoming the putative founder of Wissenschaft, Leopold

Zunz opined that no lasting reform could be achieved "until the Talmud will be overthrown."[78]

Though rejection of the Talmud was an obvious necessity to lay leaders and intellectuals, it was a somewhat difficult position for reforming rabbis to reach. One could even say that explicit and unequivocal rejection of the Talmud and its relevance for the present labeled a rabbi "extreme." Solomon Holdheim (1806–1860) evolved from more moderate religious positions to an extreme one in which he said that the Talmud was right for its time but not for the current time.[79] This issue was so divisive that when Abraham Geiger contemplated a schism between traditional and reform communities in 1832, he framed it as pro-Talmud versus anti-Talmud.[80]

The Talmud is a remarkably flexible document of legal and dogmatic precedent. A gifted Talmudist can re-narrativize a Talmudic legal scenario in a seemingly limitless number of ways: the resuscitation of a rejected position in the Talmud, a nuanced interpretation of a passage that had been understood differently, the discovery of minority positions—all have the potential to transform a ruling. Early Reform impulses were channeled within the Talmudic discourse, as rabbis trained in that discourse exercised their intellectual creativity in the discovery of new possibilities within the old rituals and institutions. Aaron Chorin (1766–1844), who penned a learned defense of certain reforms in the 1818 context of division within Hamburg, would insist as late as 1844 that only the Talmud and its discourse could sanction reform.

Abraham Geiger had a more complex and changing relationship with the Talmud. As both the most compelling Jewish Studies scholar of his day and a founding figure of the nineteenth-century Reform movement, Geiger merits closer attention. In 1836, he wrote to Joseph Direnbourg that "the Talmud must go, the Bible . . . as something divine must go."[81] While this may have been his advocated position, as a scholar Geiger produced a more sophisticated understanding of the Talmud, one that protested reigning anti-Talmudic sentiment by demonstrating the value the Talmud held for understanding the Second Temple period and the transition from biblical to rabbinic ideas. Geiger's scholarship undermined the attempt to sever the unholy Talmud from the sacred Bible. For Geiger, rejection of the Talmud went hand-in-hand with rejection of the Bible; both books needed to be historicized and understood in light of their cultural moments of production and neither possessed the authority to dictate from the divine to the present.

Reform began in Germany, was continued elsewhere in Protestant Europe, and grew much larger in the United States. Mainstream American Reform did not go to war against the Talmud. Isaac Mayer Wise achieved a compromise with Orthodox colleagues at the Cleveland conference of 1855 that included recognition of the divinity of the Bible and the authority of the Talmud.[82] David Einhorn, who had defended Geiger and attacked the *Frankfurt Reformfreunde* while he was in Bavaria, became more radical as an American Reform rabbi and strongly critiqued the Cleveland conference in unequivocally anti-Talmudic terms. The Talmud had value, Einhorn wrote, but it was obsolete, morally narrow, and focused on the letter rather than the spirit of biblical Judaism.[83] The Pittsburgh Platform, authored by Kaufman Kohler (Einhorn's son-in-law), created a foundational role for the Bible but was silent about the Talmud.[84] Although Kohler, as president of Hebrew Union College, reduced the quantity of Talmud study in the curriculum of Reform rabbinical students, the *requirement* to study Talmud was never eliminated.

Zionism

In 1962, David Ben Gurion, then Prime Minister of Israel, participated in a live debate with the writer Haim Hazaz about the importance of the Bible for the Zionist cause and Zionist education.[85] Hazaz opened the event with a profound rallying cry for the study of rabbinic literature as a paradigm for an evolved and inclusive set of Jewish literatures.

> Not by the mouth of the Bible do we live. And the Bible is not by itself all of Judaism. Judaism began with the destruction of the Temple and not with the Bible. The Oral Torah is that which made us a perpetual nation, not the book of the Bible . . . The Oral Torah is an intimate matter, the intimate jargon of God and Israel . . .[86]

Ben Gurion's response is dripping with resistance to any inclusion of rabbinic literature in the Zionist canon.

By the time of this debate, in the early 1960s, Ben Gurion's position rejecting the Talmud in the name of Zionism had been firmly entrenched.

Zionism is the Jewish version of nineteenth-century nationalism. Like other nationalisms, Zionism was nurtured by the Enlightenment notions of civic and ethnic autonomy and self-determination. Nationalisms fed off antireligious currents that allowed devotion to state and ethnicity to subtly and gradually supplant devotion to church and religious community. This alone explains some of the negative interaction between Zionism and the Talmud. For many Zionists, Zionism was a secularist ideology that was breaking from religious ideologies; the Talmud strongly embodied this religious ideology.

Beyond the general antipathy between nationalism and religion, there are uniquely Jewish aspects of Zionism as Jewish nationalism that affect the relationship between Zionism and the Talmud. Unlike many of the nationalisms that sprung up in the nineteenth century, Jewish nationalism emerged among a people geographically distanced from the homeland they would claim as the terrain of their state. Zionism needed to justify not only that the Jews were a nation (not merely an ethnicity or religious community) but that the nation was connected to its national home. The Talmud's centrality to the diasporic community and its survival marked the Talmud as shifting soil upon which to build an argument for nationhood. The Talmud as a diasporic document represented an argument *against* a national home and *for* diasporic dispersion.[87] This reality was magnified by the existence of a rival Palestinian Talmud that had been produced in the Jewish land. The Babylonian Talmud came to represent Babylonian, non-Palestinian identity, and undermined claims to the land of Israel. This was especially true when compared with the Bible, whose every story decorated another peak or desert village with a Jewish star.

The Babylonian Talmud is written in a combination of Hebrew and Aramaic but is often thought of as an Aramaic document. From a certain Zionist perspective, it did not matter that Aramaic is a cognate language of Hebrew and that it has its own important value for Jewish nationhood. While arguments raged about whether to resuscitate Hebrew or transmit Yiddish—arguments that highlighted the need to break from diasporic origins—the non-Hebrew nature of the Talmud further contributed to a distancing of the Talmud from the Zionist cause.

The Zionists were heirs to the Haskalah and (though less directly and with much antipathy on both sides) to Reform. They inherited from both parents an aversion to Talmudism, the discourse of learning surrounding—and the curricular exclusivity of—the Talmud. This aversion was magnified in Zionist hands by the Talmudic cultural celebration of the weak, wan, and intellectually agile heroic rabbi, at the expense of the physically strong Western-style man.[88] In the opening speech of the Second Zionist Congress, Max Nordau coined the term "muscle Jew" to describe the physically strong and able-bodied figure whom the movement needed to create in

order to succeed.[89] The "muscle Jew" would routinely be contrasted with the physically unimposing Talmud scholar, bent over a book and grown weak from study.

Nineteenth-century nationalisms produced elaborate mythologies that unified a sometimes-divided populace and provided both a shared origin story and a clear national goal for which to strive. Zionism also aspired to such a mythos; the Hebrew Bible took pride of place in producing it. The mythos produced out of the Bible was often at odds with the way that biblical stories had been understood in post-biblical rabbinic writings. Zionism was diametrically opposed to the Talmud in finding heroes (Bar Kokhba, the Maccabees, the Masada martyrs) precisely in those characters about whom the Talmud is silent or, even occasionally, actively critical.[90]

Just as there were Maskilim who sought to rehabilitate the Talmud and Hasidim who reclaimed the Talmud, there were Zionists who reformulated the Talmud in such a way that it could productively contribute to the Zionist mythos. The writer Haim Nahman Bialik partnered with Yehoshua Hana Ravnitzky, a publisher and journalist, to produce *Sefer Ha-aggadah* [book of the aggadah], a digest of stories from the Talmud and other books in Rabbinic literature edited and translated into modern Hebrew.[91] An alumnus of the Volozhiner yeshiva, Bialik never lost his appreciation for the Talmud and Talmudism, even as some of his best work is sharply critical of the world he left. *Sefer Ha-aggadah* was so successful that it became, alongside the Bible, a staple of the Israeli post-state bookshelf. By bypassing the legal materials associated with Talmudism, editing the stories into nationalist fable form and producing them in the language of modern Hebrew, Bialik and Ravnitzky succeeded in partially incorporating the Talmud's content into the Zionist mythos.

This chapter has ranged from the third and fourth century CE, when the Palestinian Talmud was produced, to twentieth-century Zionist resistance to the Talmud. While recognizing that each treated period is worthy of a deeper analysis and greater context, the survey is helpful in demonstrating the ways in which some of the Talmud's most significant relationships have occurred in an emblematic register. In this register, it is often the Talmud's reputation, or the social energy that surrounds it, that comes to stand for the thing itself and engender either support, or as most of the examples demonstrate, resistance. The Talmud's reputation is undoubtedly derivative of its essence as a literature and the enhancements of its discourse of reception. Even so, much of what the Talmud has endured has transpired on a plane removed from serious engagement with either the book or its literatures of reception.

Golden Old Age: Talmud in Modernity—Three Stories

The Talmud began life as a work of literature (the essential Talmud), evolved to produce an intellectual and cultural discourse (the enhanced Talmud), and came to symbolize, and even embody, the Jews and Judaism by both proponents and opponents (the emblematic Talmud). All of this had already transpired prior to modernity. But these aspects of the Talmud have all been magnified from the nineteenth century to the present. This chapter describes the Talmud in modernity by highlighting three different stories. The first is the story of technological transformations in the production of the Talmud from oral origins to the digital present. The hero of this story is the "*Vilna Shas*" [an acronym for *shisha sedrei*, or the "six orders" of the Mishnah, the text that underlies the Talmud], an edition produced by the Widow and Brothers Romm Printing House between 1880 and 1886 in Vilnius, Lithuania, that has become the Talmud's modern body. The second is the story of a love affair between the Talmud and a specific culture—the century and a half of pre-WWII Misnagdic culture in Eastern Europe. In this heartland of Ashkenazic Jewish life, the Talmud stood at the center of cultural consciousness and functioned as the ultimate form of cultural capital. The third is the story of the Talmud's popularity in the twenty-first century. In this story, the polymathic Talmud is a communal ritual calendar, the source of critical insight into history, religion, literature, and culture, and the formal model for both post-modern philosophy and American comedy. Over the past few decades the Talmud has developed both a larger quantity and a greater diversity of readers than it has ever had.

Story One: From Orality to the App

The Talmud is not unusual for having been composed and distributed orally; it is unusual because its oral mode of distribution persisted long after it might have given way to writing. The Talmud was being composed and orally transmitted by rabbis and other members of an ancient Jewish community that was simultaneously distributing the Bible as a written work in ink on parchment scrolls. The rabbis who produced rabbinic literature composed their works orally *intentionally*.[1]

By choosing to distribute the Talmud orally, the rabbis maintained a separation between the canonical authority of the written Hebrew Bible and the lesser and derivative authority of the Talmud. The commitment to oral transmission survived the initial institutionalization of the Geonic period. In the eighth and ninth centuries, students in Geonic yeshivot continued to study the Talmud orally as a memorized text even as they were involved in the process of producing written responsa that referenced the Talmud.[2] The earliest extant written text of the Talmud is a fragment of a tenth-century scroll.[3]

Scrolls were the common technological choice for book production in the Near East until the fourth century CE, when the codex supplanted the scroll.[4] The codex is advantageous because it enables the producer to write on both sides of the page (scrolls only utilize one side), and it enables the consumer to quickly move between locations in a work (a scroll requires rolling). To judge by extant materials, most of the handwritten Talmuds in the medieval period were codices. While some of these were written by professional scribes with calligraphic skills, many were written by nonprofessionals, probably for their own use. Transcribing a book was costly. Many of the transcriptions of the Talmud were of individual tractates rather than the larger orders or the entire Talmud. The much-celebrated Munich manuscript of the Talmud is unique insofar as it is a professionally calligraphed codex that transmits the text of the entire Talmud.[5]

The first printed editions of the Talmud were incunabula—editions published in the fifteenth century; these were one-volume single-tractate editions.[6] Several such volumes were published in Constantinople, Italy, and pre-expulsion Iberia. Print technology allowed early printers to include Rashi's commentary alongside the

Talmud. Since then, there has rarely been a print edition without Rashi's commentary. Joshua Solomon Soncino, a fifteenth-century Italian printer, began to print the Talmud with Rashi's commentary to the inside of the Talmud's text and a Tosafist commentary to the outside of the Talmud's text, creating a balanced symmetrical look.[7] (See Figure 5.1.) This design of a central text with surrounding commentary can be found in fifteenth-century Italian print editions of Virgil, Justinian's code, and the Bible; over time its popularity within those other contexts faded and it came to be identified specifically with the Talmud, whose printers retained this arrangement.

The Venice edition, published by Belgian native Daniel Bomberg between 1520 and 1523, is the first printed, complete set of Talmud.[8] It constitutes a first printing for those tractates that had never been printed in individual tractate form, although for some popular tractates, it is the fifth or sixth edition. The Bomberg is a luxury edition, with heavy paper and clean lines; some of the extant copies were acquired by aristocratic owners including King Henry VIII of England.[9]

The dominance of Italians in the printing of the Talmud came to an end with the Counter-Reformation's antagonisms towards the Talmud. The seizure and burning of books made the Talmud scarce in the second half of the sixteenth century. The Talmud's Ashkenazic printings, like the Ashkenazic Jews themselves, migrated from West to East.[10] Italian printing gave way to the Basel edition (1578–1581), with its modified and censored text. Subsequent editions were produced in Germany and

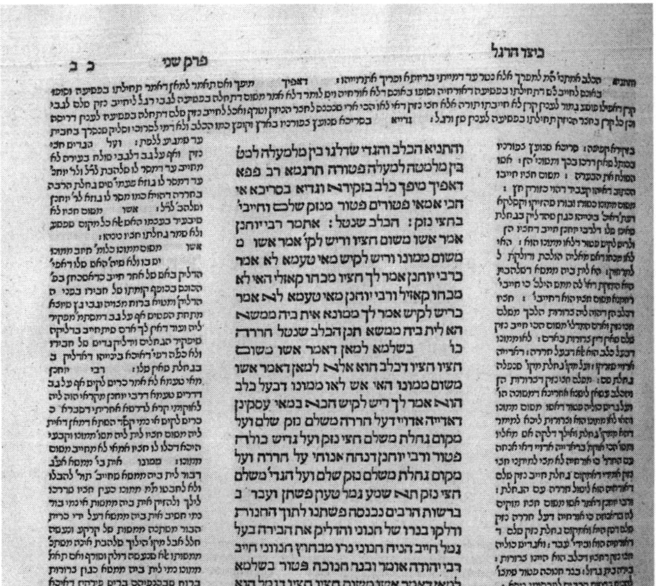

כיצד הרגל
פרק שני
כ ב

והתניא הכלב והגדי שדלגו בין מלמעלה למט
בין מלמטה למעלה פטורה תרגמא רב פפא
דאפיך טיפך כלב בוקרא וגדיא בסריכא אי
הכי אמאי פטורים פטור מנזק שלם וחייבי׳
בחצי נזק: הכלב שנטל: אתמר רבי יוחנן
אמר אשו משום חציו וריש לקי׳ אמר אשו מ
משום ממונו וריש לקיש מאי טעמא לא אמר
כרבי יוחנן אמר לך חציו מכחו קאזלי האי לא
מכחו קאזיל ורבי יוחנן מאי טעמא לא אמר
כריש לקיש אמר לך ממונא אית ביה ממשא
הא לית ביה ממשא תנן הכלב שנטל חררה
כו׳ בשלמא למאן דאמר אשו משום
חציו חציו דכלב הוא אלא למאן דאמר אשו
משום ממונו האי אש לאו ממונו דבעל כלב
הוא אמר לך ריש לקיש הכא במאי עסקינן
דאדייה אדויי דעל חררה משלם נזק שלם ועל
מקום גחלת משלם חצי נזק ועל גדיש כולה
פטור ורבי יוחנן דנחה אנוחי על חררה ועל
מקום גחלת משלם נזק שלם ועל הגדי׳ משלם
חצי נזק תא שמע גמל טעון פשתן ועבר ב
ברשות הרבים נכנסה פשתנו לתוך החנות
ודלקו בנרו של חנוני והדליק את הבירה בעל
גמל חייב הניח חנוני נרו מבחוץ חנוני חייב
רבי יהודה אומר ובנר חנוכה פטור בשלמא
למאן דאמר אשו משום חציו חציו דגמל הוא
אלא למאן דאמר משום ממונא האי אש לאו
ממונא דבעל גמל הוא אמר לך ר׳ לקי׳ הכא
במאי עסקי׳ במסככת כל הביר כולה אי הכי
אימא סיפ׳ אם הניח חנוני נרו מבחוץ חנוני
חייב ואי במסככת אמאי חייב בשעת׳ עכו׳
וסככה כל שכן דחנווני פטו׳ ובעל גמל חייב
אמר רב הונא בר מנוח משמיה דרב איקא
הכא במאי עסיקי׳ כגון שעמדה להשיל טימה
רישא

FIGURE 5.1. Daniel Bomberg's Venice Edition of the Talmud, 1520–1523. Baba Qamma 22a. Courtesy of Klau Library, Cincinnati, Hebrew Union College-Jewish Institute of Religion.

Amsterdam, then in Central Europe—in Prague, Vienna, and Budapest. Eventually, printing moved into Eastern Europe—to Cracow, Lemberg, Lublin, and finally, as far east as Slavuta (in Ukraine) and Vilna (in Lithuania).

The Council of the Four Lands organized the eastern European Jewish communities of Poland and Lithuania.[11] Among its activities, the council sanctioned book publication.[12] Until 1764, publication of the Talmud, either in individual volumes or in sets, was licensed by the council. The termination of the Council in 1764 created an unsupervised market for editions of the Talmud.

The Bomberg edition established several foundational concepts in Talmudic book production. Not only did it establish a fixed pagination for the body text of the entire Talmud (some of which was inherited from earlier editions where they existed), it also employed differences in typeface to differentiate between the central Talmud text (block type) and the surrounding commentaries (semi-cursive "Rashi" type), and produced a few additional commentaries printed as back matter in the pages following the Talmudic tractate itself. Subsequent printers accepted these foundational concepts and added features of their own. Each new edition marketed itself as having both absorbed and improved upon a prior edition.

Some of the most beautiful and expensive Hebrew books of all types were produced in Amsterdam, which had large populations of both Ashkenazic and Sefardic Jews. Joseph Dayyan's 1720 edition of Alfasi's *Halakhot* innovated the application of the Talmud's layout to Alfasi's digest; the *Halakhot* is in the center with surrounding

commentaries including a version of Rashi. A 1752 Proops Brothers edition of the Talmud employs a cleaner square type, heavy paper, and large open spaces on a tall folio page.

Eastern European printers copied the features they admired in earlier editions. The edition of Talmud that the Shapiro Press of Slavuta began to print in the first decade of the nineteenth century imitated the Proops Talmud in its size and type. The 1817–1822 Slavuta edition added the contents of the Amsterdam edition of Alfasi's *Halakhot* as back matter, making the back matter nearly as voluminous as the Talmud itself. These Slavuta editions coincided with the founding of the Volozhin Yeshiva, whose needs dictated the new editions that Slavuta printed.[13] The growth of Volozhin and the founding of new such institutions increased the market for Talmud learners and buyers.

The demise of the Council of the Four Lands officially opened the market for Talmud printing to competition. But the practice of seeking approval for publishing Hebrew books did not cease. It remained a common practice for printers (or authors) to solicit approvals from distinguished rabbis. The rhetoric of these approvals, which were printed in the volumes, included temporary monopolies backed by religious authority. The Slavuta editions of the early nineteenth century received several such approvals, which differ in the periods of time for which they guarantee the monopoly. One of the rabbis who penned an approbation for the Slavuta editions was Schneur Zalman of Liadi (d. 1812), the founder of Lubavitcher

Hasidism, who granted the Shapiros a monopoly on Talmud production for the next twenty-five years.[14]

In 1834, Menahem Romm, a printer who had recently moved from Grodno to Vilna, began to seek approbations to publish a new edition of the Talmud. This resulted in a major contretemps between the Shapiro family of Slavuta and the Romms of Vilna.[15] The Shapiros asserted their monopoly within religious law because their 1817–1822 edition was still available. The Romms claimed that there was no available stock of the Slavuta edition, and there was market demand. The fight turned ugly and, in retrospect, the specifics of the case masked a fundamental animosity between the Hasidic Shapiros and the Misnagdic Romms. Both sides began to publish a new edition. The editions are quite similar, with the Vilna printing house adopting all the features of the earlier Slavuta edition; by contemporary standards, the Vilna edition would be guilty of format plagiarism. What Vilna innovated, though, was a new square type for the central column of Talmudic text. This type was designed by Lippman Metz, a talented type designer, and became synonymous with the Romm printing house for the remainder of the century.[16] It remains a staple of Hebrew type; where prior square types emerge directly from the calligraphic tradition, the Romm Vilna typeface is a cleaner type designed for printing.[17] Unfortunately, while the Shapiros and their printers were at work on the fourth tractate of their new edition, the Slavuta press erupted in scandal.[18] The suicide of an employee of the printing house led to trumped up charges against the

Shapiro brothers, who were eventually sentenced to exile in Siberia.

The Russian government, hearing of the scandal in Slavuta, asserted control over Hebrew print in 1836 by licensing only two print houses.[19] These were the Romm press in Vilnius and a press in Kiev that would eventually move to neighboring Zhitomir and come to be controlled by the relocated heirs of the Shapiro family. The rivalry of the 1830s between the two houses was repeated in 1858 when the Shapiros of Zhitomir began producing a new edition of the Talmud.[20] The Romms in Vilna responded with a new edition of their own. The Zhitomir edition produced 3,500 copies and the Romm 2,500.[21] The competition at this point, though, was not exclusive to these two houses. Though these were the only two licensed by the Russian government, there were eight other editions being produced to their west in Central and Western Europe. Some of these editions were being made with new stereotype technology that reduced the costs of book production. The age of open competition in the Talmud marketplace was under way. Competition drove down the price, and one could now acquire a set of Talmud for fifteen rubles, the 2015 equivalent of $217 U.S.[22]

Between 1858 and the new edition they would begin to publish in 1880, the Widow and Brothers Romm press acquired stereotyping technology that could, in theory, have reduced the cost of a set of Talmud. Rather than producing a cheap edition, however, the Romm press decided to produce a deluxe set that would cost fifty rubles, or the present day equivalent of $952 U.S.[23] This edition employs the Vilna type, and adds initial print edition commentaries of important medieval authorities (Rabbenu Hananel, Rabbenu Gershom, R' Bezalel Ashkenazi), as well as commentaries of distinguished contemporary rabbis (Rabbi Akiva Eiger), and even some with Haskalah connections (Rabbi Samuel Strashoun) or protocritical methodologies (Rabbi Aryeh Leib Yellin). The first volume of the 1880–1886 edition of the Romm Vilna Shas sold more than 22,000 copies in its first year.[24] Because stereotyping technology allows one to store lead plates of the page images, the technology made it possible to reprint easily. This edition was printed repeatedly and uninterruptedly until World War I. The popularity of this edition drove various competitors out of business. Four of the eight presses that had produced competing editions of Talmud in the 1850s sold their stereotype plates to Romm for the cost of the lead. [25]

The occupation of Vilnius during World War I generated rumors that the Romm printing house had been destroyed. Photo-offset printing technology enabled publishers in England, the United States, and Canada to quickly step in and cheaply reproduce the Vilna Romm edition. (Whether this violated the existing copyright laws of Lithuania or any of these other countries, it was certainly a violation of Jewish law that protected the work from the outright theft of intellectual property.) The creation of these photo-offset editions furthered the association of the Talmud with the specific page image of the Romm edition. Over time, this page image would become iconic and would come to be dissociated from the specific printing house itself as if the image belonged to the public domain as the Talmud.

One of the most fascinating editions of the Talmud is the so-called "Survivors' Talmud."[26] In 1946, a delegation of Displaced Person rabbis approached the United States military about the unavailability of the Talmud for the many Jews displaced by the Nazis. Requisitioning a German printing house in Heidelberg, a committee brought two sets from New York and created a beautiful photo-offset edition. The dedication on this edition demonstrates the work's very important symbolic function:

> This special edition of the Talmud, published in the very land where, but a short time ago, everything Jewish and of Jewish inspiration was anathema, will remain a symbol of the indestructibility of the Torah.[27]

The editions that served as the models for the Survivors' Talmud were, naturally, Vilna editions.

By the end of World War II, the Talmud had become synonymous with a specific edition. More specifically, it had come to be identified with the page layout of the Talmud as it appears in the Vilna edition. In 1967, Adin Steinsaltz began producing an edition designed to make the Talmud more accessible to modern Hebrew speakers. Among his innovations, Steinsaltz vocalized the Hebrew/Aramaic text of the Talmud itself, produced a paraphrastic translation of the Talmud's text into modern Hebrew, and added various notes based on historical scholarship. While these features might seem to be

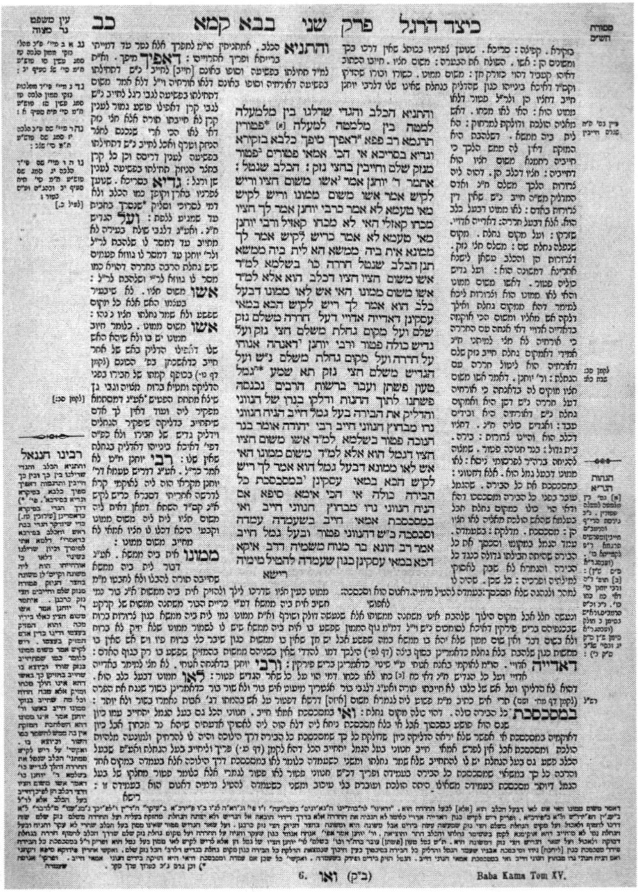

כיצד הרגל פרק שני בבא קמא כב

והתניא הכלב והגדי שדלגו בין מלמעלה למטה בין מלמטה למעלה [א] *פטורין תרגמא רב פפא "דאפיך טיפך כלבא בוקרא וגדיא בסריכא אי הכי אמאי פטורים "פטור מנזק שלם וחייבין בחצי נזק: הכלב שנטל: אתמר ר' יוחנן אמר "אשו משום חציו ור"ש לקיש אמר אשו משום ממונו ור"ש לקיש מאי טעמא לא אמר כרבי יוחנן אמר לך חציו מכחו קאזלי האי לא מכחו קאזיל ורבי יוחנן מאי טעמא לא אמר כר"ש לקיש אמר לך ממונא אית ביה ממשא הא לית ביה ממשא תנן הכלב שנטל חררה כו' בשלמא למ"ד אשו משום חציו חציו דכלב הוא אלא למ"ד אשו משום ממונו האי אש לאו ממונו דבעל כלב הוא אמר לך ר"ש לקיש הכא במאי עסקינן דאדייה אדויי דעל חררה משלם נזק שלם ועל מקום גחלת משלם חצי נזק ועל גדיש כולה פטור ורבי יוחנן "דאנחה אנוחי על חררה ועל מקום גחלת משלם נ"ש ועל הגדיש משלם חצי נזק תא שמע *"גמל טעון פשתן ועבר ברשות הרבים נכנסה פשתנו לתוך החנות ודלקו בנרו של חנוני והדליק את הבירה בעל גמל חייב הניח חנוני נרו מבחוץ חנוני חייב רבי יהודה אומר בנר חנוכה פטור בשלמא למ"ד אשו משום חציו חציו דגמל הוא אלא למ"ד משום ממונו האי אש לאו ממונא דבעל גמל הוא אמר לך ר"ש לקיש הכא במאי עסקינן 'במסכסכת כל הבירה כולה אי הכי אימא סיפא אם הניח חנוני נרו מבחוץ חנוני חייב ואי במסכסכת אמאי חייב בשעמדה עמדה וסכסכה ב"ש דחנוני פטור ובעל גמל חייב אמר רב הונא בר מנוח משמיה דרב איקא הכא במאי עסקינן כגון שעמדה להטיל מימיה רישא

6. ואו (ב"ק) Baba Kama Tom XV.

FIGURE 5.2. Widow and Brothers Romm Edition of the Talmud, 1880–1886. Baba Qamma 22a. Courtesy of Klau Library, Cincinnati, Hebrew Union College-Jewish Institute of Religion.

inherently modernizing, the aspect of his edition that generated the most criticism, particularly from ultra-Orthodox scholars, was Steinsaltz's decision to maintain the general formatting look of the Talmud's layout (central text with surrounding commentary), while changing the type and standard pagination from the Vilna edition, and relocating the commentary by Rashi to the lower half of the inside commentarial column in order to make space for his own translation. In certain circles, this was considered an egregious violation of the sacred page image of the Talmud.[28]

When ArtScroll set about to produce its translation of the Talmud into English in the 1990s, it sought to shield itself from the criticisms that had beset Steinsaltz.[29] An earlier English translation, the Soncino Hebrew-English edition, had produced its translation as a facing page to the Vilna page image.[30] The problem with this technique is the density of Talmudic language; because it is nearly impossible to fit the entire English translation on the facing page, the Soncino Hebrew-English edition carries the English text over to a back section, like the articles in some magazines "jump" to a page further back. ArtScroll, by contrast, solved the problem of Talmudic density by allowing the quantity of the English to determine the number of Vilna pages required. The Schottenstein edition from ArtScroll reprints the Vilna image multiple times to afford the English sufficient space. It is not unusual for it to be repeated five or six times. While this technique seems wasteful and makes each volume much longer than otherwise necessary, it both testifies to, and cements the relationship between, the Talmud and its Vilna image.

Revised editions of the Steinsaltz Talmud in both Hebrew and English have appeared in the past few years; they now also feature the classic Vilna page.[31] The critical editions of chapters of the Talmud produced by the Society for the Advancement of the Talmud copy the technique of duplicating the Vilna page multiple times.[32] Even The Responsa Project digital database, one of the earliest providers of digital Judaica texts, has made it possible in its newest releases to consult a Vilna page image instead of a digital Talmudic text; the Talmud is the only book in this vast digital library that has this feature. Several websites make it possible to see the Talmud specifically in its Vilna page form.[33]

The concretization of the Talmud in its Vilna page image has canonized the form of the image as specifically Talmudic. In 1995, Avraham Holtz published an edition of S. Y. Agnon's story "The Bridal Canopy" utilizing the format of central text and surrounding commentary.[34] A reviewer in an ultra-Orthodox Jerusalem weekly criticized the edition because it employs the sacred form of the Talmud's page image for nonsacred purposes.[35] The association of the Talmud's sacredness with its form has enabled the backdoor entrance of the Talmud into Orthodox education for women and girls.[36] Within Israeli ultra-Orthodox circles, prohibitions on access to Talmud by females are strictly enforced, but they are enforced specifically with respect to the Vilna edition and its image. Girls in ultra-Orthodox schools are kept away from the Vilna Shas and its image, but they are permitted to study from worksheets onto which the Talmud's digital text has been pasted.

Among Orthodox Jews in the United States and Israel today, there is a standard practice for the bride's family to present a groom with a full set of the Talmud as a wedding gift, sometimes referred to as a *Choson* [bridegroom] *Shas*. This practice was known already in Hungary before World War II.[37] Then, as now, only a Romm Vilna edition qualified for the gift.[38] Such sets often languish on bookshelves unused, but they certify that the groom can study the Talmud and the bride comes from a family that supports a husband who studies.

Several apps for the Talmud are available on both the Android and iOs (Apple) platforms. These have overlapping features—access to the entire text, commentary, and translation. What they all share is the ability to call up the "*tzuras hadaf*," the page image of the Vilna Shas.

The achievement of a fixed physical form is both the effect and cause of symbolic meanings. Insistence upon the Vilna Shas canonizes not just the essential Talmud but also the enhanced Talmud. The Vilna page includes not only the Talmud itself but several layers of commentary with indices to direct a reader to relevant passages in the code literature. The resistance to digital text or repagination is partly a function of the *effect* of reading the Talmud in those other contexts; if one reads the Talmud without the commentaries, one may have access to the essential Talmud, but the enhanced Talmud is lost.

Long ago the rabbis resisted putting the Talmud into physical form as a book and insisted upon its orality. At the time, the Bible was undergoing a process of ritualization in which it was being canonized not only as a work of literature, but also as a sacred object utilized in ritual in important ways that became even more important with the destruction of the Second Temple. Now that the Talmud has achieved a fixed physical form, it too is susceptible to the kinds of ritualizing and fetishizing that the Bible has long received (as we will see in Story Three below). The page image of the Vilna Shas has become a Jewish icon.

Story Two: Talmud as Cultural Capital

Isaac Bashevis Singer's short story "Yentl the Yeshiva Boy" is set in nineteenth-century Poland.[39] The eponymous protagonist is a woman who crosses genders and enrolls in a yeshiva to study Talmud. The tale's *avant garde* handling of transgender issues gives the story prescient shock value.[40] Leaving aside the rich and worthy issues of Yentl/Anshel's complex sexuality, the story's surface plot presumes a desire to study Talmud for its own sake, strong enough to motivate the renunciation of gender identity and the possibility of family. Singer's readers were not surprised by this plot assumption because the cultural ubiquity of the Talmud rendered this kind of devotion familiar.

Nineteenth-century Eastern Europe's Jewish culture venerated the Talmud; the Talmud represented the highest form of cultural capital.[41] Individual worth was adjudged based on Talmudic aptitude, and even the illiterate aspired—through veneration of the learned, acquisition of books, or supporting the enterprise of Talmud study—to a relationship with the Talmud. Yentl's desire motivates her to do something extreme—to transgress social roles to acquire direct access to the Talmud at a time when her gender limited her to indirect access—but it is not categorically distinct from the desires of her cultural contemporaries. Though Yentl is a fictional construct, historical figures such as Rayna Batya (wife of Rabbi Naphtali Zevi Yehudah Berlin) communicate the suppressed voice of a contemporaneous woman who wanted the direct access to which women were denied.[42]

If anything distinguishes Yentl in her pursuit of inclusion in the Talmudic discourse, it is the purity of that pursuit. Yentl is not motivated by the prospect of a beautiful or wealthy bride; in fact, the story draws considerable humor from Yentl's being forced to play to gendered expectations for such motivations. The Talmud in nineteenth-century Eastern Europe was the intellectual discourse of elite traditional Jewry and it served, alongside and in cahoots with regular economics, to divide Eastern European Jewish society into two strata: the haves and the have-nots.

Talmud study was in theory a vehicle for social striving; a poor youngster who displayed Talmudic aptitude could parlay that reputation into a higher socioeconomic position. In truth, the disparate qualities of Eastern European educators made it unlikely that a truly poor young boy could gain the necessary background education to excel in Talmud even if he managed to attain basic exposure to the material.[43]

Despite the socioeconomic bifurcation in which the Talmud participated, even those who were not part of the so-called "beautiful people" (the term for those with wealth or Talmud knowledge) embraced the cultural emphasis on Talmudic aptitude through a variety of means. An unlearned person with no aspirations to have one's daughter marry a yeshiva student could still volunteer to host such a student at his or her table for a meal or for the entire Sabbath. The larger and more bureaucratized yeshivas would send out *pushkes* [alms boxes] for homeowners to contribute loose change to the cause.[44] And all classes of people took tremendous pride in the representative Talmudic genius of the local rabbi, who served as a combination pastor, judge, and yeshiva instructor.

Talmud study served as the driving religious narrative of Misnagdic Eastern Europe. Eastern European Hasidim had fully embraced a theurgic metanarrative in which all their behaviors, when intended properly, contributed to the restoration of divine energy and the expedited arrival of the Messiah.[45] The Misnagdim rejected this metanarrative in a variety of ways. In its place, they had the communal project of studying the Talmud and promoting the study of Talmud by others.

The creation of new institutional yeshivot in nineteenth-century Eastern Europe was of a magnitude that had not been seen since the Geonic period.[46] But unlike the Geonic institutions, these were not open to the community, but were closed organizations akin to universities or the military that conscript and discipline young people into a way of acting in the world.[47]

Walk through a typical Eastern European village on a Saturday afternoon with Jewish men in the late nineteenth century.[48] After a filling Sabbath lunch, the men return to synagogue to engage in all levels of study. The elite learners sit at one table studying Talmudic law with both commentaries and codes—sometimes engaging in *pilpul* [intellectual calisthenics] to create greater depth of meaning for Talmudic concepts and sometimes looking to trace a path from the early rabbinic sources to contemporary legal rules and practices. The adjacent table features a class in *Ein Yaaqov*, the digest of aggadic stories from the Talmud that inspired readers and listeners towards ethical and spiritual growth; the participants in this class are not Talmud-educated, but literate enough to follow the Hebrew/Aramaic text as a lecturer teaches them not only its literal but also its deeper meanings. Off to the side and not at a table is a group of less literate men. These cannot follow along in even the *Ein Yaaqov* class, but they long for some connection and sit with printed Talmuds in front of them to feel physically proximate. For all of these men, the Talmud is Torah.

In his novel *The Yeshiva*, Chaim Grade fictionalizes the founding of a remote outpost of Slobodka, the yeshiva Grade himself had attended in the 1920s.[49] At a pivotal moment just after a student named Chaikl (based on Grade himself) has been caught in a sex scandal, the student reflects on the importance of the yeshiva and its Talmud study in the eyes of the locals:

> On his way back through the forest, Chaikl no longer stared at the trees . . . He thought of the rabbi and how right he was that Jews love Torah. Chaikl had often seen the simple folk and even the fresh punks from Butchers Street respectfully making way for a Torah scholar: loudmouthed market women assumed a pious demeanor when they saw a Jew in a rabbinic gabardine passing by. During winter nights, old men sat in the *beth medresh* [house of study] over their books and talked about scholars while studying.[50]

We often think of the Jews of Eastern Europe as a minority. This minority, confined to the Pale of Settlement, was often a majority in the small villages in which it lived.[51] Even in big cities, the large size of Jewish communities lent them the kind of space in which to produce a culture somewhat isolated from the majority culture. And the culture that they produced was one in which the Talmud was central. There was a cultural energy in pursuit of greater knowledge of the Talmud. And the culture's understanding of the Talmud was one that included the enhanced Talmud in that definition. When Eastern European Jews spoke of Talmud as Torah they meant to include all the codes, commentary, and responsa that received and expanded the Talmud's legal content. The canonization of the discourse of the enhanced Talmud was intertwined with the power dynamics that elevated that discourse into a cultural position of political power. In Eastern Europe, Talmud was power in a way that it never had been before and never has been since.

Story Three: Unparalleled Success

Today there are more Jews studying Talmud in the world than at any point in history. Beyond this numerical fact, the Talmud has undergone profound transformations as the book has developed discourses outside of the one that continues the trajectory of its traditional reception. These discourses have expanded the range of the Talmud's readers to include non-Orthodox and even avowedly secular Jews, historians, ministers of the church, and even critical theorists. There has been a queering of the Talmud as this traditional text has come to speak to and for gay, bisexual, and transgender people. These new discourses have, in turn, opened the Talmud to new symbolic manifestations as representing Jewish success for a developing Asian economy, as modeling a format of thinking that lends itself to manipulation in the service of comedy, and as inspiring modern art that reclaims the Talmud through protest.

Elite Study Today

Elite Jewish study of the Talmud has never been more demographically significant. More students study Talmud in institutional yeshivot today than at any prior time in

Jewish history. In 2012, 130,000 military-age Israeli men received army exemptions because of their status as full-time yeshiva students studying Talmud.[52] That number does not include the approximately 8,500 *Yeshivot Hesder* [arrangement] students whose curriculum alternates a year of full-time Talmud study with a year of military service. It does not include women studying in Modern Orthodox institutions of learning, those studying the Talmud in academic programs in Israeli universities, or secular Israelis studying in new institutions that cater to the "non-religious." It does not include those studying outside Israel. In the United States, for example, there are nearly 5,000 students of Talmud at *Beis Medrash Gavoha* [advanced house of study] in Lakewood, NJ, the premier ultra-Orthodox yeshiva, and roughly 1,000 undergraduate men study Talmud at Yeshiva College, the premier Modern Orthodox yeshiva in New York.[53][54] In 2014, 169 rabbinical students were officially certified for ordination by degree-granting American rabbinical schools; 91 of these Talmud-studying students graduated from non-Orthodox institutions.[55]

Lay Study Today

Through the vehicle of *Daf Yomi* [the daily study of a page of Talmud], the Talmud has become, for the first time in its history, a lay study text on a massive scale. Rabbi Meir Shapira of Lublin presented the idea of Daf Yomi at the 1923 inaugural conference of Agudas Yisroel, an Orthodox rabbinical colloquy.[56] The niche program originally targeted educated laity, but in 1930 became part of the curriculum in Shapira's newly founded yeshiva, Yeshivat Hakhme Lublin.[57] In 1968, a *Siyyum Hashas* [commencement party] held at the Bais Yaakov girls' high school in Boro Park, Brooklyn, was attended by 200 people.[58] By 1984, there were 7,600 people in various venues, in 1990 there were 21,000, in 1997 more than 70,000, and in 2005 nearly 140,000.[59] The most recent siyyum in 2012 was attended internationally by some 600,000 people who filed into large metropolitan stadia and arenas.[60] Though the attendees do not all complete the Talmud themselves, each successive siyyum generates larger numbers of people who commit to participate in the next cycle; one recent estimate puts the international number of Daf Yomi participants at 70,000.[61] The Daf Yomi calendar is included with other calendrical information in Orthodox publications, and there is even a comic book "Daf Yomi for Kids" produced weekly in Israel.[62] While in Eastern Europe the laity studied *Ein Yaaqov*, the non-legal Talmudic digest, today the unabridged Talmud with all of its legal material is the book of choice for lay and elite alike.

The increases in elite learning and lay study are not unrelated. Both reflect a fusion of traditional Eastern European enthusiasm for Talmud with Western notions of universal education. In the past forty-five years there has been a significant growth in the number of school-age children who have been provided a middle school and high school Talmud education. For these students, the Talmud is a subject analogous to math or history, in which they are trained from basic rudiments to advanced logical thinking. These mostly male students now comprise the bulk of the elite and lay populations who engage in intense Talmud study either in a yeshiva or via the Daf Yomi program. The analogy to other curricular subjects helps to explain the way the Talmud functions in Orthodoxy—as a discourse of resistance. Through its rigor and complexity, the Talmud asks to be taken seriously as an alternative exclusively Jewish discourse that can compete with Western discourse writ large. As American Orthodoxy has grappled with exposure to higher education, it has insisted upon a rigorous Talmud curriculum alongside other subjects. The Talmud is tasked with grounding the Orthodox college student so that he (or she in some Modern Orthodox contexts) does not disappear into the undercurrents of higher education.

The Daf Yomi movement has produced a new religious reality for the Talmud. The Talmud, like the Torah before it, has become ritualized as a way of marking time, and unifying a community in study that is increasingly about breadth and completion, rather than depth. The weekly Daf Yomi sheets that are produced in the United States and Israel for adults and children make this equation quite clear—just as Jews have been unified over the years by a calendar that includes the ritualized reading of the Torah divided into weekly portions, Jews are now unified by a calendar that includes somewhat ritualized reading of the Talmud divided into daily portions. This is not to say that Daf Yomi classes are purely ritual, or that it is impossible to comprehend the depth of the Talmud at the pace of Daf Yomi (skilled practitioners might be capable), but that for all participants, Daf Yomi has religious import beyond the educational value of assimilating the Talmud's content.

It is somewhat difficult to account for the recent success of Daf Yomi given the time commitment it mandates. Perhaps an explanation can be found in broader contemporary culture. In the age of the internet, it has become common for writers to commit to daily projects that involve developing a new skill or acquiring new context. Some of these projects have resulted in books like *The Year of Living Biblically* and *The Julie/Julia Project* which inspired the movie *Julie and Julia*. Daf Yomi is the original such project. Daf Yomi provides structure. There is comfort in the regularity of daily study and in the community that surrounds such learning, both in the physical sense (classmates in a Daf Yomi class) and in the virtual sense (people around the world with whom one has kinship because of the shared project). Not surprisingly, Daf Yomi has lent itself to reproduction as a blog project like the ones referenced above. Writer Adam Kirsch has been studying the Daf Yomi since the new cycle began in 2012 and produces weekly blogs for Tablet Magazine about a secular Jew's take on the Talmud.[63] Jacqueline Nicholls, a London-based artist, is producing Draw Yomi, a website on which she posts a daily drawing inspired by the day's page.[64] Through Daf Yomi, the Talmud is being transformed from an intellectual to a ritual text (like a Torah scroll), and contributes to the calendar by helping to structure Jewish time.

New Discourses

Since the Renaissance there has been continuous non-Jewish intellectual interest in the Talmud. While much of this interest has been motivated by intellectual curiosity and friendly Hebraism, there has also been a long current of non-Jewish interest in the Talmud for specifically anti-Semitic purposes. This reigning skepticism regarding the Talmud, and its pejorative association with negative Jewish stereotypes, produced a negative valence for the noun "Talmud" and the adjective "Talmudic." Though this undercurrent continues to live on, particularly on internet conspiracy sites, this is not the extent of non-Jewish engagement with the Talmud today. The Talmud is accessed and studied earnestly and productively by a larger audience than ever before. Beyond those who study it inherently, there are many others who have been influenced by the emblematic Talmud in contemporary culture.

There have been several attempts to popularize the Talmud for an English-speaking audience via translation. The first, by Michael Rodkinson (1896–1903), translates only partial sections of selected tractates and is best considered a digest.[65] The faculty of Jews' College in London produced the first comprehensive edition, the Soncino edition of the Talmud (1935–1948), which was initially published in elegant all-English volumes before being reproduced in the aforementioned 1960 edition with a facing page of Vilna Romm.[66] While the Soncino edition is an impressive translation, it did not inspire a sizable non-Jewish readership.

Jacob Neusner, an American historian of ancient Judaism, produced a new translation of the Talmud in the 1980s.[67] The "American Translation," as Neusner dubbed this work, was part of a massive project in which Neusner and his students translated all of rabbinic literature. At the same time, Neusner and his students made inroads in American academia and intensified connections between the study of ancient Judaism and the study of early Christianity. Neusner's activities increased the profile of rabbinic Judaism within academe and, within a generation, many major institutions of higher learning in the United States would hire an expert in rabbinic Judaism to their respective faculties. The expansion of rabbinics outside of yeshivot and rabbinical seminaries invited hitherto marginalized scholars (e.g., non-males, non-Jews, non-heterosexuals), who would not have had access to the Talmud in confessional settings, to become specialists in this field. At the same time, the field of rabbinics started to shed the local textual interests emphasized within the insider discourse, and began to mimic the trends of contemporary academia, analyzing rabbinic literature through the lenses of politics, psychology, gender, and comparative religion.

Through books, courses, and personal relationships, Neusner and his students made the Talmud and rabbinic literature enticing to scholars of Christian antiquity. Academic conversations about Jesus in light of rabbinic literature had been transpiring since the turn of the twentieth century, if not earlier.[68] But Neusner's work made rabbinic literature accessible to Christian ministers and their congregants. The pinnacle of Neusner's penetration into Christian circles was his interaction with Pope Benedict XVI. As Cardinal Joseph Ratzinger, Benedict had become enamored with Neusner's *A Rabbi Talks with Jesus*, a book in which Neusner engages the book of Matthew and explains why he would not have been persuaded by Jesus had he lived in the first century.[69] As Pope, Benedict returned to Neusner's book and devoted twenty pages of his biography of Jesus to Neusner's Talmud-based perspective. [70] Neusner was invited to the Vatican and received by Benedict in 2008.[71]

Studying the Talmud in terms of its relationship with nascent Christianity is one subfield of the academic critical discourse. But academicians are also interested in using the Talmud to write ancient Jewish history, to consider the Talmud and contemporaneous cultural products from the Greco-Roman world in light of each other, to employ narratology to consider the Talmud's stories, and to engage both constructively and historically with Talmudic theology.[72] An important recent trend is a full-scale attempt to consider the Talmud in its Babylonian context. [73] The Babylonia of the Talmud's day was a post-Persian society in which the language of high society was Persian and the dominant religion was Zoroastrianism. Increasingly, scholars are sensitized to the ways in which differences between the two Talmuds can be best understood considering the cultural beliefs and behaviors of the respective surrounding cultures of Palestine and Babylonia. Scholars are developing deeper fluency in Middle Persian to try to understand the Talmud as a product of Persian culture.

The Talmud has moved beyond neighboring religions and parallel contemporaneous cultures, though. It has come to function within the broader humanities as a model for both "thinking with texts" and for pluralistic dialogical discourse. The Talmud's reputation for microanalysis has been transformed from a negative to a positive trait, and its nonlinear free association is looked upon not as an instantiation of twisted thinking, but as a paradigm for narrative organization and a critique of abstract systematization.

Three figures—Hermann Cohen, Emmanuel Levinas, and Robert Cover—provide a window through which to witness the way in which the Talmud has entered the canon of Western thought. Though Immanuel Kant died thirty-four years before Hermann Cohen was born, Cohen is often considered a student of Kant's because Cohen devoted himself to understanding and expanding upon the work of the figure often considered the founder of modern philosophy. This would become increasingly fraught for Cohen as, in his later years, Cohen embraced his Jewishness and sought to explicitly reject Kant's writings vis-à-vis Judaism. In *Religion of Reason: Out of the Sources of Judaism* (1919), Cohen moves away from Kant's notion of ethics' emerging from the autonomous self, and argues that the self is only intelligible in terms of its relation to others, to the suffering of others.[74] Jewish sources, including those of rabbinic literature, become philosophical ones in Cohen's hands; this helped to dispel the long prejudice of the irrationality of the Talmud and its way of thinking. Later in the twentieth century, the rabbi and theologian Joseph Dov Soloveitchik would merge Cohen's philosophical ideas with an even subtler and more learned understanding of Talmudic discourse.[75]

Cohen's other-centered ethics is echoed by Emmanuel Levinas, a Lithuanian-born Jew who came to be one of the leading figures of existential phenomenology and an important influence on the vibrant Paris intellectual culture of the late 1960s and 1970s. Levinas' "Other" is an entity sometimes theologized as partly divine, whose ontological status is prior to one's self, and as such makes an ethical claim that is superior to that of the self.[76] The emergence of such an extreme Other-based ethics after the Holocaust is not that surprising; what is surprising is Levinas' ability to ground this ethical position in readings of the Talmud. From 1960 until 1989, Levinas delivered an annual discourse about Talmudic texts within the context of a new colloquy known as the *Colloque des Intellectuels Juifs de langue Française* [Colloquium of French-speaking Jewish Intellectuals], designed to provide young Jews with Jewish content that was more appealing than traditional synagogue fare.[77] Though a Lithuanian by birth, Levinas only began to study the Talmud in postwar Paris under the tutelage of an enigmatic rabbi named Chouchani, who also taught the Holocaust survivor and writer Elie Wiesel.[78] Though self-conscious of his own limitations as a Talmud scholar, Levinas found instantiations of his phenomenological ethics in the Talmud. Impressed by Chouchani's knowledge, Levinas considered the Talmud an alternate intellectual discourse to the dominant philosophical discourse of Western thought. Through its narratives and the theoretical debates veiled in legal particulars, the Talmud expressed ideas that the Greek-inspired philosophical canon could not. In the Talmud, Levinas finds examples of texts that inspire the idea that one must prioritize the other before the self and, sometimes, even to the extent of negating the self.

Levinas' emphasis of ethical obligations to others is paralleled (without awareness or direct influence) in Robert Cover's legal theory. An American Jewish law professor, Cover insisted upon the value of the Jewish legal discourse centered on the Talmud for theorizing and critiquing Western constitutional law. In his most direct comparison of the two legal discourses, Cover noted the way in which Western law begins with the subject and prioritizes the subject's rights, while Jewish law begins with the other and prioritizes the obligations both individuals and communities have towards that other.[79] This other-centered lens of viewing legal theory extended to Cover's personal involvement in the Civil Rights Movement, and his continual reevaluation of the relationship between law and morality within a pluralistic democratic society comprised of multiple minority communities.[80] Cover's most famous essay, "Nomos and Narrative," draws on biblical, rabbinic, and postrabbinic Jewish law to promote a vision of law that is deeply embedded in cultural narratives.[81] Implicit in Cover's frequent dichotomies in the essay is his sense that the theoretical apparatus of law that emerges in the Talmud and out of it, has greater intellectual and ethical depth than a legal apparatus more closely and directly tied to the ability to punish the body of the legal subject.

Beyond these uses of Talmudic content to critique Western fields like philosophy and law, the form of the Talmud and other works of rabbinic literature have come to be celebrated by the field of critical theory. This field, which emerged out of a marriage between literary theory, philosophy, and psychoanalysis in the 1970s and 1980s, is deeply suspicious of essential claims and of works of cultural production (like philosophical theories) that assert such claims systematically and totally. Suspicion of systems led to a rediscovery of rabbinic midrash and talmud as nonlinear modes of interpretation that are self-deconstructing, since they deny their own monopoly on theorizing beliefs, deciding laws, and interpreting prior literature. Though Jacques Derrida had no formal training in rabbinic literature, his deconstructive mode of reading texts against the grain were understood by some to reflect a rabbinicization of Western thought, wherein the hermeneutic strategies of midrash and talmud were marshalled within Western thought.[82]

The various new academic discourses of the Talmud have inspired some secular Israelis, who generally receive no Talmud education in their middle and high schools, to reclaim the Talmud as adults. Ruth Calderon became a member of the Knesset (Israel's parliament) in February 2013. In keeping with a long-standing tradition, the new Member of Parliament addressed her fellow Knesset members.[83] This speech differed from other such speeches insofar as it was largely an ode to the Talmud and Calderon's relationship with this work. Speaking for a generation of secular Israelis who ceded the Talmud to their religious fellow citizens, Calderon drew on her own experience to make an impassioned plea for all Israeli society to re-embrace responsibility for its Jewish heritage, and to do so, specifically, by seeking out the Talmud. Calderon framed the Talmud as a work that produces meaning in the mundane, a necessary corrective to the Bible, whose mythic quality gives that corpus a greater ability to speak to momentous historic events but not to everyday life.[84]

Calderon's arrival in the Knesset and the viral success of her speech on the internet, were preceded by Calderon's personal initiation into the Talmud at institutions like the Shalom Hartman Institute and The Hebrew University, which provide access to learners without regard for their gender, sexuality, or religious identity. Drawing on that experience, Calderon cofounded Alma, an institution that can best be described as a Tel Aviv yeshiva for secular Israelis, in 1996. Those secular Israelis, who are asserting their relationship with the Talmud, no longer think of it as a diasporic book, written in a language that threatens the hegemony of Hebrew. Hebrew is solidly in place as the language of the state, and the Talmud represents a rich anthology of Jewish heritage. Moreover, the flexibility that academicians have celebrated with respect to the Talmud's meaning, is an eye-opening counter-narrative for secular Israelis whose prior relationship with the Talmud had associated that work with the Orthodox state rabbinate which they evaluate as being dogmatic and inflexible.

Like secular Israelis, LBGTQ individuals might be expected to have little reason to embrace a text that has long been considered the bulwark of a traditional heteronormative culture. But American scholar Daniel Boyarin has inspired a full-on queering of the Talmud. In his 1997 book *Unheroic Conduct,* Boyarin claimed that Jewish gender difference and Western gender difference are not identical.[85] The ideal man, promoted within the Talmud and in the context of its historical study, is not a muscled warrior and physical achiever, but a diminished male whose characteristics would be described as effeminate by Western culture. And the ideal woman, by contrast, is far more worldly and industrious than her Western analog. Connecting this insight with recent more fluid theorizations of sexuality and gender, Boyarin opened the door to a new way of engaging the essential Talmud as a potential aid in subverting heteronormative Western cultural hegemony. In 2003, Rabbi Benay Lappe founded S'vara: A Traditional Radical Yeshiva which explicitly invites students to queer the Talmud and is open to students of all religious and sexual backgrounds.

New Symbolizations

The Talmud's breadth has not been limited to the intellectual. Larry Charles, an important contributor to the long-running sitcom *Seinfeld,* once compared the sitcom to the Talmud: "I would compare writing Seinfeld to writing the Talmud—a dark Talmud. You have a lot of brilliant minds examining a thought or ethical question from every possible angle."[86] Charles' comparison points to both the Talmud's comprehensive nature and its narrow focus as models for producing television humor. These features have also been present in the works of Jewish fiction writers like Philip Roth and Saul Bellow, whose microscopic descriptions of the mundane presage the comic subjects of *Seinfeld* and *Curb Your Enthusiasm*. American Jewish cultural production in the last century demonstrates a significant degree of microscopic analysis of the divide between minority self and majority other, as exemplified in the films of Woody Allen, whose habit of casting himself made the Jewish authorial voice of this microscopic analysis—nebbishy, anxious, obsessed with non-Jewish women—quite explicit.[87] Even within non-fiction writing, ethnographic works like Irving Howe's *World of Our Fathers* echo this same cultural ability to delve microscopically and comprehensively into the everyday. The microscopic examination of the mundane from multiple angles is today a central feature of standup comedy. That genre of cultural production has long been dominated by Jews like Lenny Bruce, Joan Rivers, Jerry Seinfeld, and Sarah Silverman.

It is often difficult to make the connection between Jewish cultural producers and the Talmud. It is highly unlikely that Woody Allen or Philip Roth ever studied the Talmud.[88] And yet, there is something profoundly Talmudic to the microscopic musings of a *Seinfeld* episode and the way in which the characters free-associate in Talmudic fashion. Perhaps it is best to think about American Jewish cultural production as a manifestation not of the essential Talmud, or the enhanced Talmud, but of the emblematic Talmud. To live as an American Jew in the twentieth century was to imbibe, to some degree, a notion of the Talmud's inherent form and a cultural valuing of that form. Jewishness celebrated microscopic evaluations and distinctions because these had been the stuff of Talmudic aptitude; even when the book itself didn't appear, certain reputational features of the book and its discourse survived as part of social culture and contributed to various modes of cultural production.

A far more obvious instance of the Talmud's symbolic life is the case of the Talmud in the Far East. East Asia has never had a demographically significant Jewish population. A visitor to contemporary Taiwan, though, might find herself staying in "Talmud Hotel-Gong Yuan," a business establishment "inspired by the Talmud" that includes a copy of *Talmud-Business Success Bible* in every room. That volume competes with several other titles (e.g., *Crack the Talmud: 101 Jewish Business Rules*, and *Know All of the Money-Making Stories of the Talmud*) within a growing subdivision of popular business self-help books that credit the Talmud for disproportionate Jewish success in business.

In 1971, Rabbi Marvin Tokayer, an American rabbi living in Japan, accidentally came to coauthor a book entitled *5,000 Years of Jewish Wisdom: Secrets of the Talmud Scriptures*. This book, which retells Talmudic vignettes and collects some of the Talmud's pithy sayings, went through seventy printings and sold half a million copies in Japan, but this success pales in comparison to its reception in South Korea.[89] Koreans have translated, digested, and modified Tokayer's original work, producing illustrated versions and versions that specifically target children.[90] These versions are understood by Koreans to be the Talmud and are ubiquitous in Korean culture, available in convenience stores and book vending machines, and occupy top positions on the list of steady book sales.[91] The Korean Talmud is a book of wisdom that is consulted for comfort, advice, and insight into the success represented by Jews; it straddles a fine line between philo-semitism and anti-Semitism. Overall, Korean culture admires Jews for their success—particularly in business and the sciences—and understands the Talmud to be the necessary educational key to replicating that success. Though the Korean example is an extreme one in which "the Talmud" is not the book itself but a different book altogether, it highlights the idea of the emblematic Talmud.

Postscript: Feminist Protest Art

While Yentl is a story of desire for the Talmud and of transgender passing, it is also a feminist narrative. It is not surprising that the story was rewritten for the stage in the late 1970s and then turned into a Hollywood movie in the 1980s. The story of a fiery woman trying to gain access to a men's-only club had tremendous appeal during this heyday of American feminism. The story's tale of access was somewhat mirrored in actual life as liberal

Jewish seminaries began ordaining women as rabbis and nonliberal denominations began to provide women and girls with increased opportunities to study the Talmud.

But even these limited examples of access could not paper over the extent to which both the essential and the enhanced Talmuds were produced in entirely male societies, and that these societies were often connected to authority structures that translated knowledge of the Talmud into power—power sometimes employed in suppressing the interests of women. This emblematic register of the Talmud as gendered power has recently occasioned powerful feminist art.

From a distance, the garment in Figure 5.3 looks like the signature prop from Andrew Lloyd Webber's *Joseph and the Amazing Technicolor Dreamcoat*. The full spectrum of the rainbow is represented from the central interior red to the outside fringes of violet. The squared-off shoulders suggest one is looking at a *tallit*—a four-cornered garment to which Jews attach fringes and which they employ for ritual purposes. Looking more closely, one can see that there are no formal fringes, though there are loose threads hanging off the garment that flow like occasional wisps of otherwise controlled hair. Up close it becomes clear that this is no ordinary garment. The fabric of this dreamcoat is comprised of more than 4,300 pieces of Japanese paper printed in assorted colors and rolled into scrolls arranged and sewn one next to the other. The color effect is produced by the color of the paper, the color of the ink, and the color of the thread sewing the scrolls together. The scrolls are

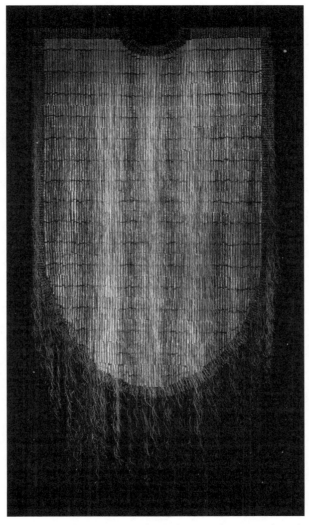

FIGURE 5.3. "If Only They Had Asked Us," Andi Arnovitz (2010)

each small but recognizable sections of the Romm Vilna edition of the Talmud.

Andi Arnovitz' arresting 2010 artwork "If Only They Had Asked Us" uses the Talmud's modern form to embody the specifically male nature of Jewish law and its history.[92] The rainbow has long represented spectral diversity, and the artwork draws a connection between the iconic black/white Vilna page and the nondiversity of the book's composers and participants in traditional discourse.

The iconic Vilna page is the perfect symbolic representation of Jewish tradition. The artwork's title imagines the production of an alternate Talmudic discourse—one that had incorporated female participation. The cloak of tradition might not have been black rabbinic gabardine, but rainbow colored and fringed. The artwork does not reject the Talmud; it reclaims it, imagining what the Talmud could have been and may still be. The Talmud is a book that generated a rich discourse and became symbolic in myriad ways. It is still becoming.

PROLOGUE: THE TALMUD—ESSENTIAL, ENHANCED, AND EMBLEMATIC

1. Chaim Potok, *The Promise* (New York: Knopf, 1969), 218–21.
2. Ibid., 325ff.
3. This point is made explicitly in the text.
4. Polemics between traditional and critical students of the Talmud in Israel transpired differently. Lower criticism (the use of manuscripts and alternate print editions to correct the basic text) did not engender a loud polemic in Israel. Though *Hazon Ish* famously resisted lower critical corrections, the practice has been common even among some Israeli ultra-Orthodox scholars for some time. Higher criticism (the positing of theories of composition to resolve tensions within a text) engendered a polemic in 2003 when some attempted to incorporate the new methodologies into Israeli high school education.

CHAPTER 1: GESTATION AND BIRTH

1. All translations are mine. Mishnah text is based on Kaufmann A50 housed in the library of the Hungarian Academy of Sciences.

2. The Soncino *editio princeps* (and all subsequent printed editions on its basis) is the only text witness that does not have "his fire" as a heading. By the rules of lower criticism, though, this is the original version and the heading was added by a later scribe for clarity.

3. Florence and Vatican 116 omit this instance of "his fire" because it is redundant in light of the heading. See previous note.

4. A homoioteleuton corrupts the original text of Vatican 116 here.

5. The implicit parenthetical was missing in the original text as evidenced by Munich 95.

6. The implicit parenthetical was missing in the original text as evidenced by Munich 95, Escorial G-I-3, Florence II-I-8, and Vatican 116 manuscripts.

7. The ellipsis is filled in with a fuller citation to the Mishnah in Escorial G-I-3, Hamburg 165 and Florence II-I-8 manuscripts.

8. The implicit parenthetical phrase is not original as evidenced by its omission in Vatican 116.

9. Munich 95, Escorial G-I-3, Hamburg, and Florence change the pronoun to a plural form from the original singular to match the noun "arrows."

10. The implicit parenthetical phrase is not original as evidenced by its omission in Vatican 116 and Munich 95.

11. The implicit parenthetical phrase is not original as evidenced by its omission in Vatican 116, Escorial G-I-3, and Hamburg 165.

12. The word is omitted in Vatican 116 but it is hard to determine whether it is original or not.

13. This is a slight simplification. The first four attempts to use statutes are the work of the anonymous narrator

and are explained away. The fifth attempt, attributed to Rava, is not explained away.

14. BT Gittin 56a–b and Avot De-Rabbi Natan A:4. The motif of escape through the ruse of a coffin is cleverly borrowed and adapted in Michael Chabon, *The Amazing Adventures of Kavalier and Clay: A Novel* (New York: Random House, 2000), 61–65.

15. A militant faction inside the walls of Jerusalem.

16. The implicit bracketed object is absent in St. Petersburg RNL Evr. I 187.

17. Several textual witnesses (St. Petersburg and two JTS manuscripts) make this entirely descriptive: "he came to him privately."

18. The implicit parenthetical word is absent from Vatican 130. It is not original to the text.

19. There is considerable instability among the text witnesses here. All have them bringing something vile smelling though the placement in the text varies. The two JTS manuscripts and the St. Petersburg manuscript have them rubbing saffron on Rabban Yohanan's face or nose (perhaps out of respect or so that he can endure).

20. The implicit parenthetical is only present in the Soncino print edition and the Vatican 130 manuscript. It is not original to the passage.

21. The implicit parenthetical phrase is absent in Arras 889 and the JTS manuscripts. It is a later addition.

22. The plural is based on Vatican 140. There is no method of establishing the original version here.

23. Vatican 140 makes the gate the subject: "the gate opened."

24. The implicit parenthetical is missing in Munich 95, Arras 889 and Vatican 140. It is not original to the text.

25. The implicit parenthetical phrase is absent in Arras 889 and Vatican 140. It is not original to the text.

26. The absence of this implicit parenthetical in Arras 889 and the two JTS manuscripts as well as the different placement in Vatican 130 strongly argue that this phrase is not original to the text.

27. The implicit parenthetical phrase is missing from the St. Petersburg and JTS manuscripts. It is likely not original to the text.

28. A number of text witnesses are missing this last midrash because of a homoioteleuton.

29. The absence of this line in Vatican 130 suggests that it was not part of the original text.

30. This parenthetical only appears in the Soncino *editio princeps* and subsequent print editions.

31. Vatican 140 changes the text to the more common Hebrew term for snake.

32. This dramatic silence is missing in Munich 95 suggesting that it has been added for effect.

33. The absence of this reference in Vatican 130, Munich 95, and Munich 153 and the change of wording in Vatican 140 all suggest that this is a later addition to the original text.

34. The two JTS manuscripts have a word change to a more common word meaning "decide."

35. Both JTS manuscripts add "at that moment" for dramatic effect before this scene.

36. This implicit parenthetical is explicated only in Arras 889 and the two JTS manuscripts. It is not part of the original text.

37. The absence of this comforting beginning in the two JTS manuscripts suggests that this is not original.

38. This implicit addition is missing in Soncino and Munich 95.

39. The two JTS manuscripts have a more archaic imperative verb "*hav*" which may be the original text.

40. Baruch M. Bokser, "Rabbinic Responses to Catastrophe: From Continuity to Discontinuity," *Proceedings of the American Academy for Jewish Research* 50 (1983) references the scholarship on this thesis before articulating a more nuanced approach that considers the passage of time as an important factor in developing rabbinic attitudes towards the lost Temple.

41. For further reading see Martin Goodman, *Rome and Jerusalem: The Clash of Ancient Civilizations*, (New York: Alfred A. Knopf, 2007), 416–19.

42. This point has been made repeatedly by Yonah Fraenkel. See, e.g., Yonah Frenel, *Darkhe Ha-Agadah Veha-Midrash*, 2 vols., Yad La-Talmud (Israel: Masadah : Yad la-Talmud, 1991), 1:235–42.

43. Much of this paragraph is influenced by the approach and ideas expressed in James Kugel, "Two Introductions to Midrash," *Prooftexts* 3, no. 2 (1983).

44. See, e.g., Ruth R. Wisse, *Jews and Power*, Jewish Encounters (New York: Nextbook : Schocken, 2007), 26–28.

45. The idea of perpetual Jewish pursuit of a vertical alliance is developed in Yosef Hayim Yerushalmi, *The Lisbon Massacre of 1506 and the Royal Image in the Shebet Yehudah*, Hebrew Union College Annual: Supplements (Cincinnati: Hebrew Union College-Jewish Institute of Religion, 1976), 37–66.

46. Jacob Neusner is the scholar most responsible for recognizing the unreliability of rabbinic stories as

historiography. He introduced this mindset in a book (Jacob Neusner, *Development of a Legend: Studies on the Traditions Concerning Yoḥanan Ben Zakkai*, (Leiden: Brill, 1970).) dedicated to the hero of the Vespasian legend, Rabban Yohanan ben Zakkai.

47. Goodman, 419.

48. Josephus, *The Jewish War* 3.8.9 399–408. Flavius Josephus, *Josephus*, trans. H. St J. Thackeray, (London, New York: Heinemann; Putnam, 1926), 114–19.

49. The Joseph story is in Genesis, beginning with chapter 37. The direct parallel is in chapters 39 and 40. Note that Josephus and Joseph are the same name.

50. Jeffrey L. Rubenstein, *Talmudic Stories: Narrative Art, Composition, and Culture* (Baltimore: Johns Hopkins University Press, 1999), 345 No. 2.

51. An overview of the sects and sectarianism can be found in Albert I. Baumgarten, *The Flourishing of Jewish Sects in the Maccabean Era: An Interpretation* (Leiden: Brill, 1997), 1–40.

52. This thesis is developed extensively in Shaye J. D. Cohen, "The Significance of Yavneh: Pharisees, Rabbis, and the End of Jewish Sectarianism," *Hebrew Union College Annual* 55 (1984).

53. Acts 5.

54. Seth Schwartz, *Imperialism and Jewish Society, 200 B.C.E. To 640 C.E.*, Jews, Christians, and Muslims from the Ancient to the Modern World (Princeton, N.J.: Princeton University Press, 2001).

55. The primary sources are collected and thoroughly treated in Saul Lieberman, *Greek in Jewish Palestine: Hellenism in Jewish Palestine* (New York: Jewish Theological Seminary of America, 1994).

56. See the glossary of terms in Samuel Krauss, *Griechische Und Lateinische Lehnwörter Im Talmud, Midrasch Und Targum*, 2 vols. (Berlin: S. Calvary, 1898), 23–47.

57. Steven Fine, *Art and Judaism in the Greco-Roman World: Toward a New Jewish Archaeology* (Cambridge; New York: Cambridge University Press, 2005), 34–46.

58. Henri Irénée Marrou, *A History of Education in Antiquity* (New York: Sheed and Ward, 1956), 98–99.

59. Ibid., 196.

60. E. J. Bickerman and Jewish Theological Seminary of America, *The Jews in the Greek Age* (Cambridge, MA: Harvard University Press, 1988); William Boyd, *The History of Western Education* (London: A. & C. Black, 1921), 61; Eliezer Ebner, *Elementary Education in Ancient Israel During the Tannaitic Period (10–220 C. E.)* (New York: Bloch Pub. Co., 1956); Nathan Morris, *The Jewish School: an Introduction to the History of Jewish Education* (London: Eyre and Spottiswoode, 1937).

61. Most prominently, the stories of Hillel and R. Aqiva.

62. Amram D. Tropper, *Wisdom, Politics, and Historiography: Tractate Avot in the Context of the Graeco-Roman near East*, Oxford Oriental Monographs (Oxford: Oxford University Press, 2004), 1–16.

63. It is true that prepositions can be tricky to translate and one could translate "at" Sinai. This is still surprising because the chain of transmission would presumably be on stronger ground if the first link, the divine, was mentioned explicitly.

64. Another common understanding of "oral Torah" is a set of hermeneutic tools that function as a cipher for the encoded written Bible. That is also not the

meaning of "Moses received Torah from Sinai" in
Ethics of the Fathers.

65. Daniel Boyarin first drew attention to some of the
connections between the rabbis and monasticism
as well as the compromises the rabbis produced as a
cultural alternative. See Daniel Boyarin, *Carnal Israel:
Reading Sex in Talmudic Culture* (Berkeley: University of California Press, 1993), 134–66.

66. David M. Goodblatt, *Rabbinic Instruction in Sasanian
Babylonia*, (Leiden: Brill, 1975), 263–85.

67. For a more developed theory of rabbinic genres see
David Halivni, *Midrash, Mishnah, and Gemara: The
Jewish Predilection for Justified Law* (Cambridge, MA:
Harvard University Press, 1986).

68. Moshe Halbertal, *People of the Book: Canon, Meaning,
and Authority* (Cambridge, MA: Harvard University
Press, 1997), 11–44; Kugel (in footnote 43 above).

69. Daniel Boyarin, *Intertextuality and the Reading
of Midrash*, Indiana Studies in Biblical Literature
(Bloomington: Indiana University Press, 1990), 1–21.

70. This was first noted in David Hoffmann, *The First
Mishna and the Controversies of the Tannaim: the High-
est Court in the City of the Sanctuary* (New York: Her-
mon Press, 1977). It has been most recently developed
within Azzan Yadin-Israel, *Scripture as Logos: Rabbi
Ishmael and the Origins of Midrash* (Philadelphia:
University of Pennsylvania Press, 2004); *Scripture and
Tradition: Rabbi Akiva and the Triumph of Midrash*
(Philadelphia: University of Pennsylvania Press, 2014).

71. The ideological implications, particularly for theology, are central to Abraham Joshua Heschel, Gordon
Tucker, and Leonard Levin, *Heavenly Torah: As*

Refracted through the Generations (New York: Continuum, 2005), 46–70.

72. Genesis did not engender tannaitic midrash because of its primarily narrative and nonlegal quality.

73. This is a simplification for presentation purposes. Much of the organization of the Mishnah is based upon mnemonic non-content organizations indicative of earlier documents that were organized according to those qualities.

74. These numbers reflect the original division of the tractates during Rabbinic times. Since then, a single tractate *Neziqin* has been divided into three parts (Baba Qamma, Baba Metzia, and Baba Batra) and Makkot was severed from its original inclusion as part of Sanhedrin. In contemporary editions, there are thirty-six tractates in the Babylonian Talmud and thirty-nine in the Palestinian.

75. Saul Lieberman, *ʿal Ha-Yerushalmi* (Jerusalem: Darom, 1929).

76. David Weiss Halivni and Jeffrey L. Rubenstein, *The Formation of the Babylonian Talmud* (Oxford: Oxford University Press, 2013); Leib Moscovitz, *Talmudic Reasoning: From Casuistics to Conceptualization*, (Tübingen: Mohr Siebeck, 2002).

77. Eyal Ben Eliyahu et al., *Handbook of Jewish Literature from Late Antiquity, 135–700 CE* (Oxford: Oxford University Press for the British Academy, 2012), 61–95; Hermann Leberecht Strack and Günter Stemberger, *Introduction to the Talmud and Midrash* (Minneapolis: Fortress Press, 1992), 225–32, 276–359.

78. David Brodsky, *A Bride without a Blessing: A Study in the Redaction and Content of Massekhet Kallah and*

Its Gemara (Tübingen: Mohr Siebeck, 2006) makes the provocative claim that Tractate Kallah and the first two chapters of Kallah Rabbati are Babylonian amoraic compositions. If this is correct, then the Babylonian Talmud is not the only literary remnant.

79. Daniel Boyarin, *Border Lines: The Partition of Judaeo-Christianity* (Philadelphia: University of Pennsylvania Press, 2004), 182ff.

80. David Stern, "Midrash and Indeterminacy," *Critical Inquiry* 15 (1988); "Anthology and Polysemy in Classical Midrash," in *The Anthology in Jewish Literature*, ed. David Stern (Oxford: Oxford University Press, 2004); Steven D. Fraade, *From Tradition to Commentary: Torah and Its Interpretation in the Midrash Sifre to Deuteronomy* (Albany: State University of New York Press, 1991), 123–64.

81. Mishnah Eduyot 1:5.

82. Boyarin, *Border Lines: The Partition of Judaeo-Christianity*, 189–201.

CHAPTER 2: ANATOMY

1. The nature of the dichotomy of halakhah/aggadah as a hermeneutic practice has been developed in Barry Scott Wimpfheimer, *Narrating the Law: A Poetics of Talmudic Legal Stories* (Philadelphia: University of Pennsylvania Press, 2011).

2. The word "nappaha" means blacksmith. This would seem to be a tale whose *dramatis personae* is determined by its content. See Shamma Friedman, "Ha-Shem Gorem: Divre He-Hakham Noflim Al Shemo," in *Ve-Eleh Ha-Shemot: Mehqarim Be-Ozar Hashemot*

Hayehudiyim, ed. Aharon Demsky (Ramat Gan: Bar Ilan, 1999).

3. The implicit parenthetical phrase is only present in Florence II-I-8 and Vatican 116 manuscripts. It is not original to the text.

4. The term used here is "*shm'ateta*" which means tradition, or perhaps, precedent. The terminology is evidence of the fact that an idea of halakhah as such had not yet formed.

5. The implicit parenthetical phrase is only present in Florence II-I-8 and Vatican 116 manuscripts. It is not original to the text.

6. The only textual witness that asserts that R' Isaac began with the aggadah is the Soncino *editio princeps*. Because of the later dominance of halakhah, I assume this is the original version.

7. The different and less elegant formulation of Hamburg 165: "from this side and this side bald" may be the original version.

8. The implicit parenthetical is missing in the Munich 95 and Escorial G-I-3 manuscripts and has been added in the margins of Hamburg 165.

9. This version found in Munich 95, Escorial G-I-3, Hamburg 165, Vatican 116 and a genizah fragment in the Taylor-Shechter collection is more likely the original. The version "Zion" found in Soncino and Florence is likely adapted based on the verse citation that follows.

10. The second clause of the verse is only found in Soncino and Escorial G-I-3. It is likely an addition.

11. Several textual witnesses add the missing "says the Lord" from the biblical verse. It was likely not originally in the text.

12. The second clause of the verse is only found in Soncino and Munich 95. It is likely an addition.

13. David Goodblatt, *Rabbinic Instruction in Sasanian Babylonia,* (Leiden: Brill, 1975), 263-285.

14. This is one of Aesop's fables. See Phaedrus Babrius, *Babrius and Phaedrus*, trans. B. E. Perry, (Cambridge, Mass.; London: Harvard University Press; W. Heineman, 1984), 234–37.

15. Joseph Heinemann, *Derashot Ba-Tsibur Bi-Tekufat Ha-Talmud* (1970), 7–28.

16. This reading was suggested to me by Tzvi Novick.

17. Jonathan D. Culler, *Structuralist Poetics: Structuralism, Linguistics and the Study of Literature* (London; New York: Routledge, 2002), 172.

18. Tzvi Novick notes that it also has permitted easy parodies of the Talmud in the literature of the Haskalah and in contemporary observance of Purim.

19. Jenny Steele and Rob Merkin, "Insurance between Neighbours: Stannard v. Gore and Common Law Liability for Fire," *Journal of Environmental Law* 25, no. 2 (2013) 305–317.

20. Though the hypothetical is outlandish, it also corresponds to a literal reading of the biblical verse. The opaque opening verb leaves the fire without an agent—it spreads seemingly on its own. This outlandish case can be understood among other things as explaining one such case of a fire's spreading on its own.

21. Louis Jacobs, *Structure and Form in the Babylonian Talmud* (Cambridge: Cambridge University Press, 1991).

22. Rashi asserts that the issue here is the fact that the fire does not belong to the dog's owner. Other

commentators have trouble with this idea. See below chapter 3.

23. The implicit parenthetical phrase is absent in Escorial G-I-3, suggesting that it is not original to the text.

24. Munich 95 and Florence II-I-8 add "and spread" here based on the ensuing few words. The movement of the word for spreading in Florence II-I-8 suggests that neither the question nor the answer had this modifier in the original text.

25. The implicit parenthetical explanation is missing in both Hamburg 165 and Florence II-I-8. It is a later addition to the text.

26. There is considerable instability in the textual witnesses surrounding this name. Escorial G-I-3 and Florence II-I-8 have the common "Rav Aha son of Rav Ikka," and Munich 95 has "Rav Aha son of Rava." Hamburg 165 eliminates the second name altogether.

27. The phrasing in the text is awkward. It literally means "he did not want to unload the load." This awkwardness generates the addition of the words "that much" in Munich 95.

28. My own term. The Talmud's Aramaic term for the concept is literally translated: "establish for him with the more severe of them."

29. The Hebrew formulation is in the singular and I have modified to the plural for clarification.

30. It should be noted that while the Talmud considers this an absurdity, Exodus 21:29 mandates (at least in theory) capital punishment for both the ox and the owner for an ox's killing of a person. This is the one case in which property's damage does invoke capital punishment. See Moshe Greenberg, "Some Postulates of Biblical

Criminal Law," in *Yehezkel Kaufman Jubilee Volume*, ed. Menahem Haran (Jerusalem: Magnes, 1960).

31. This parenthetical "would" is missing from Vatican 116 which demonstrates that it is a stylization.

32. For a more elaborate treatment of the divide between these two legal systems see Chaya T. Halberstam, *Law and Truth in Biblical and Rabbinic Literature* (Bloomington: Indiana University Press, 2009), 76-105.

33. See, e.g., BT Pesahim 30b.

34. Some medieval commentaries understand the four payments to be a sum total (and exclude a humiliation payment), but the simpler interpretation is that this refers to the four other payments (beyond restitution).

35. The revolution is credited to two of my mentors, Shamma Friedman and David Weiss Halivni. Friedman's most thorough articulation of the question of Talmudic composition is found at Shamma Friedman, "Mavi Kelali ʿal Derek Ḥeqer Ha-Sugya," in *Meḥqarîm U-Meqorot* ed. H.Z. Dmitrovsky (New York: The Jewish Theological Seminary of America, 1978). The best introduction to Halivni's thoughts on these issues is Halivni and Rubenstein, note 76 in chapter 1. A helpful methodological primer for beginners is Joshua Kulp and Jason Rogoff, *Reconstructing the Talmud: An Introduction to the Academic Study of Talmudic Literature* (New York: Hadar Press, 2014).

36. Avishalom Westreich has authored a definitive history of fire liability in his Avishalom Westreich, "Development and Exegetical Aims of Talmudic Tort Liability in Light of Unusual Cases" (Bar Ilan University, 2007), 181–224. Much of what follows is in conversation with this excellent work.

37. Ibid., 211–14.
38. Ibid., 198–99.
39. Ibid., 212.
40. Ibid.
41. In truth, these "would have" statements may be later scribal additions to the text. Munich 95 is missing both of these statements in the prologue while several text witnesses are missing the second instance but not the first.
42. David Weiss Halivni has been most responsible for attempts to date the Stam. His position on the matter has changed slightly from volume to volume of his Talmud commentary. A translation of these different positions is found at Halivni and Rubenstein, note 76, chapter 1.
43. Rava also mentions these ideas at Baba Qamma 31a-b and 58b.
44. David Weiss Halivni, *Mekorot U-Masorot*, (Tel Aviv: Dvir, 1968), ad loc.
45. Westreich, 200 references a different way of understanding Rava's impact on the topic. An attentive reader might wonder how Rava can say that he is supporting the view of R' Yohanan (as if a universal debate between R' Yohanan and Resh Laqish were known). It is possible that Rava supports the view of R' Yohanan in his other debate with Resh Laqish about transmitting fire to a child. R' Yohanan said the dispatcher is liable when sending fuel, firestarter, and flame. It is possible that when Rava says the verse and rabbinic source support R' Yohanan, he intends this other position of R' Yohanan. Rava infers from the verse that responsibility for the fire lies with the human who is directly responsible for lighting the fire. In this case that refers

to the minor or deaf person and exempts the one who
sent materials with them. By this reading, the editors of
the passage who inherited Rava's statement about one
position of R' Yohanan have cleverly repositioned it to
comment on a different and larger conceptual position
they have attributed to R' Yohanan.

46. Much of this is Westreich's theory.

47. Mishnah Baba Qamma 2:6.

48. Baba Qamma 62a.

49. Westreich, 200.

50. Moscovitz is responsible for the clearest and most
comprehensive articulation of the notion of conceptual
development within the generations of the rabbis of the
Talmud. See Moscovitz, *Talmudic Legal Reasoning*.

51. The notion of a unifying drive in the Talmud is developed in Wimpfheimer as cited in note 1.

52. Only one textual witness has this version here, but
many in Avodah Zarah 2a have it this way.

53. This version is based on Munich 95 and Vatican 108.
Other textual witnesses add the word "bar Hasa" after
"bar Hama." This could either be an orthographic
marginal correction entering the text or the addition
of a known name ending to Hama (Hama bar Hasa is
well known in the Talmud).

54. There are other ways of finding redundancy in the
text. The specific word used for "at the base" is longer
than it need be. I thank Tzvi Novick for noting this.

55. See, e.g., Jeremiah 2:2.

56. Mekhilta Massekhta Debahodesh 3, S. Horovitz and
I. A. Rabin, *Mekhilta* (Frankfurt am Main,: J. Kauff-
mann, 1931), 214.

57. It is also possible, if you rely on the preceding line in
the midrash, to understand Israel as seeking protection

from the theophany under the severed mountain. I
thank Tzvi Novick for this point.

58. For a more elaborate development of this passage see
Rubenstein, 212–41.

59. BT Sanhedrin 92b

60. BT Baba Batra 40a-b, 47b-49a.

61. This doesn't apply as effectively to scenarios of gifts.
See Rashbam at BT Baba Batra 40b.

62. BT Baba Batra 48b.

63. Ibid.

CHAPTER 3: ELECTION: HOW THE TALMUD'S
DISCOURSE DEVELOPED

1. Gerson D. Cohen, "The Story of the Four Captives,"
*Proceedings of the American Academy for Jewish Re-
search* 29 (1960); Daniel Boyarin, *A Traveling Homeland: The Babylonian Talmud as Diaspora* (Philadelphia: University of Pennsylvania Press, 2015), 9–31.

2. This section is indebted to three mentors and one
study partner. Shmuel Nacham first demonstrated to
me that the medieval Talmudists were brilliant readers.
Haym Soloveitchik provided me with an overview of
the history of the three different medieval cultures and
their interrelationship. Shamma Friedman modeled the
use of critical understandings of the Talmud for new
insights into medieval interpreters. Daniel Reifman was
my study partner for several years of intense day-long
examinations of the Talmud and its discourse. Many of
the unattributed ideas in this chapter were inspired by
these men. All mistakes are my own.

3. The definitive treatment of the Geonim is Robert Brody,
*The Geonim of Babylonia and the Shaping of Medieval
Jewish Culture* (New Haven: Yale University Press, 1998).

4. Isadore Twersky, *Introduction to the Code of Maimonides (Mishneh Torah)*, Yale Judaica Series (New Haven: Yale University Press, 1980).

5. The best treatment of these works is found in Neil Danzig, *Mavo Le-Sefer Halakhot Pesuqot: ʿim Tashlum Halakhot Pesuqot* (New York: Jewish Theological Seminary of America, 1993).

6. Twersky.

7. See, e.g., the commentary of Rabbenu Peretz cited in *Shittah Mequbezet ad loc.*

8. Isadore Twersky, *Rabad of Posquieres, a Twelfth-Century Talmudist* (Cambridge: Harvard University Press, 1962).

9. Haym Soloveitchik, "Rabad of Posquieres: A Programmatic Essay," *Studies in the History of Jewish Society* (1980).

10. Israel M. Ta-Shma, *Ha-Sifrut Ha-Parshanit La-Talmud Be-Europah Uvi-Tsefon Afrikah: Korot, Ishim Ve-Shitot* (Jerusalem: Magnes, 1999), 35–40.

11. Rashi's commentary to the Talmud is treated in Yonah Frenkel, *Darko Shel Rashi Be-Ferusho La-Talmud Ha-Bavli* (Jerusalem: Magnes, 1975); Avraham Grossman, *Rashi*, trans. Joel A. Linsider (Oxford, England; Portland, OR: Littman Library of Jewish Civilization, 2012); Ta-Shma, 40–56.

12. Ta-Shma, *Ha-Sifrut* 1:125,39.

13. The definitive treatment of the Tosafists is Efraim Elimelech Urbach, *Baʿale Ha-Tosafot: Toldotehem, Hiburehem Ve-Shiṭatam* (Jerusalem: Mosad Bialik, 1955).

14. BT Baba Qamma 55b and Mishnah Baba Qamma 6:8 respectively.

15. In fairness to Rashi, while the view that the challenge to Resh Laqish in the beginning of the passage is a bit forced within the section of the passage that questions

Resh Laqish from the dog-and-coal case, it actually is a better fit for the question that arises from the camel-and-candle case.

16. David Abraham ben, *Hidushe Ha-Rabad . . . Bava Qamma* (Jerusalem: Horeb, 1963).

17. The last clause is in parentheses in Atlas' edition but not in MS Or. 852 in the British Library from which Atlas transcribed his basic text.

18. Soloveitchik, chapter 3, no. 9.

19. Menachem Elon, *Ha-Mishpat Ha-Ivri* (Jerusalem: Magnes, 1973).

20. *Nizqe Mammon* 14:9–10.

21. *Maggid Mishnah ad loc.*

22. *Arba'ah Turim, Hoshen Mishpat* 418.

23. Eliyahu Stern, *The Genius: Elijah of Vilna and the Making of Modern Judaism* (New Haven: Yale University Press, 2013).

24. Ibid.

25. Ibid., 138–39.

26. Marc B. Shapiro, "The Brisker Method Reconsidered," *Tradition: A Journal of Orthodox Jewish Thought* 31, no. 3 (1997).

27. *Haelef Lakh Shlomo Orah Hayyim* #32.

28. *Melamed L'hoil Orah Hayim* #49.

29. *Iggrot Moshe Even Haezer* 4:28.

30. https://www.responsa.co.il.

31. "Central Conference of American Rabbis," https://ccarnet.org/rabbis-speak/reform-responsa/.

32. For a good introduction to these, see James L. Kugel, *The Bible as It Was* (Cambridge, MA: Belknap Press of Harvard University Press, 1997), 1–50.

33. Leopold Zunz, *Die Gottesdienstlichen Vorträge Der Juden, Historisch En Wickelt. Ein Beitrag*

Zur Alterthumskunde Und Biblischen Kritik, Zur Literatur-Und Religionsgeschichte (Berlin: A. Asher, 1832), 342–72.

34. This text does not appear in standard print editions of *Sheiltot*. It was recovered from the Cairo Genizah and can be found in Solomon Aaron Wertheimer, *Bate Midrashot: Yakhilu Midrashim Ketanim Mi-Kitve Yad Shonim*, 4 vols. (Jerusalem: Bi-defus M. Lilyenthal, 1893), 2:131.

35. The text does not appear in the Buber edition of *Tanhuma*. In the standard edition, it appears as a comment on Genesis 6:9. *Midrash Tanhuma* (Constantinople, 1520), 8.

36. Ritba, Shabbat 88a.

37. Ramban, Shabbat 88a.

38. *Hiddushe Hatorah* (Cracow: Joseph Fischer, 1904), 60.

39. *Aqedat Yizhaq*, Deuteronomy, Gate 92.

40. Joseph Hayyim ben Elijah al-Hakam, *Sefer Ben Yehoyada: Be'Urim U-Ferushim Al Divre Agadah She-Dibru Hazal Be-Talmud Bavli* (Jerusalem: Yeshivat ha-Rabanim u-Vet ha-Keneset a.sh. Ezra ha-Sofer, 1963), Shabbat 88a.

41. Harry Austryn Wolfson, *The Philosophy of the Kalam*, Structure and Growth of Philosophic Systems from Plato to Spinoza (Cambridge, MA: Harvard University Press, 1976), 1–111.

42. Mashhad Al-Allaf, "Islamic Theology," in *The Bloomsbury Companion to Islamic Studies*, ed. Clinton Bennett (London: Bloomsbury, 2014).

43. Lenn E. Goodman, "Saadiah Gaon Al-Fayyumi," in *History of Islamic Philosophy*, ed. Seyyed Hossein; Leaman Nasr, Oliver (New York: Routledge, 1996).

44. Alexander Broadie, "Maimonides," ibid.

45. *Or Hashem*, 2:5:6. For elaboration see A. Ravitzky, "Crescas' Theory on Human Will: Development and Sources," *Tarbiz* 51, no. 3 (1982).

46. Bernard Septimus, *Hispano-Jewish Culture in Transition: The Career and Controversies of Ramah*, Harvard Judaic Monographs (Cambridge, MA: Harvard University Press, 1982).

47. Moshe Idel, "Maimonides' Guide of the Perplexed and the Kabbalah," *Jewish History* 18, no. 2–3 (2004).

48. Gershom Scholem, *Origins of the Kabbalah* (Philadelphia; Princeton: Jewish Publication Society; Princeton University Press, 1987), 199–364.

49. Ibid., 365–475.

50. *Major Trends in Jewish Mysticism* (Jerusalem: Schocken, 1941), 156. Boaz Huss and Yudith Nave, *The Zohar Reception and Impact* (Oxford; Portland: The Littman Library of Jewish Civilization, 2016), 112–47.

51. Ḳalonimus Kalman Shapira, *Esh Kodesh: Imrot Tehorot Mi-Shenot Ha-Shoʾah She-Neʾemru . . . Be-Geto Varsha* (Jerusalem: Vaʿad haside Pyasetsnah, 1960), 52.

52. Barukh Shalom Ashlag, *Dargot Ha-Sulam* (New York: Bne Barukh, 1996), #383.

53. Marc Saperstein, *Decoding the Rabbis: A Thirteenth-Century Commentary on the Aggadah*, Harvard Judaic Monographs (Cambridge, MA: Harvard University Press, 1980).

54. An earlier example of these kinds of works is Rabbenu Nissim's *Hibbur Yafeh Mi-hayeshuʾah*, an Arabic collection of Talmudic aggadah.

55. Marjorie Suzan Lehman, *The En Yaaqov: Jacob Ibn Abib's Search for Faith in the Talmudic Corpus* (Detroit: Wayne State University Press, 2012).

CHAPTER 4: RIVALS, NAYSAYERS, IMITATORS, AND CRITICS

1. Talya Fishman, *Becoming the People of the Talmud: Oral Torah as Written Tradition in Medieval Jewish Cultures*, Jewish Culture and Contexts (Philadelphia: University of Pennsylvania Press, 2011).

2. Haym Soloveitchik, "The People of the Book since When?", *Jewish Review of Books* (Winter 2013).

3. *Becoming the People of the Talmud* makes the mistake of conflating technological change, jurisprudential shifts, and hermeneutic transformations. It is tremendously ambitious to assert that the change from orality to writing was contemporaneous with both a shift to the Talmud as the centerpiece of practical jurisprudence, and a shift to a Tosafist style understanding of the Talmud as a coherent work of legal literature. This ambition makes it easy for Soloveitchik to chip away at the complex picture by showing a misreading of a core source about practical jurisprudence or an overreading of a claim about orality and writing. Soloveitchik's corrections undermine some of this most ambitious triple claim, but they do not contradict the basic and important insight that the Talmud's cultural significance differs in different regions and different times.

4. Michel Foucault, *Discipline and Punish: The Birth of the Prison* (New York: Pantheon Books, 1977).

5. Tractate counts are complicated by the changing definitions of a tractate throughout history. This

count is based on a scholarly reconstruction of the original mishnaic tractates. Thus, Baba Qamma, Baba Metzia, and Baba Batra are one tractate and Sanhedrin-Makkot is one tractate.

6. Yaakov Sussman, "Veshuv Liyerushalmi Neziqin," in *Mehqarei Talmud*, ed. Yaakov Sussman and David Rosenthal (Jerusalem: Magnes, 1990); Alyssa M. Gray, *A Talmud in Exile: The Influence of Yerushalmi Avodah Zarah on the Formation of Bavli Avodah Zarah* (Providence, RI: Brown Judaic Studies, 2005). See also the methodology for analyzing stories in both Talmuds as explained in Rubenstein, chapter 1, no. 50, pp. 25–26.

7. Yaakov Elman, "Classical Rabbinic Interpretation," in *The Jewish Study Bible*, ed. Adele Brettler and Marc Berlin (Oxford: Oxford University Press, 2004); Moscovitz, 343–65.

8. Robert Brody, *The Geonim of Babylonia and the Shaping of Jewish Medieval Culture* (New Haven: Yale University Press, 1998); Marina Rustow, *Heresy and the Politics of Community: The Jews of the Fatimid Caliphate* (Ithaca: Cornell University Press, 2008).

9. Lieberman, chapter 1, no. 75.

10. This is the 1523 Venice edition published by Daniel Bomberg.

11. This issue was most forcefully articulated in Saul Lieberman's review of Jacob Neusner's translation of the Palestinian Talmud: Saul Lieberman, "A Tragedy or a Comedy?" *Journal of the American Oriental Society* 104, no. 2 (1984). The critique is relevant for the new ArtScroll Schottenstein as well. There have been some commentaries like *Noam Yerushalmi* or *Hiddushe Haritzad* that have attempted to resist Bavli-centrism.

12. Nathan Shur, *Toldot Hakaraim* (Jerusalem: Bialik, 2003), 33–70.

13. Rustow, 52–57.

14. Ibid.

15. Ibid.

16. Ibid.

17. Brody, 86.

18. Brody, 87–88; 96. Full responsum in Brody, *Teshuvot Rav Natronai Gaon* (Cleveland: Makhon Ofeq, 1994), # 258.

19. Exodus 32:9.

20. The Palestinian Aramaic form is influenced by the author's familiarity with Targum Onkelos. See Scholem, *Major Trends in Jewish Mysticism*, 164.

21. Arthur Green, *A Guide to the Zohar* (Stanford, CA: Stanford University Press, 2004), 71–76.

22. Daniel Abrams, "The Zohar as a Book: On the Assumptions and Expectations of the Kabbalists and Modern Scholarship," *Kabbalah: Journal for the Study of Jewish Mystical Texts* 12 (2004); "The Invention of The 'Zohar' as a Book: On the Assumptions and Expectations of the Kabbalists and Modern Scholars," *Kabbalah: Journal for the Study of Jewish Mystical Texts* 19 (2009).

23. Huss and Nave, chapter 3, no. 50: 112–47.

24. Gershom Scholem, *Sabbatai Sevi: The Mystical Messiah, 1626–1676* (Princeton, NJ: Princeton University Press, 2016), 691–92.

25. The best overview of this subject is in Chen Merchavia, *Ha-Talmud Bi-Re'i Ha-Natsrut: Ha-Yaḥas Le-Sifrut Yisra'el Shele-Aḥar Ha-Mikra Ba-ʿolam Ha-Notsri Bi-Yeme-Ha-Benayim (500–1248)* (Jerusalem: Mosad Bialik, 1970).

26. For recent recognition of the slow process of separation between these two movements, see Boyarin, *Border Lines: The Partition of Judaeo-Christianity*, 1–33.

27. Ora Limor, "Christians and Jews," in *The Cambridge History of Christianity: Christianity in Western Europe C.1100- C.1500*, ed. Miri Rubin and Walter Simons (Cambridge: Cambridge University Press, 2009).

28. Alex J. Novikoff, *The Medieval Culture of Disputation: Pedagogy, Practice, and Performance*, The Middle Ages Series (Philadelphia: University of Pennsylvania Press, 2013), 170–218.

29. Peter Schäfer et al., *Toledot Yeshu ("The Life Story of Jesus") Revisited: A Princeton Conference* (Tübingen, Germany: Mohr Siebeck, 2009), 3–18.

30. Recent scholarship on Christian intellectual life in Sasanian Babylonia shows intriguing structural parallels between Christian and Rabbinic learning communities. See Adam H. Becker, *Fear of God and the Beginning of Wisdom: The School of Nisibis and Christian Scholastic Culture in Late Antique Mesopotamia* (Philadelphia: University of Pennsylvania Press, 2006).

31. The few passages are taxonomized and framed in: Peter Schäfer, *Jesus in the Talmud* (Princeton, NJ: Princeton University Press, 2007).

32. Novikoff, 182.

33. Merchavia, 93–127.

34. Jeremy Cohen, *The Friars and the Jews: The Evolution of Medieval Anti-Judaism* (Ithaca: Cornell University Press, 1982), 33–50.

35. Ibid.

36. Robert Chazan et al., *The Trial of the Talmud: Paris, 1240* (Toronto: Pontifical Institute of Mediaeval Studies, 2012), 1–92.

37. Saadia R. Eisenberg, "Reading Medieval Religious Disputation: The 1240 "'Debate' between Rabbi Yehiel of Paris and Friar Nicholas Donin" (University of Michigan, 2008), 168–75.

38. Eisenberg calls this "autonomy" at ibid., 168.

39. Chazan et al., 130.

40. Ibid.

41. Caroline Walker Bynum, *Holy Feast and Holy Fast: The Religious Significance of Food to Medieval Women*, The New Historicism: Studies in Cultural Poetics (Berkeley: University of California Press, 1987), 255–59.

42. Susan L. Einbinder, *Beautiful Death: Jewish Poetry and Martyrdom in Medieval France* (Princeton, NJ: Princeton University Press, 2002), 76.

43. Ibid., 75.

44. On this subject see Boyarin, *Carnal Israel: Reading Sex in Talmudic Culture*, 134–66.

45. Bavli Yevamot 63b.

46. Robert Chazan, *Barcelona and Beyond: The Disputation of 1263 and Its Aftermath* (Berkeley: University of California Press, 1992), 57–59.

47. Cohen.

48. Chazan et al., 98–101.

49. Ibid., 30–31.

50. Amnon Raz-Krakotzkin, *The Censor, the Editor, and the Text: The Catholic Church and the Shaping of the Jewish Canon in the Sixteenth Century* (Philadelphia: University of Pennsylvania Press, 2007), 27.

51. David Price, *Johannes Reuchlin and the Campaign to Destroy Jewish Books* (Oxford: Oxford University Press, 2011), 131–35.

52. Raz-Krakotzkin, 32.

53. Ibid., 54.

54. Marvin J. Heller, *Printing the Talmud: A History of the Earliest Printed Editions of the Talmud* (Brooklyn, NY: Im Hasefer, 1992), 241–65.

55. Johann Andreas Eisenmenger, *Entdecktes Judenthum*, 2 vols. (Frankfurt, 1700).

56. Alexander McCaul, *The Old Paths; or, a Comparison of the Principles and Doctrines of Modern Judaism with the Religion of Moses and the Prophets*, 2d ed. (London: The London Society, 1846).

57. Eliyahu Stern, "Catholic Judaism: The Political Theology of the Nineteenth Century Russian Jewish Enlightenment," *Harvard Theological Review* 109, no. 4 (2016).

58. Gershom Scholem, *Sabbatai Ṣevi; the Mystical Messiah, 1626–1676*, revised and augmented translation ed., The Littman Library of Jewish Civilisation (London: Routledge & K. Paul, 1973), 691–92.

59. *Major Trends in Jewish Mysticism*, 325–50.

60. Mordecai L. Wilensky, "Hasidic-Mitnaggedic Polemics in the Jewish Communities of Eastern Europe: The Hostile Phase," in *Essential Papers on Hasidism*, ed. Gershon David Hundert (New York: NYU Press, 1991), 262.

61. There were groups, such as the Hasidim of Przysucha, who were extremely devoted to the Talmud and halakhah. See Raphael Mahler, "Hasidism and the Jewish Enlightenment," in *Essential Papers in Hasidism*, ed. Gershon David Hundert (New York: NYU, 1991), 454. One should distinguish between early and late Hasidism in this regard. By

the mid-nineteenth century (ibid., 428) there was a change of heart within Hasidism regarding the Talmud and its study.

62. Wilensky, 261-266.
63. Paweł Maciejko, *The Mixed Multitude: Jacob Frank and the Frankist Movement, 1755–1816* (Philadelphia: University of Pennsylvania Press, 2011).
64. Ibid.
65. Ibid.
66. Ibid.
67. Jacob Shavit, Mordechai Eran, and Jacob Shavit, *The Hebrew Bible Reborn: From Holy Scripture to the Book of Books: A History of Biblical Culture and the Battles over the Bible in Modern Judaism* (Berlin; New York: Walter de Gruyter, 2007), 38. In the nineteenth century the Bible gained not only the status of an alternative to the Talmud, but also as its opposition.
68. Moshe Pelli, *The Age of Haskalah: Studies in Hebrew Literature of the Enlightenment in Germany*, Studies in Judaism in Modern Times (Leiden: Brill, 1979), 48–72.
69. Ibid.
70. Ibid.
71. See Shmuel Feiner, *The Jewish Enlightenment* (Philadelphia: University of Pennsylvania Press, 2004), 91.
72. Pelli, 48–72.
73. Ibid., 55.
74. David Philipson, *The Reform Movement in Judaism* (New York: The Macmillan Company, 1907), 158.
75. Ibid., 160.

76. Isaac Disraeli, *The Genius of Judaism* (London: Edward Moxon, 1833), 265.

77. Michael A. Meyer, *Response to Modernity: A History of the Reform Movement in Judaism* (Oxford: Oxford University Press, 1988), 122.

78. Ibid., 52.

79. Ibid., 81.

80. Ibid., 90.

81. Susannah Heschel, *Abraham Geiger and the Jewish Jesus* (Chicago: University of Chicago Press, 1998), 77.

82. Meyer, 243.

83. Ibid., 249.

84. Ibid., 387–88.

85. Anita Shapira, *Ha-Tanakh Veha-Zehut Ha-Yissreʾelit* (Jerusalem: Magnes, 2005), 141–58. Mira Balberg alerted me to this source.

86. Ibid., 143–44.

87. Boyarin, *A Traveling Homeland: The Babylonian Talmud as Diaspora*.

88. For a review of this concept and a strong critique, see *Unheroic Conduct: The Rise of Heterosexuality and the Invention of the Jewish Man* (Berkeley: University of California Press, 1997), 271–312.

89. Paul R. Mendes-Flohr and Jehuda Reinharz, *The Jew in the Modern World: A Documentary History* (Oxford: Oxford University Press, 2011), 547.

90. Boyarin, *Unheroic Conduct: The Rise of Heterosexuality and the Invention of the Jewish Man*, 273–74.

91. Hayyim Nahman Bialik and Yehoshua Ḥana Rawnitzki, *Sefer Ha-Agadah: Mivhar Ha-Agadot Sheba-Talmud Uva-Midrashim*, 6 vols. (Krakow: Y. Fisher, 1907).

1. On rabbinic orality, see Martin S. Jaffee, *Torah in the Mouth: Writing and Oral Tradition in Palestinian Judaism, 200 BCE-400 CE* (Oxford: Oxford University Press, 2001); Yaakov Sussman, "Torah Sheb'al Peh Peshuto Kemashma'a: Koho Shel Quzo Shel Yod," *Mehqare Talmud* 3, no. 1 (2005).

2. Daphna Ephrat and Yaakov Elman, "Orality and the Institutionalization of Tradition: The Growth of the Geonic Yeshiva and the Islamic Madrasa," in *Transmitting Jewish Traditions: Orality, Textuality and Cultural Diffusion*, ed. Yaakov Elman and Israel Gershoni (New Haven: Yale University Press, 2000).

3. The scroll's unique orthographic features are discussed by Shamma Friedman, "An Ancient Scroll Fragment (B. Hullin 101a-105a) and the Rediscovery of the Babylonian Branch of Tannaitic Hebrew," *The Jewish Quarterly Review* (1995).

4. Frederick G. Kilgour, *The Evolution of the Book* (Oxford: Oxford University Press, 1998), 54–56.

5. Bayerische Staatsbibliothek Cod. hebr. (Munich) 95. This is the manuscript that was the basis for Raphael Nathan Nata Rabbinovicz, *Dikduke Sofrim*, 15 vols. (Jerusalem, 1959).

6. Marvin J. Heller, *Printing the Talmud: A History of the Earliest Printed Editions of the Talmud* (Brooklyn: Im Hasefer, 1992), 15–133.

7. This innovation was introduced by Gershom Soncino.

8. An excellent introduction to this edition is Sharon Liberman Mintz et al., *Printing the Talmud: From Bomberg to Schottenstein* (New York: Yeshiva University Museum, 2005).

9. Heller, 155.

10. After the Iberian expulsion, the Talmud was printed in Fez, Salonika, and Constantinople. These Sefardic editions sometimes do not match the Bomberg pagination.

11. See literature cited at Gershon David Hundert and Gershon C. Bacon, *The Jews in Poland and Russia: Bibliographical Essays* (Bloomington: Indiana University Press, 1984), 13, #26.

12. Israel Halpern, "The Council of the Four Lands in Poland and the Hebrew Book," *Kiryat Sefer* 9 (1932–33).

13. Mordechai Breuer, *Oholei Torah: The Yeshiva, Its Structure and History* (Jerusalem: Zalman Shazar, 2003), 269.

14. Samuel Meir Feigensohn, "L'toldot Defus Romm," in *Yahadut Lita*, ed. Haim Bar Dayyan (Tel Aviv: Association of Lithuanian Jews in Israel), 271.

15. Michael Stanislawski, "The 'Vilna Shas' and East European Jewry," in *Printing the Talmud*, ed. Sharon Liberman Mintz et al. (New York: Yeshiva University Museum, 2005).

16. Feigensohn, 271.

17. Aliza Dzik graciously discussed Hebrew type with me and it is her observation that the Vilna type is less calligraphic.

18. For a more elaborate account of this episode, see Saul M. Ginsburg and Ephraim H. Prombaum, *The Drama of Slavuta* (Lanham, MD: University Press of America, 1991).

19. Feigensohn, 275.

20. Ibid., 276–77.

21. Ibid., 276.

22. Ibid., 277.

23. Ibid., 284. Using a conversion rate of 1/1.3 rubles to dollars ($38.46 in 1880) and an inflation adjuster from 1880.

24. Ibid., 285.

25. Ibid. In 1912 the Romm press acquired plates from the press at Piotrkov, which had published an edition of the Palestinian Talmud in 1899–1900. Romm then embellished the Piotrkov plates rather than resetting the entire edition. This is why the central type in Romm's Palestinian Talmud does not fully share the elegant look of its Babylonian Talmud.

26. Mintz et al., 294.

27. Ibid.

28. Sue Fishkoff, "Steinsaltz Completes Talmud Translation with Global Day of Learning," *Jewish Telegraphic Agency*, October 31, 2010. Uziel Fuchs, "Limmud Be'steinsaltz'—Be'etzem Lama Lo?", *Da'at*, no. 4 (1997). See Shpigel, *Amudim*, vol. 2, page 525.

29. The first volume of the ArtScroll edition was Hersh Goldwurm and Nosson Scherman, *Masekhet Makot = Tractate Makkos: The Gemara: The Classic Vilna Edition, with an Annotated, Interpretive Elucidation*, The ArtScroll Series (Brooklyn, NY: Mesorah Publications, 1990).

30. Isidore Epstein, *Talmud Bavli* (London: Soncino Press, 1960).

31. Adin Steinsaltz, *Talmud Bavli: Masekhet Pesaḥim, Sheḳalim* (Jerusalem: Ḳoren, 2013); Adin Steinsaltz et al., *Koren Talmud Bavli* (Jerusalem: Koren Publishers, 2012).

32. Moshe Benovitz, *Me-ematai Korin et Shemaʿ: Berakhot, Pereḳ Rishon Min Ha-Talmud Ha-Bavli: ʿim*

Parshanut ʿal Derekh Ha-Mehkar (Jerusalem: Society for the Interpretation of the Talmud, 2006).

33. E.g., e-daf.com, shas.org, hebrewbooks.org.

34. Shmuel Yosef Agnon and Abraham Holz, *Marʾot U-Meḳomot: Mahadurah Muʿeret U-Meʾuyeret Shel Hakhnasat Kalah Le-Shai ʿAgnon* (Jerusalem: Schocken, 1995).

35. M. Halevi, "Miperot Beit Hamidrash Lerabbanim: Agnon Im He'arot," *Yom Hashishi*, July 5, 1996. My thanks to Avraham Holtz for sharing this with me.

36. Tamar El-Or and Haim Watzman, *Next Year I Will Know More: Literacy and Identity Among Young Orthodox Women in Israel* (Detroit: Wayne State University Press, 2002), 220.

37. David Weiss Halivni, interview by Barry S. Wimpfheimer, December 29, 2014.

38. Ibid.

39. Isaac Bashevis Singer, *Short Friday and Other Stories* (New York: Farrar, 1964), 131–59.

40. Singer wrote the story in the 1950s.

41. Shaul Stampfer, *Families, Rabbis and Education: Traditional Jewish Society in Nineteenth-Century Eastern Europe* (Portland, Or.: The Littman Library of Jewish Civilization, 2010), 146–66.

42. Don Seeman, "The Silence of Rayna Batya: Torah, Suffering, and Rabbi Barukh Epstein's 'Wisdom of Women,'" *The Torah U-Madda Journal* (1995–96), 91–128.

43. Stampfer, 165–66.

44. Ibid., 106.

45. Scholem, *Major Trends in Jewish Mysticism*, 325–50.

46. Shaul Stampfer, *Lithuanian Yeshivas of the Nineteenth Century: Creating a Tradition of Learning* (Portland,

Or.: The Littman Library of Jewish Civilization, 2012), 1–12.

47. On modern disciplining organizations see Foucault, chapter 4, no. 4.

48. This paragraph paraphrases a description found in Ephraim Deinard, *Zikhronot Bat ʿami : Le-Korot Ha-Yehudim Veha-Yahadut Be-Rusya Be-Meshekh Karov Le-Shivʿim Shanah = Sichronoth Bat Ami: Memoirs of Jewish Life in Russia*, 2 vols. (Arlington, NJ: s.n., 1920), 1:86–87. Eliyahu Stern alerted me to this source.

49. Chaim Grade, *The Yeshiva*, trans. Curt Leviant, 2 vols. (Indianapolis: Bobbs-Merrill, 1976).

50. Ibid., 354.

51. Stern, *The Genius: Elijah of Vilna and the Making of Modern Judaism*, 63–82.

52. Gili Cohen, "Despite Mandatory Conscription," *Haaretz*, June 9, 2013.

53. Josh Nathan-Kazis, *The Forward*, April 22, 2013.

54. http://www.yu.edu/yeshiva-college/mission-history/.

55. http://www.jta.org/2014/03/18/news-opinion /united-states/whos-leading-the-u-s-rabbinical -school-scene/.

56. Jeremy Stolow, *Orthodox by Design: Judaism, Print Politics, and the ArtScroll Revolution* (Berkeley: University of California Press, 2010), 36.

57. Breuer, 90.

58. Stolow, 36–37.

59. Ibid., 37.

60. Sharon Otterman, "Orthodox Jews Celebrate Cycle of Talmudic Study," *New York Times*, August 1, 2012.

61. http://www.nytimes.com/2012/08/02/nyregion /nearly-90000-jews-celebrate-talmud-at-metlife -stadium.html/.

62. Yoel Finkelman to *The Talmud Blog*, October 21, 2013, https://thetalmudblog.wordpress.com/2013/10/21/daf-yomi-4-kids-a-simulacrum-of-a-simulacrum-of-talmud-study-guest-post-by-yoel-finkelman/.

63. Adam Kirsch, "*Daf Yomi*," http://www.tabletmag.com/tag/daf-yomi.

64. Jacqueline Nicholls, October 22, 2015, 2012-, http://drawyomi.blogspot.com/.

65. Michael Lewy Rodkinson and Isaac Mayer Wise, *New Edition of the Babylonian Talmud*, 2d ed. (New York: New Talmud publishing company, 1901).

66. Isidore Epstein, *The Babylonian Talmud* (London,: Soncino Press, 1935).

67. Jacob Neusner, *The Talmud of Babylonia: An American Translation*, Brown Judaic Studies (Chico, Calif.: Scholars Press, 1984).

68. e.g. Albert Schweitzer and W. Montgomery, *The Quest of the Historical Jesus: a Critical Study of Its Progress from Reimarus to Wrede* (London: A. & C. Black, Ltd., 1931).

69. Jacob Neusner, *A Rabbi Talks with Jesus: An Intermillennial, Interfaith Exchange* (New York: Doubleday, 1993).

70. Benedict XVI, *Jesus of Nazareth* (New York: Doubleday, 2007), 103–23.

71. Jesus Colina, *Zenit*, January 21, 2010.

72. For an excellent overview of all of these methods, see Charlotte Elisheva Fonrobert and Martin S. Jaffee, *The Cambridge Companion to the Talmud and Rabbinic Literature* (Cambridge; New York: Cambridge University Press, 2007).

73. Yaakov Elman, "Toward an Intellectual History of Sasanian Law: An Intergenerational Dispute in

Hērbedestān 9 and Its Rabbinic Parallels," *Bakhos and Shayegan, The Talmud in its Iranian Context*; Shai Secunda, *The Iranian Talmud: Reading the Bavli in Its Sasanian Context* (Philadelphia: University of Pennsylvania Press, 2014).

74. Hermann Cohen, *Religion of Reason: Out of the Sources of Judaism* (New York: F. Ungar Pub. Co., 1972). I am indebted to Kenneth Seeskin for this formulation.

75. Joseph Dov Soloveitchik, *The Lonely Man of Faith* (New York: Doubleday, 1992).

76. This formulation is also indebted to Kenneth Seeskin.

77. These are available in Emmanuel Lévinas, *Beyond the Verse: Talmudic Readings and Lectures* (Bloomington: Indiana University Press, 1994); Emmanuel Lévinas and Richard A. Cohen, *New Talmudic Readings* (Pittsburgh, PA: Duquesne University Press, 1999); Emmanuel Levinas, *Nine Talmudic Readings* (Bloomington: Indiana University Press, 1990).

78. Chouchani has been unmasked as Hillel Perlman, a student of Rav Abraham Isaac Kook.

79. Robert M. Cover, "Obligation: A Jewish Jurisprudence of the Social Order," *Journal of Law and Religion* 5, no. 1 (1987).

80. Robert M Cover, *Justice Accused: Antislavery and the Judicial Process* (Yale University Press, 1984).

81. Robert M. Cover, "The Supreme Court, 1982 Term—Foreword: Nomos and Narrative," *Harvard Law Review* 97, no. 4 (1983).

82. Benoît Peeters and Andrew Brown, *Derrida: A Biography* (Cambridge, UK ; Malden, MA: Polity Press, 2013).

83. Rabbi Yehoshua Looks, "The Knesset as Beit Midrash: A Model of Hope for a Better Israel," *Haaretz*, February 25, 2013.

84. David Hartman, *Israelis and the Jewish Tradition: An Ancient People Debating Its Future*, The Terry Lectures (New Haven: Yale University Press, 2000). Elie Stern showed me this reference.

85. Boyarin, *Unheroic Conduct: The Rise of Heterosexuality and the Invention of the Jewish Man*, 1–29.

86. Michael Flaherty, "The Seinfeld Chronicles: An Obsessive-Compulsive Dissection of 169 Episodes," *Entertainment Weekly*, May 30, 1997.

87. It is perhaps worth noting that Marcel Proust, famous for a literary style associated with mundane details, was descended from a prominent Jewish family on his mother's side.

88. Derrida noted this problem about himself—he had never studied Talmud. See Peeters and Brown, 503.

89. Ross Arbes, "How the Talmud Became a Best-Seller in South Korea," *The New Yorker*, June 23, 2015.

90. Ibid.

91. Ibid.

92. Andi Arnovitz, http://andiarnovitz.com/work/if-only-they-had-asked-us-2/.

Paris, 178, 180, 183–85, 238
Passover Haggadah, 170
Passover Seder, 170
Pentateuch, 35, 44. *See also* Torah
Persia, 72, 88, 98, 168, 236
Pfefferkorn, Johannes, 185
Pharisees, 25
Philo, 150–51
philosophy, ix, 28, 35, 97, 101–2,
    105, 110, 131, 144, 150–54, 158,
    166, 187, 196–97, 210, 237–40
Pittsburgh Platform, 204
Place de Grève, 178
Plato, 150–51
Podolia, ix, 193–94
Poland, 103, 137, 141, 157, 214, 224
polysemy, 34, 39–40
Portugal, 135
Posquières, ix, 102
Potok, Chaim, 4–5, 8
Prague, 214
prayer, 34, 144, 192
Promise, The. See Potok, Chaim
Proops Edition, 215
Provence, ix, 100, 102, 106, 109,
    116–17, 129–30, 135–36, 140,
    144, 148, 154–55, 167, 171
pseudepigraphy, 155–56, 171–72
Pugio Fidei. See Martini,
    Raymundi
Pumbedita, 32, 106
Purim, 97–98, 145, 149, 153, 157,
    260n
purity law, 22, 48

Qairouan, viii, 102, 125, 131.
queering of the Talmud, 229,
    242

Rabad, ix, 109, 116–18, 127–30,
    133, 135, 139, 155
Rabbah, 31
Rabbanites, 168–71
Rabbi Talks with Jesus, A. See
    Neusner, Jacob
Ramerupt, 102
Rashi, ix, 65, 109, 118–30, 133,
    135, 167, 211–12, 214–15, 221,
    260n, 266n
Ratzinger, Joseph. *See* Bene-
    dict XVI, Pope
Rav, 31
Rava, 31, 52, 66–68, 78–83, 86,
    88–91, 97–98, 251n, 263n,
    264n
Ravina, 31
Ravnitzky, Yehoshua Hana. See
    Sefer Ha-aggadah
Rayna Batya, 225
redaction, viii, 35, 78, 83, 105,
    166. *See also* editorial work,
    Stam, structure of the Tal-
    mud, unattributed material
Reform Judaism, 142, 188, 195,
    199–204, 206
Reformation, 185–86
*Religion of Reason: Out of the
    Sources of Judaism. See*
    Cohen, Hermann
Renaissance, ix, 187, 234
Resh Laqish, 10–14, 30, 51–57,
    60, 62–63, 67, 69, 73–77, 79–
    80, 82, 91–92, 110–13, 115, 122,
    125, 128, 263n, 266n, 267n
responsa, ix, 105, 107–9, 129,
    130–32, 135, 141–42, 160, 211,
    228

Responsa Project, 142, 222
restitution, 47, 66, 70, 262n
Reuchlin, Johannes, 185
rhetoric, 14, 26, 63, 66, 79–80,
　　90, 97, 107, 114–18, 132–33,
　　138, 140, 170, 215
ritual law, 13, 34, 48, 135, 142,
　　188
ritual murder, 181
Ri Migash. *See* Joseph ibn
　　Migash
Rivers, Joan, 243
Rodkinson, 234
Rome, 17, 23, 186
Romm Edition. *See* Vilna
　　Edition
Romm, Menahem, 216–18
Roth, Philip, 243
Russia, 103, 188, 198, 217

Saadiah Gaon, 152, 154. See also
　　Sefer Emunot V'Deot
Sabbateanism, 173, 188–191,
　　193–95. *See also* Shabtai Zevi
Sabbath, 85, 92, 130, 142, 144,
　　226–27
sacraments, 34
sacrifice, 20, 34, 152
Salonika, 159, 279n
Sanhedrin, 257n, 271n
Saragosa, ix, 102
Sasportas, Jacob, 190
Schneur Zalman of Liadi, 215
scholasticism, 1, 24, 26, 30–32,
　　39, 107, 126, 160
Scholem, Gershom, 191
Schottenstein Edition, 221, 271n
Second Zionist Congress, 206

sectarianism, 19, 24–25, 27,
　　168–69
Sefarad, 101–3, 106, 109, 125,
　　129, 144, 189, 214
Sefer Emunot V'Deot, 152. *See
　　also* Saadiah Gaon, Mutazi-
　　lite school
Sefer Ha-aggadah, 207–8
Sefer Mizvot. *See* Anan ben
　　David
sefirot, 154, 156, 189. *See also*
　　Kabbalah
Seinfeld, 242–43
Sepphoris, 32
sermon, 144, 146, 149, 158, 175.
　　See also homiletics
Seville, 102, 129
Shabtai Zevi, 173, 189–91. *See
　　also* Sabbateanism
Shammai, 30
Shapira, Rabbi Kalonymous
　　Kalman, 156–57
Shapira, Rabbi Meir, ix,
　　230–31
Shapiro family, 215–17
Sheiltot, 14, 268n. *See also* Ahai
　　Gaon, R.
Sherira Gaon, Rav, viii, 131
Shittah Mequbezet. *See* Bezalel
　　Ashkenazi
Shulhan Arukh, ix, 135, 137–38,
　　141
Shushan, 88, 98, 157
ShutSMS, 142
Silverman, Sarah, 243
Simeon bar Yohai, R., 30, 155.
　　See also Zohar
Simon ben Gamaliel, Rabbi, 30

Yom Kippur, 61
Yom Tov ben Avraham, 129

Zhitomir Edition, 217
Zion, 43, 182–83, 259n. *See also* Jerusalem

Zionism, 142, 188, 195, 204–8
Zohar, 155–57, 171–73. *See also* Moses de Leon, Simeon bar Yohai
Zoroastrianism, 175–76, 236
Zunz, Leopold, 201–2